HINDUISM
INVADES AMERICA

By

WENDELL THOMAS
B.S., M.A., Ph.D., S.T.M.

Published by

THE BEACON PRESS, INC.
318-324 WEST 39TH STREET
NEW YORK CITY

HINDUISM
INVADES AMERICA

PRINTED IN THE UNITED STATES OF AMERICA

FOREWORD

This work is not an attack on Hinduism. It is not meant to inflame American citizens by pointing to a foreign menace. Nor is it a defense of Hinduism. Nor is it a defense of Christianity or anything else. It is simply a study of the amazing adventure of an Eastern faith in a Western land. Accordingly, it is not a collection of curious or sensational anecdotes about a few of the many Hindu *swamis* and *yogis* visiting these shores, but an account of the serious impact on American life of Hindu philosophy and culture especially in the form of organized religion.

Several years of study and teaching in India have somewhat prepared me to write on Hinduism in America. For expert help in this modern study I am grateful especially to Professor Hervey D. Griswold, formerly of the Panjab University, Lahore, who guided my researches in Hinduism, and to Professor Herbert W. Schneider, of Columbia University, New York, who advised me concerning the subject and form of the book. I wish also to thank the many accomplices who kindly answered my questions by letter, and several Hindu friends in New York, who gave me every possible encouragement.

WENDELL THOMAS.

New York, April 1930.

INTRODUCTION

In the imagination of the great majority of Americans, foreign missions has been an altogether one-sided affair. Taking for granted the superiority of Christianity, they have pictured the Christian movement as going out to overspread the world.

To thoughtful minds, it has long been obvious that there would soon come a time when the great Eastern religions, sure of the superiority of their spiritual life over the mechanized living of the Western world, would come to us with the deep conviction that they were the heralds of the world's true gospel.

Mr. Thomas's book, so far as I know, is the first thoroughgoing treatise setting forth with patient research both the direct and the indirect invasion of Western thought by Hinduism. The book makes clear, what it has long been evident would sometime be inevitable, that there can no longer be a sharp distinction between the so-called "home" and "foreign" fields in religion. Christianity is at work in India and Hinduism is at work in the United States. There is no possibility of Indian religion escaping the influence of Jesus Christ, and there is no possibility of American religion escaping the influence of the great Indian faiths.

Mr. Thomas's book therefore is of primary importance, and it is to be hoped there will be a popular understanding and appreciation of its significance.

HARRY EMERSON FOSDICK

CONTENTS

CHAPTER I

HINDU MOVEMENTS IN AMERICA, AN EXPRESSION OF YOUNG INDIA

An old faith is now invading a new country. The new country is the United States of America. The old faith is Hinduism. The invasion began when the first Christian colonists from Europe set foot on the American continent, for there are traces of Hindu sentiment in both Catholic and Protestant creeds. As soon as students in America began to study Plotinus, Thomas Aquinas and Spinoza, Hinduism began to spread, and when Emerson and his like-minded friends received a generous hearing, Hinduism became more firmly established in America than in Europe. Theosophy, Christian Science and similar religious movements further extended its sway, and when Hindu *swamis* and *yogis* themselves began to appear on the horizon in robes of the color of this book-cover, Hinduism suddenly advanced in all its pristine glory. But the end of the invasion is not yet in sight, for apart from the *swamis* and *yogis,* a goodly throng of academic lecturers and organization directors are slowly but surely conducting Hindu ideas into the very center of American culture.

Of course Hinduism reminds us of Mahatma Gandhi and his inspired movements of "non-violent non-coöperation." We should understand at the outset, however, that Hinduism in America has little to do with non-violent non-coöperation, for the non-violent part of his program Gandhi took over from the Sermon on the Mount and the *ahimsa,* or non-injury, practice of Buddhism and Jainism, while the non-coöperation part is the obvious political and economic weapon of a rebellious and disarmed people. Again, Hinduism reminds us of Katherine Mayo and her startling book *Mother India*. But the Hinduism that comes to America is no more a reflection of the culture portrayed by Miss Mayo than the Christianity carried to India by American missionaries is a reflection of free love, race riots and racketeering. As far as I have been able to discover, Hinduism appears in America in the following forms:

1. Hindu cults, such as the Ramakrishna movement, and the Yogoda Sat-sanga Society of America.

2. Hindu cultural movements, such as the Threefold Movement, and the International School of Vedic and Allied Research.

3. Learned Hindu lecturers, such as Tagore and Radhakrishnan.

4. Popular lecturers on practical Hinduism, such as "Super-Akasha Yogi Wassan," a Panjabi Hindu, and "Yogi Ramacharaka," an American.

5. American impostors passing for Hindu popular lecturers, such as "Prem Lal Adoris," and "Joveddah de Raja."

6. Hindu professors and students in America.

7. Oriental cults of partly Hindu origin, such as Buddhism and Sikhism.

8. American cults of partly Hindu origin, such as Theosophy and Christian Science.

9. Hindu influence on Western thought in such thinkers as Schopenhauer and Emerson.

No doubt there are Hindu movements in America that I have not discovered, and even as I write new forms of American Hinduism may be arising. Every year sees the advent of new Hindu teachers of one kind or another. Certainly Hinduism is invading America wave after wave. Will it eventually overwhelm Christianity? Such is the claim of some of its champions. And this claim cannot lightly be set aside. If our view of the world is so changed by science and the law of evolution that the Heavenly Father of Christianity becomes a useless idol—at best a harmless creation of religious imagination, and at worst a superstitious drag on progress—then Hinduism, with its conception of vital evolutionary progress toward a divine goal, will be just the religion we need to keep us from atheism in a scientific age. Thus disillusioned Christians, and for that matter all modern men will finally see the truth of Hinduism, and eagerly seek its universal embrace. So reason the champions of Hinduism.

And to orthodox Christians who shudder at this prospect, these Hindus are ready to explain that Hinduism is not a missionary religion, and makes no attempt to convert people to an exclusive sect or creed. So it should cause no alarm. *Hinduism,* they point out, is after all a word of Western coinage, whereas the proper term for their religion is *Dharma,* which simply means the universal progressive principle of every man. To acknowledge the upward urge and divine goal of this principle, they say, is not to exchange Christianity for Hinduism, but to find a bigger and better Christianity.

Whatever the outcome of Hinduism in America may be, we cannot understand it without a knowledge of certain facts pertaining to the history of its past and present achievements. These facts I have endeavored to present in two ways: first, by means of a careful study of the two most imposing Hindu cults in America, namely, Vedanta and Yogoda; and second, by means of a brief survey of all the other Hindu movements.

The study of Vedanta occupies chapters three to five, chapter three dealing with its patron saint in India, chapter four with its first missionary to America, and chapter five with its growth and expansion in the United States.

The study of Yogoda occupies only chapter six. Vedanta has received more space than Yogoda because it has spent much more time in America, is more classic, orthodox and representative, and is perhaps the first modern missionary movement of any Eastern religion to the West. The facts here presented are based mainly on Hindu sources, and have been checked by the Hindu leaders themselves. The judgments I pass on these facts are intended to be sympathetic, yet critical and constructive.

The survey of all the other Hindu movements occupies chapter seven. Several of these movements are very important, more important perhaps than Vedanta or Yogoda, but limited time and space forbids a more extensive treatment. In chapter eight, which is the last, I aim to present a brief resumé of the causes and effects of the Vedanta and Yogoda movements in American life, and a brief opinion of the American prospects of the Hindu faith in general.

Since the meaning of Hinduism in America cannot be grasped without some knowledge of Hinduism in India, I offer in chapter two a short account of classical Vedanta, the basic philosophy of Hinduism, which forms the general heritage of all Hindu movements in America, and not merely the heritage of the particular Ramakrishna movement which labels its American centers "Vedanta," and which I also call "Vedanta" in order to pair it nicely with Yogoda. Furthermore, since this modern revival of classic Hinduism cannot be properly understood without some knowledge of modern India, I now set down a few facts about modern India that are relevant to our purpose.

* * *

Hindu missionaries to America have come not from ancient India, of course, but from modern India, and modern India is a child of East and West. In 1600, just before the Pilgrim Fathers set foot on the shore of America, the East India Company of London ventured forth to the land of India. It found an ancient and long-suffering people, inured to repeated invasions from the Northwest, but dimly remembering golden days of commerce, science, art and religion. This Western trading company gradually gained control over the whole land of India, and in 1858, after the Mutiny, yielded the government to the Crown.

In 1857 the three great universities of Calcutta, Bombay and Madras were founded, modelled on the University of London. They did all their work in English. The establishment of these and other institutions of higher learning marks the transition of young India from infancy to childhood. In spite of their somewhat old-fashioned methods and paucity of Indian culture, creating a gap between the "national" and the "English" Indian, the universities have served as a bridge between East and West whereon the Indian student catches the vision of freedom shining in English literature, and hastens to embody this vision in the organization of his country. With almost perfect command over the English language, and familiarity with the best works of European literature and science, a small but increasing section of the population is moving in touch with the outer world so closely as to be keenly sensitive to every breath of Western thought and feeling. East and West have met, and never the twain shall part.

In addition to Western education, the highly centralized British government has imposed on the oriental culture of India a modern system of manufacture and commerce, involving a well-paid civil and military service, trunk roads, railways, telegraph and postal services, law courts and hospitals. Partly because of this Western culture, partly in reaction against it, the movement of Indian nationalism has increased step by step until it has now taken on a world-wide significance. Young India is becoming of age.

India may be divided into ten distinct language areas, two types of government—democratic and monarchic—and five religious communities: Hindu, Muslim, Christian, Sikh and Parsi. Moreover, we find lines of cleavage between the liberal North and the conservative South, between the priestly Brahmans and the insurgent non-Brahmans, between the complacent castes and the depressed outcastes, between the learned university graduates and the illiterate peasants, and between the free-moving men and the more or less shut-in women. These lines, however, are being effaced as rapidly as age-long custom will permit.

The religious development of modern India can best be understood as the reaction of her communities to the impact of Western Christianity. Toward the close of the eighteenth century, when the British power was rising in India, C. F. Schwartz of Germany established the Reformed Church in the South, near Madras, while William Carey of England started the work of the Baptist Mission in the North, near Calcutta. To Hindus and Muslims alike they preached the gospel of salvation from sin through Jesus Christ, supported by the doctrines of one Book, one God, one Savior, and one Brotherhood.

The Muslims as a rule turned a deaf ear to this appeal, for they also belonged to a dominant missionary minority. For six centuries in India they had spoken to command and not to obey. Moreover, they also had their doctrines of one Book, one God, one Prophet and one Brotherhood, which, as they firmly believed, had superseded the doctrines of Christianity. Most of all, they were the world's fiercest propagandists, and would tolerate no defection from their creed. Hence only a very few of the most sensitive and courageous members of the Muslim community dared leave the Crescent for the Cross. But these few became the pillars of the Church.

While the Hindus likewise refused to break their age-long bonds of caste to join the Christian Church, they did not refuse to listen to the Christian message. They could afford to be more tolerant, for they were in the majority. Not merely for six centuries, but for thirty-six centuries or more had their religion flourished in India and developed an immense variety of forms. Like a vast *banyan* tree it had sent forth from its branches many aerial roots, each of which had grown down into the soil and become a new tree trunk sending forth in its turn new branches and new roots. So the Hindus listened. Many even read the Bible, translated by the arduous toil of scholarly missionaries. But for a long time they did not understand. The missionaries had not yet learned to present the gospel from the Hindu point of view. But they refused to lose heart, and established the two great aids to preaching, namely, healing and teaching.

The ministry of healing, with its hospitals, dispensaries and asylums, directly imparted the doctrine of Christian love even to the most hostile or degraded. It naturally made its greatest appeal to the Hindu outcastes, comprising over fifty millions of people, almost as many as in the whole Muslim community. When these dealers in filth and carion felt the healing touch of love, they were not slow to trust themselves to their benefactors. Especially in the heart-breaking times of famine, when the missionaries laid aside their usual work to save the poor from starving, whole communities in great mass movements followed their village chiefs into the Christian Church.

Here they have been welded into a powerful lever which is shaking the social structure of Hinduism. For note this fact: once an outcaste becomes a Christian, he is magically transformed from a despised Hindu untouchable into a member of the ruling community, a fellow churchman of the King-Emperor. Moreover, a majority of the five million members of the Christian community, the third largest in India, have risen from the ranks of the outcastes. Roused by the fear of thus losing to the Christians (and also to the Muslims) a huge section of their community, the Hindus are now striving to purify and take back into the fold of caste (or at least community) these long-neglected and long-suffering brothers. But once the barrier between caste and outcaste is demolished, what will become of the barriers betwen caste and caste?

The ministry of teaching, with its schools and colleges, naturally made its greatest appeal to the upper-caste Hindus, who gladly sent their youths to drink at the spring of modern culture provided by Government and influenced by missions. Three results may be noted. First, a few of these Hindu intellectuals have become outstanding Christians. Second, a number of vigorous Hindu liberals have adopted on the basis of reason the ethics of Jesus and a monotheistic faith expressed by certain selections from the Hindu scriptures. The great pioneer in this movement was Prince Ram Mohan Roy, who founded the *Brahma Samaj,* or Divine Society, just a century ago in Calcutta. Most of the Indian social reform of the past century has come from this "unitarian church" and its sympathizers, warmly supported by the Christian missionaries.

A third result of the Government's more or less Christian education has been to stimulate the orthodox Hindu communities to appreciate their own rich heritage and defend it against the invasion of Christianity. And it is chiefly from these orthodox communities that the Hindu missionaries to America have emerged. The Brahman pandits, whose business has ever been to treasure up India's sacred lore in their Sanskrit books and memories, had become so exclusive, that even the educated classes did not know their country's scriptures until Western orientalists like Max Müller presented them in English, which after all was the all-Indian learned language of the Indian intellectual. This kind of research was taken up also by Indian scholars, trained in Western methods, but saturated with the spirit of the East from their childhood. Then with growing national self-respect the orthodox Hindu religious leaders began to delve into their own scriptures in order to find something to express their national character and to offset the Christianity brought to them by men of originally foreign culture and usually domineering ways.

They did find something, which in the strange course of future events proved to be a weapon of spiritual aggression as well as defense. But what was it they found? What is the character of the religious heritage of the Hindus? It is revealed in the dominant Hindu philosophy known as "Vedanta," which Hindu leaders are popularizing in America today. This Vedanta, or Vedantism, will now be explained in the following chapter; but whoever is not especially interested in the ancient classical foundation of American Hinduism may pass directly to chapter three, where the story of Vedanta's invasion of America will begin.

CHAPTER II

CLASSIC VEDANTA, THE ESSENCE OF HINDU FAITH

1. THE BACKGROUND OF VEDANTA

The oldest sacred scriptures of the Hindus are the four *Vedas,* a mass of hymns, chants and spells composed orally about 1300 to 800 B.C., during the time of the Aryan occupation of the Panjab. The hymns of the *Rigveda,* the chief of the four, are for the most part vital prayers addressed to the powers of nature, such as Indra, the storm, and Agni, the fire.

Very soon the philosophic quest for unity began. One way of unifying the gods was by identification. Just as the different tribes use different words to designate the same thing, so must there be *Tad Ekam* (that One), of which the various gods are but various names.

The sages call that One in many ways, they call it Agni, Yama, Matarisvan.[1]

But this identification did not destroy the individuality of each god, which a worshiper might select from the heavenly substance, and praise for the moment as God absolute. This early distinction between the philosophic One and the popular Many is the key to Vedanta.

The Aryans of this time were like the Greeks of Homer's time: free, fresh, natural, wholesome and happy. Their gods were *devas,* or shining ones, and their life was strong and open. There was no hint of world sorrow, or desire to escape from life's problems. The system of caste, or hereditary class, had not yet been formed, and vegetarianism was not practiced. Beef eating was common. *Karma,* or the chain of action, and *sansara,* or the cycle of birth and death, were conceptions not yet invented, and God was still made in the image of man.

However, by the time of the *Upanishads,* or secret comments on the *Vedas,* breathed from master to disciple in the forest retreat about 800 to 600 B. C., the worldly joy of this vigorous culture had almost faded out. The distinctions of color and occupation between the invading Aryans and the native Dasyus had developed into a set of four *varnas,* or orders, of (1) *Brahmans,* or priests and teachers, (2) *Ksatriyas,* or warriors and rulers, (3) *Vaisyas,* or farmers and merchants, and (4) *Sudras,* or servants and toilers. This lowest order was composed of the dark-skinned aborigines, who were excluded from the rites of the "twice-born," or three higher orders. At the time of Manu, the greatest Hindu lawgiver, near the Christian era, these orders solidified into strict castes and sub-castes.

The dogma or principle of the "wheel of life," named transmigration, palingenesis, metempsychosis, reincarnation, or rebirth, is absent from the *Rigveda,* but present in the *Upanishads.* The actions, deeds, or works of the soul, such as sacrificial rites, charity, austerity, and the general performance of social duty, which originally led it to complete salvation in the highest heaven, now merely chain it to the meaningless, monotonous cycle of rebirth. No matter how high up in the moral scale the soul may go, it is bound to come down again, for life is a Wheel. And no matter how desirable human intercourse in the world of nature may seem now and then, here and yon, its final monotony will steal away all zest. Thus life is no longer a thrilling adventure to be welcomed, but a dreary round to be renounced. Here is a basis for *acosmism,* literally "no-world-ism," the doctrine that the world is futile and unreal. To achieve salvation, we must be negative to the world, but positive to a realm above, in which the world melts.

The central task of the *Upanishads* is to point out the path from the world to this upper realm of "Reality."

> From the unreal lead me to the real.
> From darkness lead me to light.
> From death lead me to immortality.[2]

Contrary to the previous Vedic literature, the *Upanishads* (which come at the end of the *Vedas*) show a distrust of "works" and a trust in "knowledge." Hence the great effort to grasp the key of the universe, that one principle by which a knowledge of all things can be gained. Of what nature is the ultimate reality? On the answer to this leading question depends man's course of salvation. Like the *Vedas* on which they depend, the *Upanishads* teach a variety of doctrines, which may be grouped into three fundamental positions: a pantheistic monism, a vitalistic dualism and an individualistic pluralism. These three inconsistent positions form the basis of later Vedanta; for, as we shall see, when they are combined with an emphasis on the monism, we get the pantheistic acosmism developed by Sankara, but when they are combined with an emphasis on the pluralism, we get the theistic determinism developed by Ramanuja. These are the two great classic forms of Vedanta (or Vedantism), both of which appear in America, not only in the "Vedanta" movement, but in the "Yogoda" and other movements as well.

It seems that the *risis,* or seers of the *Upanishads,* in seeking the key of knowledge to unlock the gate of salvation, did not want to explain the world so much as to explain it *away.* They themselves were not in the social world of industry, but apart from it; not low-caste men, but mostly Brahmans, the exclusive possessors of religious learning, supported by the manual toil of the inferior orders of society. Their teachings were avowedly secret, and not meant for the masses, who had neither the mind to understand them nor the opportunity to carry them out. For the masses, the "lower," common-sense knowledge and the way of "works," or social and ceremonial duty, would have to suffice.

But the masses were not content with a second-rate salvation. They cried out for the best, and their cry was heard. Two popular leaders arose with deeply pondered answers on their lips: Gautama Buddha, who preached salvation by the new morality of love and service to all mankind, and the unknown author of the *Bhagavad Gita*, or "Song Celestial," who fastened the sanction of *Upanishad* teaching to the increasingly popular cult of loving-devotion to a God who was in mankind, to be sure, but essentially above and beyond.

In Siddhartha Gautama Sakyamuni, born in the sixth century B. C., and later called the *Buddha* or Enlightened, a noble youth of warrior line of the *Sakya* clan near the border of Nepal in the Himalayas, the factor of an outstanding historic personality first enters the history of Hindu religion. The bitterness of war and plunder, the misery of old age, sickness, death, and poverty, and the monotonous futility of life in general, set forth in the law of *karma* and rebirth, had existed before Gautama, but never before had any seer brought these evils so vividly to the mind of his people. To the keen and sensitive nature of this original thinker, suffering is the overpowering fact of life. After prolonged meditation on the cause and cure of this evil, he becomes convinced of four basic truths:

1. Individual life is suffering
2. The origin of suffering is worldly desire

3. Escape from suffering lies in freedom from this desire
4. Freedom from this desire comes from right thinking and action

Desire and thinking are one. Worldly desire causes suffering because we think the world is worthy, because we value what is transient and perishable. Since action springs from thinking, the pain of action can be cured by right thinking. We need neither priests nor austerity. We will renounce our cravings individually and of our own accord when once we realize the truth that all things are worthless. Man is an ever-changing stream of consciousness, while nature also is a continual process of change without abiding reality. With this knowledge, individuality will cease in *Nibbana* (the Buddhist *Nirvana*), a cool, calm state of ineffable joy, experienced even in this life. This is the doctrine of the "middle path" that seeks to avoid the extremes of self-indulgence and self-mortification.

Buddhism taught two ways of uprooting sorrow and attaining this state of bliss: the *Arhat* ideal of individual renunciation and meditation, and the *Bodhisattva* ideal of social love and service, which overpasses the bounds of caste and takes all life into its embrace. This latter ideal resembles the Christian, but its background is considerably different. The Buddha himself was *Arhat*, but, out of pity for the world, remained to teach it. This *but* shows the essential opposition between the two ideals of individual detachment and social sympathy.

Then came the *Bhagavad Gita,* or the *Lord's Song,* some time perhaps between 200 B. C. and 200 A. D. Like Buddhism, the *Gita* rejected austerity as a way of salvation, but unlike Buddhism, it was wise in its own generation, and so refrained from preaching love for the world, or anything that smacked of the *old-fashioned* way of works discarded by the *Upanishads*. Yet it did preach love—love for a personal God. Driven from the broad realm of social intercourse, love took refuge in the narrow province of private devotion.

The *Gita* accepted completely the ways of knowledge (*jnana*) and meditation (*yoga*) laid down in the *Upanishads*. But it made another contribution all its own: the way of *bhakti*, or "loving-devotion" to God, together with detached or meritless works, consituting a new kind of *karma*. The secret ways of knowledge and meditation may do for the exclusive Brahmans who have the time and mentality for such otherworldly practices, but they cannot benefit the toilers who live in the thick of the world and support the Brahmans, for they cannot possibly renounce the objects of sense. How can these commoners find salvation?

The *Gita* is an answer to this deep question. The common man must work and love, but ordinary work and love will not do, for this only binds him more firmly to the wheel of action. Just here the popular worship of the divine hero Krishna makes its contribution. Let the common man work not for the world, but for the Lord. Let him love not kin but Krishna. To achieve release a man must work without regard to the personal consequences of his deeds, without fear of punishment or hope of reward. He must learn not to be attracted by the attractive or repelled by the repellent, but envisage both as illusory manifestations of the adorable Lord. In the midst of turmoil he must rest in the Lord of Peace, discharging every duty to the fullest, not because he seeks to benefit mankind, but because his duty is to obey the eternal law of caste.

Prince Arjuna, a warrior by caste, appearing on the field of battle to vindicate his brother's title to the throne and

free the land from oppression, feels a sudden pang, a
sharp demand for peace on earth, when he sees kinsmen
and beloved comrades in the ranks of both the opposing
army and his own.   How can he slay those to whom he
owes the duty of honor and affection and trample on the
sacred ties of kinship? Krishna, his divine charioteer, then
tells him how.   When duties conflict, caste duties must
prevail, for they belong to *Dharma,* the very order of the
universe.   The warrior must fight.   Identified with the
Lord by devotion, he must enter the fray without hatred,
and slaughter his kinsmen without remorse.   Such action
welds no bonds, and so the soul is free.

2.   THE MEANING OF VEDANTA

Some time after the writing of the *Bhagavad Gita,* perhaps, the *Vedanta Sutras* were composed.   The term Vedanta is made up of two words, *Veda* (revelation) and
anta (end), and literally means, "the end of revelation,"
or the final aim of the *Veda.*   In this sense it has sometimes been taken to include "the six systems of philosophy" based on the *Upanishads,* and even the *Bhagavad
Gita.*   More specifically, however, the term Vedanta refers to just one of these systems, embodied in the *Vedanta
Sutras,* or Vedanta Aphorisms.   As the only system that
posits an absolute God, the Vedanta is the boldest and
most characteristic form of Indian philosophy.

Several thinkers who start from the *Upanishads* and
Vedanta Sutras, such as Sankara, Ramanuja and Madhava,
are often called Vedantins (or Vedantists), but I shall
limit the term Vedanta to the positions of Sankara and
Ramanuja, for only these two thinkers seek to maintain
an absolute God.   Aside from the *Vedanta Sutras,* which
provided the systematic foundation for both of them, Sankara based his pantheistic acosmism chiefly on the mystic
declarations of the Upanishadic sage Yajnavalkya, the

renunciatory aspect of Buddhism, and the *Gita's* ways of knowledge and meditation, while Ramanuja's theistic determinism depends mainly on the individualistic *Katha* and *Svetasvatara Upanishads*, the old-fashioned Vedic way of merit-making "works," and the *Gita's* way of "loving-devotion."

Yet below their differences, Sankara and Ramanuja have many points in common.

(1) Both were ardent defenders of the Hindu faith, and welcomed the doctrine of release from the wheel of life. That is, both depicted a universe in which every individual soul with its subtle "causal body" containing the "seeds of action" repeatedly returns to rebirth in forms determined by the deeds of every previous life. The form of rebirth may be plant, animal or human, the subconscious self being retained. The human form, in turn, is divided into the four great castes which may not intermarry or interdine, and the outcastes. And both maintained that *Sudras,* or members of the lowest caste, are excluded from salvation in this life because they cannot be admitted to the study of the *Vedas,* lacking the initiation of the sacred thread common to the three higher castes.

(2) Both were Brahmans and natives of South India where Brahmans are much more exclusive than in the North. They alone studied the Vedas with satisfaction. While the three upper or "twice-born" castes were permitted the sacred study, only the Brahmans actually did so as a rule, since the others would find small use for such learning in everyday life. Such books as the *Pancatantra* show that the education given to princes was in many cases much more practical. As a result, the working out of philosophic theories became almost the exclusive task of a certain hereditary order. Since, moreover, this philosophy was especially directed to the elaboration of

"Sruti," or Revelation, composed of early hymns, ceremonies and forest meditations, it was not especially concerned with industry, art, ethics, politics or science. India
had indeed developed many sciences, such as medicine and
mathematics, but these were not considered departments
of religious philosophy; political and ethical precepts were
laid down in the *sastras,* or law books, as divinely fixed
once and for all, and did not evolve under despotic rule,
while art and industry were manual labor beneath the
function of a priest. Hindu philosophers were not merely
an exclusive set: they even dealt with exclusive problems.

(3) So we are not surprised to learn that Sankara and
Ramanuja both rejected "sense-perception" and "logical
inference" in favor of "scriptural authority" as the source
of supreme knowledge, or the knowledge of God, which
was considered a matter of experience or intuition. Sankara recognized intuition, or *anubhava,* as final only if
based on the word and sanction of scripture. As for
reason, it was held to be useless as a means of dealing
with ultimate reality, for it cannot yield the "higher"
knowledge, which is the experience of the "higher" God.

> The fact of everything having its Self in Brahman cannot be
> grasped without the aid of the Scriptural passage "That art
> thou." [3]

Thus Sankara and Ramanuja were at bottom very much
alike, for in life and thought they both emphasized the
sharp distinction between the creative and the blissful
God, between the laity and the priesthood, and between
reason and revelation.

3. SANKARA VEDANTA

Sankara, who was born in the very south of India about
800 A. D., became in childhood a prodigy of Vedic lore.
Rejecting the ways of the world at an early age, he turned

sannyasi; wandered over India, preaching and disputing, and established four *mathas,* or monasteries, at the four points of the compass: Badarinath in the Himalayas to the north, Sringeri in the south, Puri in the east and Dvaraka in the west. From these monasteries would sally forth in good weather his order of preaching friars, or *sannyasis* like himself, to proclaim his message. In this organization he followed Buddhism. His monks were called *dasnamis,* or "Ten Named," because each monk had for his surname one of ten names, such as Puri or Giri. Thus each name came to denote a suborder. On initiation into the order, every man would take a new first name standing for one of Sankara's main doctrines, and put on an ochre, saffron, or flame-colored robe, signifying the fire of knowledge in which ignorance and impurity are consumed. The color of the robe, still worn today by sannyasis, or swamis, is like the color of this book-cover. Castes also, along with property, ordinary clothes and family ties, were "burnt up" in this order of renunciation and meditation. But what did these friars preach? What was Sankara's system?

Weary of the nihilistic doctrines spread abroad in India by Buddhism, the Hindu community longed for a return to Vedic authority. This meant a return to the *Upanishads,* which by their own dictum had fulfilled the earlier parts of the *Vedas.* But what did the *Upanishads* teach? There was no common view. The *Vedanta Sutras* were comprehensive but cryptic. So an intelligible authority was the urgent need of the day. How to make the *Upanishads* teach one main doctrine, then, is Sankara's great problem. And he solves it with a genius as subtle as rare. In the *Upanishads* he sees the "lower" Brahman known by the "lower" knowledge, and the "higher" Brahman known by the "higher" knowledge.[4] Taking this sharp distinction as his guide, he fixes the "higher" knowledge as the standard authority of infallible scripture, and treats the "lower" knowledge as an accommodation to men of lower position on the cosmic wheel.

The "lower" knowledge gives us a creative, time-including God and the manifold regulations for ceremonial worship and social duty enjoined by Hindu tradition. All this Sankara sanctions as a wise propagandist. The "lower" knowledge is true indeed, but only relatively true. The "higher" knowledge gives us the God of formless bliss. In this bliss alone is full salvation, attained by the *sannyasi,* the one that renounces the world to meditate on his "inner divine nature."

With this plan in mind, Sankara constructs his system. His first act is to lay down the proposition that object and subject, the "thou" and the "I," are absolutely distinct and cannot be identified in any respect. This is supposed to be self-evident. The subject is God, the object the world. The trouble with most men, says Sankara, is that they are unaware of this simple truth! They naïvely say, "I am cold," or, "I am hot," when in reality it is impossible for the self to be anything finite at all. For cold and heat are qualities of objects, whereas the self is the subject, which is quite another thing. My *body* may be cold or hot, but I myself can be neither.

This transference of the qualities of the object to the subject, says Sankara, is man's innate or natural error based on his cosmic forgetfulness of his original, quality-less Self. And since the subject is the only reality, as the *Upanishads* reveal, it is incorrect to think of the object as real in itself. Hence the world as we usually know it, is the result of ignorance, or *avidya.* It does not really exist as it appears to exist. Therefore it is illusion. In the dusk we see a snake. But as we approach, we find it a rope. The snake is an illusion, banished by knowledge. So with the world.

As a matter of fact, Sankara's course was *away* from illusionism, and not toward it: all he desired was consistent authority. His spiritual grandfather Gaudapada had written a commentary on the *Mandukya Upanishad* to show that waking life is no more than a dream. But Sankara took great pains to point out the relative reality of the waking life compared to dreaming. The world, said he, is not a private, but a public illusion, and real for all practical purposes. Indeed, the illusion is produced by God himself, the great Illusion-Maker. Hence the way of final salvation is the knowledge of God as the absolute Self, and the everyday world as illusion.

The complete comprehension of Brahman is the highest end of man, since it destroys the root of all evil such as false knowledge, the seed of the entire process of transmigration.[5]

When *vidya,* or true knowledge, begins, then *avidya,* or false knowledge, ceases. Hence the two views of God, practical and intuitive, cannot possibly conflict, for they cannot exist in the same person at the same time.

The man who has once comprehended Brahman to be the Self does not belong to this transmigratory world as he did before. He, on the other hand, who still belongs to this transmigratory world as before, has not comprehended Brahman to be the Self. Thus there remain no unsolved contradictions.[6]

Now, the comprehension of Brahman as the solitary Self demands private intuition as the completion of public authority. After the devotee is convinced of the scriptural verity "That art thou," he must also "realize" by inner experience that he truly *is* that Brahman. Even before a member of the faithful begins his *sadhana,* or "realization," he must form a stable character by means of common sense, practical logic, and the ordinary religion of ceremony, works and duty. Thus the "lower" knowledge has a distinct place as an educative agency for the "higher" knowledge. Then he must fit himself for the direct intuition of *Sat-cit-ananda,* or "Reality-consciousness-bliss," by traversing four stages:

(1) Discrimination between God and the world;
(2) Renunciation of the world, called *sannyasa;*
(3) Six mental disciplines:
  (a) Restraint of the outer senses;
  (b) Restraint of the inner senses;
  (c) Retraction of the mind from the senses;
  (d) Fixation of the mind on the "Self";
  (e) Indifference to pairs of opposites, such as cold and heat, gain and loss, pleasure and pain;
  (f) Complete trust in the scriptures and *guru,* or master.
(4) Keen desire to escape all bondage.[7]

After the student is thoroughly trained in these four stages with their *yoga* practice, he is ready to follow the final three stages.

(1) Learning the meaning of the text "That art thou" from a *guru* who has himself really experienced this truth.
(2) Testing this truth by means of practical doubt and experiment.
(3) The final constant bliss of intuition.[8]

This final rapturous experience can never be communicated: it must be private. Indeed, according to Sankara, the Vedic texts do not even aim to implant truth: they merely direct our attention to it. Knowledge springs up in the mind "of itself" as a direct perception of the Eternal, in which all limitations vanish, and the soul obtains *mukti,* or liberation, here and now.

That which is real in the absolute sense, immutable, eternal, all-pervading like akasa, exempt from all change, all-satisfying, undivided, whose nature is to be its own light, in which neither good nor evil, nor effect, nor past nor present nor future has any place, this incorporeal is called liberation.[9]

By taking mental discipline as one of the means of liberation, Sankara embraces the *yoga* practice as presented

in the *Upanishads*[10] and developed in the classic system
of Patanjali.[11]   The word *yoga* means yoke.   Thus *yoga*
means the yoking, or restraint, of the senses.   But if the
yoking be taken as a way to God (in contrast to the position of the *Sankhya* system of philosophy), it comes to
signify union—union with God.   Patanjali taught the *raja-
yoga* or "kingly" way of restraint, as distinguished from
the *hatha-yoga* and the *mantra-yoga*.   The *hatha-yoga* is
a system of bodily exercises for warding off diseases and
making the body fit to bear with perfect calm all sorts of
privations and strains.   The *mantra-yoga* is a course of
meditation on certain "mystic" syllables leading to the
audition of certain "mystic" sounds.

The *raja-yoga*, which of all these is the most important
and the system taught most in America, is a discipline of
gradual restraint and final annihilation of all mental
states for the sake of salvation.   It tells how the senses
may be withdrawn from the objects of sense, and reduced
to stillness in the *anta:karana*, or inner central organ;
and how this central organ in turn may be so wholly
centered in the *atman*, or soul, as to lose itself in the bliss
of "superconscious" unity.   But this goal of deliverance
can be reached only through a series of stages in which
external aids play a large part.   Various bodily attitudes,
named *asana*, are prescribed, as well as the control of
breathing by means of counting and holding the breath,
and the fixation of attention on various parts of the body,
such as the navel or the tip of the nose.   All this is meant
to reduce natural activity to a minimum.   Sometimes tears
flow from the eyes, the body becomes cataleptic, or as stiff
as a piece of wood, and the devotee or *yogi* falls into
yoganidra, the hypnotic sleep that precedes complete
emancipation.   One method that is useful in producing a
state of death to the world and awaking to bliss consists
in extending the tongue, bending it round, and inserting

the tip into the opening of the throat, while gazing stead-fastly on the spot between the eyebrows.

A development of Patanjali's method is the *surtsabda* (or "spirit word") *yoga,* built on to the more classic way. Before achieving his bliss, the *yogi* hears in his heart or throat or some other part of the body various sounds, such as the rolling of a drum, the roaring of the sea, the tolling of a bell, the hum of a bee or the singing of a lyre. These sounds are given tremendous, "cosmic" significance.

When the *yogi* earnestly perseveres in the correct method, so we are told, he can both heal his body and employ marvelous powers such as making himself in-finitely small or invisible, swelling to an immense size so as to touch the moon with the tip of his fingers, or trans-porting himself anywhere by a simple act of will. His mind is so concentrated and intense that he can see through walls or read the minds of other men. He can look into the past or future, and hold converse with de-parted spirits. Yet we are told that *the true yogi never uses these powers:* they are mere distracting handicaps to his escape from the world and the attainment of heavenly peace. As the snake sheds its skin, so does the soul shed its body, and rest in the bliss of Brahman.

Such is the outcome of Sankara's message to the faith-ful, to the orthodox sects he represents. Here his authority is intuition based on scripture. But his message to the heretical sects he opposes, such as Buddhism and the Sankhya position, must be couched in different terms and rely on a different authority. Since these sects do not accept the Vedanta revelation, he must convince them by reason alone—he must meet them on the plane of the "lower" knowledge where they dwell.

(1) When the Buddhists, for example, deny the sub-stantial self maintained by the Vedanta, Sankara must prove the substantial self exists. But how can he? How

can anyone know the self exists, when knowledge (according to the common, traditional belief) is the apprehension of an *object*, and the self is not an object at all, but only the subject? Says Yajnavalkya, the knower cannot know *itself*. Sankara himself raises this question, and replies that the subject is a necessary *presupposition* of all knowledge.

It cannot be denied, for of that very person who might deny it, it is the Self.[12]

Moreover, the Self, or God, is known intuitively.

The existence of Brahman is known on the ground of its being the Self of everyone. For everyone is conscious of the existence of his Self, and never thinks "I am not." If the existence of the Self were not known, everyone would think "I am not." And this Self is Brahman.[13]

(2) Again, to convince the Sankhyas that the ultimate reality is intelligence or consciousness, Sankara proceeds to demonstrate that the efficient or material cause of the world is the Self, or Brahman. To show that Brahman is the efficient cause, he uses the argument for design.

A non-intelligent thing, which, without being guided by an intelligent being, spontaneously produces effects capable of subserving the purposes of some particular person, is nowhere observed in the world. We rather observe that houses, palaces, couches, pleasure grounds, and the like—things which according to the circumstances are conducive to the attainment of pleasure or the avoidance of pain—are made by workmen endowed with intelligence. Now look at this entire world . . . of which the most ingenious workmen cannot even form a conception in their minds, and then say if a non-intelligent principle is able to fashion it![14]

To show that Brahman is the material cause, he uses the argument from causality.

With regard to ether and air, the possibility of an origin has been shown. But in Brahman's case there is no such possibility; hence the cases are not parallel. Nor does the fact of other effects springing from effects imply that Brahman also must be an effect; for the non-admission of a fundamental causal substance would drive us to a *regressus in infinitum*. And that fundamental causal substance which as a matter of fact is generally acknowledged to exist, just that is our Brahman.[15]

The relation of God to the world is defined more precisely in terms of substance and modes.

The omniscient Lord of all is the cause of the origin of this world in the same way as clay is the material cause of jars and gold of golden ornaments. . . .[16]

In both these arguments, Sankara develops the genuinely monistic strand of the *Upanishads* into a kind of theism. The Self, or God, is not distinct from the world (as in the dominant dualism), but its very substance or being. This is the "lower" God, known by the "lower" knowledge. Here there is no basis for acosmism: God creates the world out of Himself with careful purpose. Again, it is the *individual,* living in the strife and change of the *world* that is "conscious of the existence of his Self," and never thinks "I am not." This means that the ordinary man knows his Self, or God, without all the paraphernalia of renunciation and steps in meditation. As a matter of fact, when Sankara relies on reason, he is a monistic theist, but when he takes refuge in revelation, he is an acosmistic pantheist. And this he is fundamentally, for as a defender of that particular faith known as Hinduism, he must take its scripture as final authority, and relegate reason to the comparative unreality of the "lower" knowledge.

4. RAMANUJA VEDANTA

As Sankara in the ninth century fulfils the teachings of the Upanishadic sage Yajnavalkya, so does Ramanuja in the eleventh century fulfill the teachings of the *Svetasvatara Upanishad* and the *Bhagavad Gita.* And as Sankara was influenced by Buddhism, Ramanuja was influenced by the Alvars, or Visnuite saints, whose Tamil hymns of "loving-devotion" had voiced the aspirations of the masses that worshiped the god Visnu. So sings Yamunacarya, the spiritual grandfather of Ramanuja:

> Oh, fie on me, foul shameless wanton brute
>   Craving the rank of servantship to Thee,
> Which lieth far, O God! beyond the chief
>   Of saintliest souls, Brahman or Mahadeo!
>
> * * *
>
> Lord Madhva, whatever mine may be,
>   Whatever I, is all and wholly Thine.
> What offering can I bring, whose wakened soul
>   Seeth all Being bound to Thee for aye? [17]

Like the *Svetasvatara Upanishad*,[18] these hymns express a sharp difference between God and the individual soul, as well as between God and the world. Finally, just as Sankara's chief opponent was the *Sankhya,* Ramanuja's chief opponent was Sankara himself. Although Ramanuja also became a *sannyasi,* and toured South India preaching release, he was always a champion of the Visnu cult of divine grace which stressed the distinction between devotee and Lord. Early in life, so runs the legend, the will of God came to him in this verse:

> I am the supreme reality. My view is *distinction.* Self-surrender is the unfailing cause of salvation, individual effort not being essential. Release will come in the end. . . .[19]

While both Sankara and Ramanuja are Vedantins, Ramanuja is more moderate than Sankara. He does not perfect a device[20] to divide revelation into "lower" and "higher," but labors to harmonize all teachings in one doctrine. Rather than stand forth as an independent thinker, he follows a long tradition of Vedantic expositors. He agrees that salvation is release from *karma* and rebirth, and that release comes through knowledge, but he takes knowledge as meditation on the supreme, loving Person.[21]

Such knowledge is really *bhakti,* or "loving-devotion," in response to which God graciously reveals Himself, and so rewards the devotee. As the *Bhagavad Gita* says,

> To those who are constantly devoted and worship with loving-devotion I give that knowledge by which they reach me.[22]

Since this devotion can be cultivated only by certain definite duties and ceremonies,[23] Ramanuja, unlike Sankara, makes good works integral to the knowledge of God.

While God is the one and only reality, the basis of the origination, subsistence and reabsorption of the world, He is also a loving Person. Although Ramanuja was not original in treating ultimate reality as personal, he was indeed the first Hindu thinker to define a person clearly in common sense terms as one who has the power to realize his purposes. God alone is unconditionally a person, since He alone has complete power to realize His purposes. Man has only a limited amount of this power, and so is only conditionally a person.

Following his favorite *Upanishad,* the *Svetasvatara,* Ramanuja insists that Nature (*prakriti*) and individual souls (*jivas*) are substances in themselves. Souls are one with God not in *being,* but in *kind.* Individual souls are divine in nature, but are separate and distinct from the universal Soul. They are atomic; it is infinite. It creates; they only enjoy. Yet Ramanuja wants to keep monism. So he calls individuals "modes of God" in the sense that they come under his personal control. Accordingly they are members of the body of which God is the Soul.[24]

> Any substance which a sentient soul is capable of completely controlling and supporting for its own purposes, and which stands to the soul in an entirely subordinate relation, is the body of that soul. . . . In this sense, then, all sentient and non-sentient beings together constitute the body of the Supreme Person, for they are completely controlled and supported by Him for His own ends, and are absolutely subject to Him.[25]

Thus Ramanuja, like Sankara, wants to make God both the material and the efficient cause of the world. But to Ramanuja, God is also the final cause. To Sankara, the creation of the world is God's playful illusion, utterly devoid of purpose; and *karma,* or work, has no integral connection with release from rebirth. But to Ramanuja, God creates all beings in order that as a *reward* for their good works in the world, individual souls may enjoy eternal divine communion.

While Ramanuja thus sees God in every way the cause of the world, he is yet careful to keep God free from the world and its evil. God is in the world but not of it. He is embodied, but not subject to the actions of the body, to the good and evil deeds of the world. He creates with purpose, to be sure, but only in play or sport, unattached to results. God never *completely* absorbs the world, he tells us: the world becomes subtle and gross in endless cycles, but remains ever distinct from God. How can the impure reveal the Pure? God has really two forms: a worldly form distinct from Him, and a heavenly body of His very own, which from time to time He incarnates, or thrusts into His worldly body, for the sake of His devotees.[26]

With the aid of these incarnations, the soul finally achieves communion with its Maker. Not the bliss of union, but the love of communion. However high the soul may rise, there will always be an "other" for it to cherish and adore. And since God is really separate and aloof from the world, the soul that would love Him eternally must also be separate from the world. For Ramanuja there is no *jivanmukti,* no release in this life. The soul attains God only after exhausting all *karma* and casting off the body entirely.

While Sankara and Ramanuja thus differ in emphasis, they are yet alike in the main structure of their thinking, which is a dualism between God and the world. To be sure, they both get a spurious monism, Sankara by treating the world as unreal, and Ramanuja by linking it with God through God's power, but their basis remains dualistic. These two dogmatic philosophers or theologians—India's best—are like two artists painting the landscape of the *Upanishads*. Ramanuja brings into prominence the broad green and red of "work" and "loving-devotion," Sankara suffuses the canvas with the white and yellow of "knowledge" and "meditation," but the outline and figures are the same.

Both proclaim the monistic doctrine of substance and modes, but fail to maintain it in its purity to the end. Sankara virtually consigns it to the limbo of false knowledge, while Ramanuja vetoes it by calling God separate from the world. As a matter of fact, both thinkers are loyal to two dogmas. The first dogma is the "wheel of life," which demands that salvation be conceived as release from the world. The second dogma is the final authority of scripture, which imposes the difficult task of reconciling its contradictory doctrines of monism and dualism.

These two dogmas, developed by a priestly caste aloof from science and industry in a land of glorious culture, yet inured to invasion, hardship and despotic rule, compose the framework of the Hindu religious tradition inherited by the modern Hindu. This does not mean that his religion is limited to his Hindu heritage. Life is more than logic, and present religion more than a summary of past dogma. In practice, the modern Hindu may be strongly influenced by Western ideas. Yet the clearest way to trace the direction of a religious movement is to understand its definite past positions. We are now ready to study the more immediate source of the American "Vedanta" movement in Ramakrishna, the brilliant, illiterate, naked saint of Bengal.

CHAPTER III

SAINT RAMAKRISHNA, A CHILD OF
MOTHER KALI

The first Hindu cult in America was founded by Vivekananda in New York in 1894, and Vivekananda's inspiration came from Ramakrishna, a modest saint who never left India. The Hindu heritage did not come to Ramakrishna in books, for he was ignorant of both Sanskrit and English as well as the higher literature of his native speech, Bengali. He was just a country lad, simple and singleminded. But his perfect piety and perfect artistry, coupled with his contact with devotees of most of the Hindu sects, made him virtually an epitome of Hindu orthodoxy, plus a dash of tender love. In the words of "Mahatma" Gandhi,

The story of Ramakrishna Paramahansa's[1] life is a story of religion in practice. . . . His sayings are . . . revelations of his own experience. . . . In this age of scepticism Ramakrishna presents an example of a bright and living faith which gives solace to thousands of men and women who would otherwise have remained without spiritual light. His love knew no limits. . . .[2]

The life of Ramakrishna may be divided into five periods, each with its own distinct character.

(1) From his birth in Kamarpukur, Bengal, in 1836[3] till he reached the age of seventeen, he lived the happy, carefree life of a talented village boy.

(2) From his arrival in Calcutta in his seventeenth year until his twenty-third year, he assisted his brother Ram Kumar as a household and temple priest, and developed a passionate worship for the goddess Kali.

(3) From his twenty-third until his thirty-fifth year, a period of twelve years, he strove with the utmost intensity and rigor to gain visions of Kali and other Hindu divinities.

(4) From the time he fulfilled this desire and attained mental peace at the age of thirty-five, until his thirty-ninth year, he experimented with various religious ideals, including Islam and Christianity.

(5) From 1875, when at the age of thirty-nine he met Keshab Chandra Sen, the leader of the Brahma Samaj, until his death in 1886 at the age of fifty, he devoted most of his time to teaching his many disciples. A section will now be devoted to each period.

1. THE VILLAGE PET

Our hero made a wise choice of parents. Although his Brahman forebears, named Chatterji, were poor in this world's goods, they were honest and generous. Their small village was far from the nearest city, yet on the road to the holy Puri, where Saint Sankara had founded his eastern monastery. The family had its idol, and the village had one too. The child was marked for religion.

According to the story, his father's[4] function in conception was fulfilled by both Visnu and Siva, the gods of the two great Hindu sects. While the father Khudiram was lodging in sacred Gaya[5] whence he had gone to offer barley balls to his ancestors,[6] he dreamed he was in the temple of Visnu beholding a luminous God enthroned, who spoke to him sweetly as follows:

I am well pleased at your sincere devotion. I am born again and again to chastise the wicked and protect the virtuous.[7] This time I shall be born in your cottage and accept you as my father.

While Khudiram was thus off in Gaya, his wife Chandra Devi, back in Kamarpukur, was also beholding a strange vision. One day, standing with her friend Dhani, a woman blacksmith, before the Siva temple next to her house, "she saw a flood of celestial light issue from the Lord Siva and dart towards her." As the light entered her body, we are told, she fell down senseless. On regaining consciousness, she felt as if she were with child. In similar manner, so runs tradition, were the classic Hindu incarnations conceived: Rama, Krishna, Buddha, as also Sankaracarya.

After the child was born, it is supposed to have slipped into an oven, and lain there without a cry, half covered with ashes. Perhaps this foretold a life of renunciation. The father rejected the "proper" zodiacal name, and called his son Gadadhar, one of the names of Visnu. Gadadhar Chatterji became Ramakrishna at the age of thirty-five when he passed through his initiation into *sannyasa,* and became a *swami.*

The child grew to be a village favorite. When about six years old, he fell into his first trance at the unspeakable joy of seeing a flock of white cranes fly across a dark mass of wind-swept clouds. Later on, the death of his father convinced him of the impermanence and futility of the world. Already the seeds of Sankara's renunciation and rapture! He associated with Sankara's *sannyasis,* or with *sadhus* like them, and began to imitate their ways. Like Sankara, he was a prodigy of Hindu lore, solving a scriptural problem for the learned *pandits* at the tender age of ten. Playing truant with the village lads in good old Krishna style, he taught them amateur religious drama.

Once while impersonating the God Siva in a village play, the character so filled his mind that he rose to ecstasy, and had to be carried off the stage. Owing to his amazing memory and fondness for acting, his mind became saturated with the stories of Hindu gods and heroes. He often imagined himself a *gopi,* or milkmaid, sporting with the divine young cowherd Krishna, and impersonated a woman so well as to deceive everybody. Both men and women enjoyed his graceful dancing, his clever merriment and jest. He enjoyed modelling images of the gods, and became an expert in this line. But in all his play he felt a sense of mission, and resigned himself to Rama, his household god.

2. THE YOUNG PRIEST

At the age of seventeen, Gadadhar joined his eldest brother Pandit Ram Kumar in Calcutta, and helped him perform his priestly duties. But he did not share his brother's concern for the family income, and stubbornly refused to attend school. "What shall I do with a mere bread-winning education?" he demanded, "I would rather acquire that wisdom which will illumine my heart, and getting which, one is satisfied forever." [8] True to his Hindu heritage and emotional temper, the boy wanted to fly the world. To prevent just such immature renunciation and social loss, the great lawgiver Manu had laid down the four stages of life, in which renunciation comes only after a man is old and grey and has already performed his social labors. But the youth Gadadhar had many a striking precedent in such saints as Gautama and Sankara.

Two years later a wealthy Bengali lady named *Rani* Rasmani opened a palatial temple for the goddess Kali on the Hugli River at Daksinesvara, four miles north of Calcutta, and appointed Ram Kumar as chief priest. For all her wealth, the Rani was only a Sudra, or member of the lowest order of Hindu society, and so Gadadhar, like the pious Brahman he was, protested against this service of a low-caste woman. But he finally yielded to a decision by lot. Even then he refused to eat within the temple walls until his brother told him that no place on the banks of the sacred Ganges could remain "unclean."

Mathur Nath Biswas, the Rani's son-in-law and agent, fascinated by the artistic temper of Gadadhar, favored him with the request to assist his brother in the temple service. The youth consented only on condition that his nephew Hriday (who was about his own age) assume the burden of the work and responsibility. Gadadhar himself then took charge of the dressing and decorating of the image of Kali.

All through his life, Sri Ramakrishna showed an utter disgust for service of any kind. Conquest of the cravings of flesh, and renunciation of wealth were, in his opinion, the *sine qua non* of divine realization. . . . To engage one's mind to serve another is to divert a part of one's attention from the contemplation of God. . . . Besides, Sri Ramakrishna would often say that to accept service was to demean oneself. . . .[9]

The pious boy now had free rein to indulge in devotion, and he spent four precious years worshiping his mother Kali. This goddess, it seems, was originally a blood-thirsty female demon of an aboriginal tribe. But the Brahmans took her into the Hindu pantheon by making her the consort of Siva, who in his different aspects is the great ascetic, the eternal creator, the patron of outlaws, and the wild carouser. Kali is his *sakti,* or outpouring energy; she it is that makes him "dance." She is the mother of the universe, half humane, half terrible. Her image stands in the Temple of Daksinesvara.

The Mother wears a gorgeous Benares cloth, and is decorated with ornaments from head to foot. From Her neck hangs a garland of skulls and round Her waist is a girdle of human arms—made of gold. In Her lower left arm She holds a decapitated human head, also made of gold, and in the upper a sword. With Her lower right arm She is offering boons to Her devotees and with the upper one She says, Fear not! The skulls and the sword represent Her terrible side, and Her right arms offering boons and fearlessness bring out Her benignant side. She is both terrible and sweet—just like Nature alternately destroying and creating.[10]

This is the Mother with whom our hero would eat and drink, talk and sing by the hour, till he became unconscious of the world. In spite of Gadadhar's further adventures in religion, it seems that this goddess Kali remained as the dominant influence in his life. At a later time, his favorite disciple Vivekananda probably felt the same loyalty. In times of crisis, both would turn to this "Mother of the Universe" for comfort and guidance. And in so far as both Hindu teachers were affected by the worship of this principle, at once terrible and humane, they would not be likely to spend much effort in making their environment more humane and less terrible. In other words, any moral effort would tend to be sporadic and confused.

In the state of devoted ecstasy to Kali, the boy priest would pass into that form of trance known as the classic *samadhi,* or union with the divine, according to the *yoga* practice based on Sankara's teaching. His body would become rigid, his pulse and heart beat imperceptible. Moreover, we are told that he had the power of inducing such a state in another at any time by means of a single touch. While uttering the various *mantras,* or sacred chants, he could "see and feel" those things that most priests can only "imagine."

Thus while chanting the mystic syllable *rang* which directed the priest to conceive a wall of fire around him, Sri Ramakrishna really felt himself in the midst of a circle of fire guarding himself and the place of worship from all evil influences. Again he could actually feel the mystic power called Kundalini or the "coiled up," rushing up from its place of rest at the lower extremity of the spinal column along the channel of Sushumna to what the Yogis call Sahasrara, or the thousand petalled lotus in the brain. He really visualized it passing through the six centres of the body in the spinal column. As it struck the "lotuses" of those centres, the hanging buds were turned into erect, full blown flowers.[11]

This ceremony of the *Kundalini* is described in the *Tantras*, or devotional manuals compiled from many sources some time before Sankara, and used chiefly by the Sakta cult of the Sivaite sect.

At the death of his elder brother the priest, the boy went nearly mad with grief, and spent all his time praying to get a vision of the Mother. If She is really my Mother, he said to himself, She will come to me. But for a long time She did not come. Just as he was about to kill himself with a ceremonial sword, the vision came: he plunged into an ocean of otherworldly consciousness whose shining billows kept rushing at him with a terrible noise, eager to swallow him up. After this he gained repeated visions both in trance and waking life. . . . He lost his individual impulses, and felt himself completely at the mercy of an outside impetuous force. Like other ecstatics who have wished to shirk service, he felt absolutely unable to perform his sacred duties. Mathur Nath, acting for the temple owner, allowed this strange worship to continue, while the faithful Hriday took over all the work.

Now that the youthful visionary had seen Mother Kali by following *bhakti*, or the path of loving-devotion, he craved to follow the same path to get a vision of Rama, the dutiful son and the hero-god of the great epic *Ramayana*. Caring nothing for the fact that Kali is worshiped by the Sivaites but Rama by the Visnuites, the boy applied the same method to each—the method of tears and unearthly yearning. From among the five *bhakti* relations between devotee and "Chosen Ideal," he now selected the relation of servant to master, called *dasya*, or service, and pictured himself as Hanuman, the monkey-god servant of Rama.

By a constant meditation on the glorious character of Hanuman [he recalls] I totally forgot my personal identity. My daily life and style of food now strangely resembled those of Hanuman.

I did not feign them, but they naturally came to me. I tied my cloth round the waist, hanging a portion of it in the form of a tail, and jumped from place to place instead of walking. I lived on fruits and nuts only, and these too I preferred to eat without peeling the skin. I passed most of the time on trees, and in a solemn voice used to call out, "Raghubir!" [a name for Rama]. My eyes too looked restless like those of a monkey, and what was most wonderful, I had an enlargement of the Coccyx by about an inch. It gradually resumed its former size after that phase of the mind had passed away on the completion of the course of discipline. In short, everything about me was more like that of a monkey than a human being.[12]

During this period of *sadhana*, or "realization," the boy's health decayed. From time to time he suffered severe burning sensations over his skin, for which he knew no remedy. But one day a vision gave him relief from a six months' siege. A red-eyed black man, the "man of sin," came out of his body, reeling as if dead drunk. Soon after, there emerged a saintly ascetic of placid mien, wearing the saffron robe, who killed the black man with his trident. Alarmed at Gadahar's condition, his mother and brothers now took him home, and tried to cure him of his premature otherworldliness by marrying him off. The eccentric youth yielded to the usual marriage ceremony, but not to the usual marriage relation. His wife, who happened to be a child of five,[13] returned to her father's home, and never lived with her husband as a sex mate, although she came to him later as a disciple and clung to him loyally till the end. Since he would regard her only as his mother, she came to be called the Holy Mother.

3. The Mad Saint

On his return to Daksinesvara, our hero was again seized with devotional madness. By again neglecting his duties he lost his position altogether, and betook himself to a nearby wood. Twelve years he spent in tempestuous meditation, and for the first six years, we are told, he got no sleep. His one fixed idea was to get rid of lust and wealth, so as to gain the power of beholding Mother Kali at will. After many weary years, the first person to understand him was a Brahmani nun, or *sannyasini*, who came and resided for some time in the temple. She had given up home and name, and was known only as "Bhairavi Brahmani," that is, a Brahman woman who worships the "Bhairavi," or "Fearful One," who is Siva. Out of her vast mental storehouse of sacred lore she drew a cure for his madness. "The people are right," she told him in effect, "You are indeed mad. But mad after God. It was the same with Chaitanya.[14] You are both incarnations of God!"

She cured the burning of his skin with an application of sandalwood paste. A mother-and-son worship soon sprang up between them that relieved all his tension and trouble. Then she instructed him in *yoga*, that discipline of posture, breathing and attention aiming at "superconscious" detachment from the world. She also put him through the paces of the *Tantras*, those old manuals written for the worship of Kali by the Saktist cult. The main idea of this worship, we are told,[15] is to induce the struggling soul to look on all sense-objects as visible representations of the Lord, so that the soul's undue attachment to these things may be curbed. The common practice was to indulge in wine and women with the utmost abandon. But the saintly Gadadhar, so his admirers declare, introduced an element of purity all his own, and passed through all tests unscathed. When he beheld a woman of the streets, she would only remind him of the "Divine Mother" in another form. Filthy words came to him only as a group of separate letters, each a symbol of God. Besides, after inspecting the degraded practices of the Vallabha cult of the Visnuite sect, our hero concluded that a man may be engaged in some reprehensible form of *sadhana* or "realization," and yet progress spiritually and ultimately attain the goal if only he is sincere.[16] Thus, acording to this Hindu teacher, the only moral distinction in life is between sincerity and insincerity, between tears and no tears!

Such things he learned from his Brahmani. But her greatest contribution to his cause was the open and valiant proclamation that he was an *avatara* or incarnation of God. This claim was later tested and verified by two famous Hindu pandits who saw in his mind and body the marks of divinity according to Hindu canons. From henceforth he was no longer the mad Gadadhar, but the incarnate Lord Visnu. And as such, his fame was spread abroad by hosts of visiting mendicant monks and strolling devotees. After the Bhairavi Brahmani helped her spiritual son with all she knew, she departed from his sight forever. But the son was still dissatisfied. He had not sucked enough milk from her spiritual breasts. He yearned for higher knowledge.

As if in response to his longing, the "naked one" wandered in—a tall, strong ascetic named Totapuri, who used a sacred fire but no clothing. After forty years of forest meditation, he had at last experienced God according to the "non-dualistic" Vedanta ideal of Sankara.

Said Totapuri to the Lord Visnu incarnate, "You seem to be an advanced seeker after truth. Would you like to learn Vedanta?"

"I don't know," was the reply, "It all depends on my Mother."

"All right," said the naked friar, "go and ask your Mother."[17]

So the son went silently into the temple, and returned with Mother Kali's permission! Then the sage told his pupil that before commencing to learn Vedanta, he must have an intense desire for renunciation, he must be ini

tiated into the sacred order of *sannyasa*.[18] This demand,
of course, was just grist for Gadadhar's mill. Already he
had renounced all but a loin-cloth, and he came out of
the initiation with a loin-cloth plus a saffron robe. Moreover, he got a new name—Ramakrishna. Prostrating himself before his *guru* or sacred teacher, the novice sat down
to receive instructions.

"Brahman," began the master, "is the only Reality,
ever-pure, ever-illumined, ever-free, beyond the limits of
time, space, and causation. Though apparently divided by
names and forms through the inscrutable agency of Maya,
that enchantress which makes the impossible possible,
Brahman is really one and undivided. Because when a
seeker is merged in the beatitude of Samadhi, he does not
feel even a trace of time and space or name and form—the
products of Maya. Whatever is within the domain of
Maya is unreal,—leave it off. . . . Dive deep in the search
for Self and . . . you will realize your identity with
Brahman, the Existence - Knowledge - Bliss absolute."[19]
Then he urged his pupil to taste this bliss for himself by
plunging into *samadhi*, or devoted trance. The pupil
tried once and failed. For "the familiar, radiant form
of the Divine Mother intervened." Then he tried again
and succeeded. Three days and nights he sat motionless,
his body stiff, his face serene.

"Is it really true?" asked Totapuri in breathless wonder,
"Is it possible this man has achieved in a single day what
took me forty strenuous years?"[20]

He then aroused his precocious pupil by sounding a
holy *mantra* in his ear. Soon he departed from the temple,
for he had no more to teach. Indeed he himself received
instruction. Mother Kali, said Ramakrishna, is not an
illusion but real, the very *sakti*, or forth-going power of
Brahman.

When the Supreme Being is thought of as inactive—creating,
sustaining or destroying—I call Him *Brahman* or *Purusha*, the
Impersonal God. When I think of Him as active—creating, sus-

taining and destroying—I call Him *Shakti* or *Maya* or *Prakriti* or the Personal God. . . . The Impersonal and the Personal are one. . . . You can't conceive a gem without its lustre. Such is the relation between Brahman and the Divine Mother.[21]

When left alone, the new *sannyasi* attempted his new kind of trance. With what result? We are told that for six months he remained practically dead to the world, and came back to his senses only after a siege of dysentery that lasted another six months.

4. THE CULT TASTER

Ramakrishna now felt peace of mind and breadth of view. He had reached his God by many different paths: by worshiping Kali of the Shivaites, Rama of the Visnuites, and Brahman of the Vedantins; by practicing *yoga*, *bhakti* and *jnana*, all by the way of trance. But here came Govinda Rai, a Hindu convert of the Sufi, or ecstatic sect of Islam, the religion of the Muslims, or Muhammadans. "Is not Islam also a path to God?" asked the saint, "Let me try it!" So he got initiated by Govinda, wore Muslim clothing, and ate his food in Muslim style. The cooking, however, was done by a Brahman. He was willing to eat beef, the food no orthodox Hindu will taste, but refrained at the earnest entreaty of Mathur "Babu," the owner of the temple. Says Ramakrishna:

I used to repeat the name of Allah, wear my cloth in the fashion of the Muslims and recite the Namaz[22] regularly. All Hindu ideas being wholly banished from the mind, not only did I not salute the Hindu gods, but I had no inclination even for visiting them. After passing three days in that way, I realized the goal of that form of devotion.[23]

The goal he "realized" was the trance state. First he saw a radiant Person with a long beard and grave appearance, presumably Muhammad, and then his mind, passing through the realization of Brahman with attributes, was finally absorbed in Brahman without attributes. [24]

In like manner he tried Christianity. He read the Bible with his friend Sambhu Charan Mallik,[25] and loved to look at the picture of the Madonna and Child in the home of his friend Jadu Nath Mallik. The picture, we are told, overwhelmed his Hindu ideas and evoked a deep love for Christ. As in his trial of Islam, he fell into a trance after three days, and saw a vision. Beholding a divine-looking man with beautiful large eyes, he said to himself,

This is the Christ who poured out his heart's blood for the redemption of mankind and suffered a sea of agony for their sake. It is none other than the Master-Yogin in eternal union with Godhead—Jesus, the embodiment of Love![26]

Then he felt Jesus enter his soul. Plunging into a trance, he realized his union with the Brahman *with* attributes. Thus was he convinced that Jesus Christ was an incarnation of the Lord.

He also sympathized with the ideals of the Buddhists, Jains and Sikhs. On account of this wide range of spiritual interest, and the speed with which he supposedly absorbed the various ideals as they were presented to him, he came to regard himself as a divine incarnation whose achievements were for the sake of others. His was the "Bodhisattva" ideal without the usual service. Hence, while he lived in union with God, and was free from all worldly desire, he was not free from the world itself: he would be born again and again to free others from the world until all were free.

Since he had experienced ecstatic bliss by way of his ideals of several religions or cults, he concluded all religions were true. Each system of doctrines, he believed, was a different path to the same God. And the three great systems of Hindu theology known as Madhava's dualism (*dvaita*), Ramanuja's "modified non-dualism" (*visistadvaita*) and Sankara's "non-dualism" (*advaita*), are but three stages in man's progress towards the divine goal. Dualism, he believed, with its matter, music and idols, fits the ordinary man; "modified non-dualism," with its systematic range of thought, is for the man of intellect; but final "non-dualism," with its transcendence of all distinctions, is best for the saint.

The *advaita* is the last word about Realization. . . . A man who has got absolute purity of mind naturally goes beyond action. He cannot work even if he tries to, or, the Lord does not allow him to work.

5. THE PREACHER

In 1875 Ramakrishna met Keshab Chandra Sen, the leader of the Brahma Samaj, that Hindu-Christian reform society. The two men fell in love with each other. The simple saint was so struck with the modern leader's breadth and sincerity, that he told him he could enjoy divine bliss in spite of his interest in the world. And for all his modernism, Keshab's Hindu heart so glowed with reverence for one who had fully realized the Hindu ideal, that he followed him as his *guru* or sacred teacher. An act of world-wide importance. Just as the Bhairavi Brahmani introduced our hero to Bengali Hindus, Keshab introduced him to English-speaking people in general. He welcomed him to the meetings of the Brahma Samaj, and published his fame abroad by conversations, speeches and writings.

Gripped by the saint's simple notion that all religions are equally true, Keshab announced himself as the divinely appointed leader of the "New Dispensation" in which all religions are one. But Keshad did not follow his *guru* completely. The tolerant Hindu allowed everyone to follow his own religion without disturbing him in the least. Keshab, on the other hand, true to his critical Western training, set up one composite religion, apparently centering in the supremacy of Christ as the God-man. Yet he still clung to his master's Hindu view that religious ways are indifferent. "Our position," he says, "is not that truths are to be found in all religions; but that all the established religions of the world are true."[27]

While Ramakrishna thus modified the character of Keshab's endeavor, Keshab in return directed the flow of Ramakrishna's teaching into a new channel. Aroused by the reformer's interest in the saint of Daksinesvara, educated men from Calcutta began to go up the river to see him. And it was mostly from this company that the affectionate saint selected his little group of disciples that later preached his ideals to the world. For seven years, until his death in 1886, the new world-teacher talked almost incessantly. All his life he wrote nothing, never having learned, but his disciples took down his sayings as they fell from his lips. Let us join the circle and hear the words of the master.

Like unto a miser that longeth after gold, let thy heart pant after Him.[28]

What is the strength of a devotee? He is a child of God, and tears are his greatest strength.

Knowledge and Love of God are ultimately one and the same. There is no difference between pure knowledge and pure love.

A true devotee who has drunk deep of the Divine Love is like a veritable drunkard, and cannot always observe the rules of propriety.

The soul enchained is "man" (Jiva) and free from chains is "God" (Shiva).

At one time I am clothed, at another naked, so Brahman is at one time with attributes, and at another time without.

Maya may be compared to a snake that is active and moving, while Brahman is like the snake absolutely still. . . .

As one and the same material, water, is called differently by different peoples . . . so the one Sat-chit-ananda, the Everlasting-Intelligent-Bliss, is invoked by some as God, by some as Allah, by some as Jehovah, by some as Hari, and by others as Brahman.

Every man should follow his own religion. A Christian

should follow Christianity, a Mahomedan should follow Maho-
medanism, and so on. For the Hindus, the ancient path, the
path of the Aryan *Rishis* is the best.

A truly religious man should think that other religions also
are paths leading to truth. We should always maintain an attitude of respect towards other religions.

The disciple should never criticize his Guru. He must im-
plicitly obey whatever the Guru says. . . . In the words of a Bengali couplet,

> "Through my Guru may visit tavern and still,
> My Guru is holy Rai Nityanand still."

And so he speaks on and on to the increasing crowds
of men and women that come to see him at the Temple
of Daksinesvara. As a result of this incessant labor, he
began to suffer from "clergyman's sore throat," which
later developed into cancer. He was taken to Calcutta
by his loving disciples, and attended by the best physicians, who were men of Western training. They advised
him to keep the strictest silence. But his childish, affectionate heart was wrung by the needs of his followers,
and so he spoke on and on. Even when his throat almost
closed against liquid food, he continued his efforts with
dauntless cheer till he passed into his last long *samadhi*,
from which he never returned.

6. A Little Child Shall Lead Them

As we ponder this amazing man, we are at once struck
by his utter sincerity. To the best of his ability he practiced what he preached. Of course, he could not practice
renunciation completely. While he scorned the body and
its needs, he trusted himself to physicians, whose life work
is the body's care. While he worked up such a hatred
of money that he would convulse at the touch of a coin,
he was yet very pleased with the food and sweets his
disciples got for money—and at his own request! While

he never grew tired of berating sex, his favorite religious cry was, Mother! And while he was praised as master of the art of attaining tranquillity, he would often worry and fret like a child, and pester his friends without mercy. Yet he acted in all faith and sincerity.

The fact is, he was not a man of intellect, but a man of emotion. This is the key to his mesage. At the dawn of his life, his fond parents allowed their winsome boy to pursue his smiling, wayward course, undisciplined and unchecked by the stern demands of the world. Thus he grew up to be a kind of artist, but no kind of scientist. He was an imitator, an impersonator, a man of penetrating appreciation, a perfect instrument for any ideal or character. With equal ease, he could play mother or child, mistress or monkey. He would not *strive* to absorb the ideal, but fall a victim to seizure or "possession."

In temper or behavior he could be either male or female, but he always remained a child. When he left his own mother, he worshiped the Mother Kali. When she proved too elusive to give him peace, he found relief in the lap of the beautiful Brahmani, his adopted mother. After her departure he took his own wife as his mother, and prospered famously under her maternal care. He never really grew up, but remained in a state of "mother-fixation."

Child that he was, he felt no sense of responsibility. He shuddered at the prospect of managing an estate, and even balked at his moderate priestly duties. He would rather use a soiled coverlet on his bed than take the trouble to get a clean one. He was unable to plan ahead, and loathed manual service of any kind. He failed to see any social problem. Passing a group of hungry villagers one day, he had his rich disciples feed them, and then went his way serene and satisfied that all was well with the world. In reply to the plea of a Brahma Samajist for the education and social liberation of women, our pious friend exclaimed: "Go thou fool, go and perish in the pit that your women will dig for you!"[29] He failed also to make moral distinctions. He worshiped prostitutes without teaching them, praised a degraded cult without improving it, and used obscene language without any shame. One day he alone ate all the lunch of a party of four without any apology but the remark, "I'm satisfied!" Another day he happened upon a group of winebibbers in a roadside tavern, and joyfully cheered them with cries of "Bravo! Excellent!"

Such a responsive and childlike mind was eminently fitted to absorb with simple piety every Hindu ideal that came along. In this way our saint became in turn a Sivaite, Visnuite and Advaitin, a follower of *yoga, bhakti* and *jnana,* in short, an epitome of Hindu devotion. He held all cults to be true, because each one seemed to lend itself to his familiar trance, which as a typical Hindu he regarded as the highest "realization" of God.

He could thus harmonize every Hindu cult with his simple logic of emotion because they were already in fundamental or structural accord. There is not an orthodox Hindu cult that does not regard the *world* as the result of an undesirable causal cycle, and *reality* as the realm of painless bliss. The highest good, then, is obviously some kind of escape from the world into bliss. Since the *advaita* or acosmistic pantheism of Sankara gives the simplest and most uncompromising presentation of this ideal, our simple and uncompromising devotee naturally gave this position first place in his esteem, and in his own unlettered way became a Vedantin.

Indeed, it is impossible to harmonize *advaita,* or acosmism, with other Hindu positions without giving it first place as the all-embracing whole of truth. For Sankara can explain all the other positions as true according to his "lower" knowledge of practical intellect, while his *advaita* rises above them in the "higher" knowledge of divine intuition. Thus in uniting Hindu positions, Ramakrishna was compelled to give first place to the teaching of Sankara.

This teaching he regarded as "truth," and all other Hindu and non-Hindu cults, including Islam and Christianity, as just "paths" to this truth. But this "truth" after all is only a part of the Hindu *Dharma* in general. It is the bliss of relief from the wheel of life, the freedom that follows law, the final stage of *Dharma,* or universal duty. Everyone has his cosmic caste, his position on the wheel of life, his *svadharma,* or individual duty. His place in society, determined by birth, is just an instance here and now of this *svadharma,* and fixes the kind of cult he needs to progress towards the "truth." Hence, every man should follow the cult into which he is born. Otherwise, he will sidestep his *dharma* and spoil his *karma.*

Now *Dharma,* according to the Hindu conception, is the absolute religion which includes both *karma,* or action, and "truth," or rest. In this one absolute religion there are many relative religions which help us in our progress towards the "truth." A relative religion may be called a *sampradaya*[30] or cult, a combination of *marga,* or path, with *mata,* or doctrine. When the Hindu saint says "every man should follow his own religion," for all are "paths leading to truth," he means by religion not *Dharma* of course, but *sampradaya.* He thinks of Sivaism and Visnuism, Islam and Christianity as distinct *sampradayas;* but as for *Dharma,* that is religion itself. Not for one moment does our pious provincial think of this *Dharma* as just Hinduism, one of the eleven living religions of the world, noted for its dogma of release from the wheel of life; to him, this *Dharma* is cosmic fact. The law of gravitation may be questioned, but not *Dharma!* To the pious Hindu,

Dharma is not a theory, an explanation, an interpretation, a dogma, a myth, a solution. It just *is*.

If *Dharma* is all in all, then Islam and Christianity are of course only special paths of Hinduism in general, like the various Hindu cults in particular. Hence it was quite in keeping with our saint's own duty to try out his trance on these other paths. He did so, and found that he could get visions of the Prophet and Christ as well as of Kali and Rama. Both Hindu and non-Hindu cults he harmonized on the basis of Hindu *Dharma*. But in this way he learned nothing radically new from Christianity and Islam, and always remained within the pale of conservative Hinduism. He ate his food in Muslim style, to be sure, but he employed a Brahman cook, and he never ate beef. He adored the picture of Jesus, but all his life he openly despised humble service.

As a matter of fact, the Hindu ecstatic never had the opportunity of getting these two great world religions at first hand. The man who "initiated" him into Islam belonged to the Sufi cult which is Hindu-like in some of its views, and besides, he was a convert from Hinduism. His "Christian" tutors had love and respect for Jesus, but were likewise Hindu at heart, and most probably Hindu by community. The Muslim Sufi and Christian mystic both treasure the visionary trance, but so does the Hindu Bhakta. In sum, Ramakrishna experienced Islam and Christianity only in so far as they coincided with conservative Hinduism.

Yet the Christian stress on love, service and sacrifice, together with the Buddhist "Bodhisattva" ideal, must have encouraged the simple, childlike affection that was his by nature and nurture. And this human affection was further developed by his friendship with Keshab Chandra Sen, that Hindu lover of Jesus Christ. It was Keshab's example that made him admit a man could know God while still in the world—a flat contradiction of Sankara, who said that the same man could not be in God and the world at the same time. And it was Keshab's enthusiasm that made him a teacher. Not by his own Hindu-minded investigation of Christianity, but by his contact with Christian culture did Ramakrishna come to place a certain Christian stress on Hinduism. Only when he began to teach did he begin to serve, and he served in this new way with utter self-sacrifice to the end. Only by his anxious parental love for his youthful disciples did he shake himself free from the Hindu notion that attachment to the world is bad, and lay stress on the immanence of God in man. It was this love that held those English-educated students who later spread his fame abroad in Western lands.

As a strict Hindu, Ramakrishna stands today as a protest against modern education, material prosperity and Western intolerance. But he is more than a strict Hindu. He is a child. And of such is the Kingdom of Heaven. Even the rigors of ancient Hindu practice could not deprive him of his simple, childlike love. This happy affection, so fresh in the morning of his life, so clouded over at noon by ascetic practice, bloomed forth in his life's evening glow with a fragrance his followers could never forget. Ramakrishna is now the inspiration of a world-wide cult that preaches love and service as well as renunciation and meditation.

CHAPTER IV

VIVEKANANDA, A CHAMPION OF MOTHER INDIA

1. THE AMBITIOUS YOUTH

Swami Vivekananda, who founded the Vedanta Society in America in 1894, was the favorite and foremost disciple of Saint Ramakrishna. His original name was Narendra Nath, meaning "Lord of Men," and his family the "lordly Dattas" from Simla, of the Kayastha caste, possibly of the Ksatriya, or warrior, order. His grandfather renounced the world soon after marriage. His one child, Visva Nath, became Narendra Nath's father, a wealthy lawyer of the Calcutta High Court, who lived as fitfully as the wind that blows. "He was always at odds with life," yet felt himself greater than the farce of it all. He took pride in his family, made himself a kingly and most surprising host, and lavished gifts on the poor. He sometimes read the Christian Bible and the Muslim poet Hafiz. His wife Bhuvanesvari was a queenly woman of power and reserve, who knew by heart whole passages from the old Hindu epics *Ramayana* and *Mahabharata*. She had two daughters, but like every Hindu mother, longed for a son!

Once for a whole day she meditated on the God Siva in His character of "Lord of monks." His form is white with ashes, His matted locks covered with the spread hood of the cobra of wisdom. About His loins He wears a tiger skin, while above His head shines effulgent the new crescent moon. In Him the worlds move, yet, unconscious of all, he meditates in silence sublime. But in the evening, so the story runs, Siva slipped from His meditation, and took form in the longing mother even as her own son.

Several months later, the boy was born—in Calcutta on January 12, 1863,[1] the day of the harvest festival of "Mother Ganges" the sacred river. The child grew up self-willed and turbulent. Often would he "tear the family peace into shreds." He was a frightful tease, and made the most horrible faces. His mother kept two nurses over him constantly, but in spite of this (or because of it) she often had to duck his head under cold water to get him back to normal. He conceived a special fondness for *sannyasis,* or *swamis,* and would often embarrass his family by giving the holy beggars whatever they wished. His nights were strange indeed. He could never get to sleep without first merging in the big ball of light that rolled towards him. He attended an old fashioned Indian school, and there became a wild gang-leader. With his astounding memory, he naturally imbibed an immense amount of Hindu lore. In his high school, called the Metropolitan Institution, he was always first in his class, both in studies and pranks.

In the University of Calcutta he kept up this record. At first he attended the Presidency College, the Government institution, but soon joined the "General Assembly's Institution," founded by the Scottish General Missionary Board, and now known as the Scottish Church's College.[2] In his studies he showed a keen interest in philosophy and mathematics. But he was also a voracious reader of all kinds of current literature, a sweet singer of Bengali lyrics, and a winner in the art of fencing with the *lathi,* or staff. His friends remember him as imperious and self-conscious, a lion among the students, and defiant in thought. He was vehement, vigorous, untiring, and—so we are told— always successful in argument and debate. His ambition was to be a great orating lawyer, with power and wealth and influence over men.

At that time, Keshab Chandra Sen, the Christ-loving leader of the Brahma Samaj, was the idol of young Calcutta. Under his spell Naren (short for Narendra Nath) felt the burden of caste and the ignorance of Indian women, and joined the progressive Samaj.[3] But he soon came to believe in a more conservative kind of reform, a gradual evolution by inner awakening. The idea of evolution was no doubt augmented by the works of Herbert Spencer, who was then "all the rage." So he joined also a movement of young Bengalis who desired the unity and education of the great Indian masses, irrespective of caste, race or creed.

One Sunday at a meeting of the Brahma Samaj, when our young hero was singing in the choir, the congregation was startled by the cry of "Naren!" and in the rear of the hall saw a stranger with only a cloth around his loins, and a pained expression on his face. Naren recognized Sri Ramakrishna, and hastened to meet him.

"My boy! My boy!" exclaimed the saint, "Why have you not come to see me? I have been waiting in anguish. . . ."[4]

As the two left the hall, the lad wondered why this brain-sick old man had made such a fuss in meeting. He had met him first when his uncle had taken him to Daksinesvara, and had since humored the saint by calling on him now and then, but scorned his *advaita* teaching as so much atheism.[5] But one day came a miracle. As the master was deep in a trance of love, his foot touched the boy, and he too went off into ecstasy, seeing nothing but "God." Even after he got home to Calcutta, he was unable to shake off his comatose state. The street cabs and himself seemed all of one stuff, and he nearly went under the horses' hoofs.

A CHAMPION OF MOTHER INDIA 67

After the miracle, a catastrophe. He had just passed his B. A. examination and entered law school, when he was overwhelmed by the news of his father's death. As with the young Gadadhar, this loss of a dear father made life seem more illusory. Besides, Naren's father had left his family very little money. From lordly comfort, his son was suddenly thrust into the direst poverty, and for years faced shame and starvation. Family disputes arose. While studying law, the would-be breadwinner went about looking for work. Day after day he would trudge over the hot streets with an empty stomach, but not even a loophole showed itself to his penetrating and anxious search. His heart sank. Bengal is fertile, but so are Bengalis. The country is overpopulated and many people undernourished. There is also an oversupply of university graduates. They have swarmed over India seeking clerical and educational posts, and still swarm into underpaid jobs in Calcutta. Naren was not the only "B. A." unemployed.

When the clouds were darkest, he fled from it all. Figuratively and liberally. He ran all the way to the Garden of Daksinesvara, and reached the master with torn garments, exhausted body and despairing mind. Prostrating himself before his *guru* he cried, "What shall I do? If you have power, then save me from this awful fate!"[6]

"Go, my boy," answered the saint, "Go to the temple there and pray to Mother! She will grant you whatever you ask!"

The boy obeyed. When he returned, his face was transfigured. Henceforth he would be a *swami!*

2. THE YOUNG SWAMI

Once more the flight from the world! Once more the conviction of "illusion" that has dogged Hindu thought from the time of the *Upanishads*. A brilliant, ambitious youth reduced to starvation by the blows of circumstance, and then—renunciation as the only alternative to crime or death or undignified labor. Renunciation, because the climate of India can support it. Renunciation, because of its now hoary sanction.

No wonder this youth forever after called this world a hell! He was not used to being crossed in purpose. Like Gadadhar, his early home life had been one of playful and innocent license. Like his father, he was proud and fiery. And so he rebelled.

Before him were the examples of his grandfather's renunciation, his father's scorn for the world, and the *swamis* he used to admire in childhood. And so he fled the world he could not conquer. Now at last he could appreciate the message of the master. His forsaken family? Oh, it managed somehow.

Owing to his talent and mystic temper, the young recluse soon became Ramakrishna's foremost pupil. And when common devoted service to their master in his mortal illness sealed the bonds of love among the disciples, Narendra Nath became the leader of the little band. While he surpassed his fellows in otherworldly emotion, his reason kept them fairly sane. The master encouraged all this. "Making Narendra Nath the fit instrument for the propagation of his ideas, [he] entrusted to him the charge of his flock."[7]

An inner circle was formed consisting of those who would renounce the world completely and live at the country house at Baranagar practising devotion. In the outer circle would work the supporting laymen, or "householders." Then the master initiated the youths of the inner circle as monks, and the foundation was laid for the future Ramakrishna Mission in India, and the Vedanta Society in America. The old saint then plunged into *samadhi* and passed on from this life, his hair standing on end, his gaze fixed on the tip of his nose.

Six of these sorrowing young swamis, weeping over the body of their beloved master in 1886, will go to preach to America: first Vivekananda (bliss of discrimination), whose name, as we know, was Naren; then Saradananda (bliss of wisdom), the former Sarat; Abhedananda (bliss of unity), the former Kali; Turiyananda (bliss of waking sleep), the former Hari; Trigunatita (transcendence of the three elements), the former Sarada; and Nirmalananda (bliss of purity), whose name was Subodh. But just now these boys are too bewildered to know what to do. Ecstasy mingles with pain. What nights they spend! Meditation, song, rapture and sorrow in turn fill their hearts. Sri Ramakrishna they treat as if still in the body.

One night Vivekananda and another swami, walking in silent meditation in the garden, suddenly beheld a Shining Figure before them. Was it the master? Both saw it at once. Yes, it must be he. Before the others could come at their call, the Figure had vanished! But in its stead an inner Presence lingered, radiating power and bliss. Verily the glorified Ramakrishna moved among them!

As they beheld their risen master even like the disciples of Jesus long ago, so also they had their Pentecost. In the quiet little village of Antpur, whither they had journeyed by bullock cart at the invitation of the mother of one of the boys, they gathered together in the open one starry evening before a raging big fire. They felt of one body, one mind and one soul, and all meditated on the master.

After a while their leader filled the silence with the story of the Lord Jesus he had heard in his college days. The young monks lived with Jesus in imagination, and

"adored Him even as they adored their own master."[8]
They saw His triumph and arrest, His sacrificial death
and glorious resurrection. "The Pentecostal fire of the
early Christians devoured their souls," and the names of
Christ and Ramakrishna resounded on the midnight air.
From this height of vision, Vivekananda charged his
brothers "to become *themselves* Christs, to aid in the redemption of the world." And standing there in the light
of the flames they took the vows of eternal *sannyasa* before
God and one another. The Order was now definitely
formed, the *matha,* or monastic order, of *gurubhais,* or
teaching brothers. And they suddenly remembered—it
was Christmas Eve!

Before retiring to the monastery at Baranagar, they all
went on a pilgrimage to the famous Temple of Tarakes-
vara Siva, where they worshiped the "Lord of monks."
At Baranagar again, life was ecstasy over-reaching ecstasy.
Often a *sankirtan,* or chorus, would begin in the morning
and go on till evening, everyone forgetting all thought of
food and rest. "In their burning desire for God-vision,
some one or another would think, as did Narendra, of
giving up the body in *prayopavesana,* that is, starving
oneself to death without rising from the meditation seat
if the Goal was not reached."[9] Yet they all did keep
body and soul together, and lived by chance begging.

What a strange mixture of Hindu asceticism and Christian service, each pulling against the other! At last something new under the sun? No, only primitive Buddhism
revived in India after a lapse of twenty-four hundred years.
Gautama, we recall,[10] preached both renunciation and
service, but never reconciled the two ideals, with the result that even today they divide the Buddhist world between them. And now we have to deal with another
compound or dual cult—the Ramakrishna Order. Even
its members admit this dualism.

The Ramakrishna Order . . . fulfils the dual mission of *"Siva and Seva";* or to put in another way, to the immemorial Hindu ideas of the life of meditation and pure and retiring monasticism, it has added the ideals of service and works of mercy; it also combines within it the dual ideal of personal freedom in the monastic order for the individual monk . . . with the principle of compact monastic brotherhood and organization as witnessed in the Western world.[11]

From their past Hindu heritage and present hard times, these Calcutta youths had welcomed the ideal of renunciation. From Ramakrishna's contact with the Christian Bible and Keshab Chandra Sen, from their own unusual menial service to their master, and from Vivekananda's career in a Christian college they imbibed the ideal of service. But they did not reconcile the two ideals in their thinking. They just added one to the other, and let them lie there side by side unarticulated and unexplained.

While Swami Vivekananda was convinced that "in India, the accumulated learning of the ages, divorced from the concrete value of the racial experience of the masses was meaninglessly abstract," he nevertheless held to this learning in the main. And while he believed the Gospels in so far as he understood them, he missed their main message, and would "vanquish" Christian missionaries "with a brilliance of logic all his own." He realized that India needed Christ to quicken her civilization, but on account of his national pride, he refused to surrender to Christ any fundamental Hindu doctrine. As might be supposed, the favorite book of the order was the *Bhagavad Gita.*

While some of the swamis remained socially at the monastery like Buddhist and Christian monks, others, in line with pure Hindu tradition, wandered nameless and alone over the length and breadth of their country, sometimes on pilgrimages to sacred shrines, sometimes to solitary retreats. Youth must be served: like most boys they had the wanderlust, and like the German Wandervögel of today, they enjoyed their freedom from the stuffy bourgeois air of the modern city. After living with the group for about four years, the leader himself broke from his brothers in 1891, and wandered alone for two years, sightseeing and brooding.

3. THE SON OF MOTHER INDIA

Finally the swami wended his way towards Madras, a center of orthodox learning and culture. On the way he met a high government official who invited him to his home in the city. The news spread abroad: "An English-speaking Sannyasin has come!" Such was our hero exactly. The English in him preached mass education, social equality and national reconstruction to his bigoted brothers, but as a *sannyasi,* he clung to the main message of old Mother India. He had heard vaguely of a World's Parliament of Religions to be held in Chicago, America, some time in the year 1893, and longed to preach to the West. By a counter-offensive he would defend his native land from ruthless foreign invasion. To his friends in Madras he exclaimed:

The time has come for the Hinduism of the Rishis to become dynamic. Shall we stand by whilst alien hands attempt to destroy the fortress of the Ancient Faith? . . . Shall we remain passive, or shall we become aggressive, as in the days of old, preaching unto the nations the glory of the *Dharma?* . . . In order to rise again, India must be strong and united, and must focus all its living forces. To bring this about is the meaning of my *sannyasa!*[12]

And his friends saw with him the imperative need of preaching the *Dharma* . . . . Said they, "It must be done, Swamiji, and you are the man to do it. You will work wonders." Thereupon they went forth to raise subscriptions for the cause. Soon they collected in rupees the value of about a hundred and fifty dollars. But the swami grew fearful, and gave the money away to the poor till he could learn the will of Mother Kali. He waited for "illumination."

In the meantime, friends of his Madras friends begged him to come to the city of Hyderabad, the capital of Hyderabad, the largest native state in India, and one ruled by a Muslim. A message was sent ahead, and when he arrived, he was surprised to find five hundred admirers at the station. In a similar way, the Vedanta Society was later propagated in America. To vast assemblies and to individuals of rank and wealth including the Nizam or Muslim prince himself, the son of Mother Kali spoke of his mission to the West. The money was raised from the upper and middle classes, and in a dream the Mother gave her consent through the master.

The Swami saw the figure of the Master walking from the seashore into the waters of the ocean, and beckoning him to follow him! He awoke. A great peace and joy filled his whole being; and his mind seemed to have been impressed with the authoritative word, "Go!" . . . All his doubts . . . were cleared away . . . All his nervousness left him.[13]

On the last day of May, in 1893, with Mother Kali above him and Mother India behind him, Vivekananda sailed from Bombay for the Pacific Ocean and America. He sailed by the fastest line, in the first-class cabin, equipped with plenty of money and costly silk robes and turbans of various colors. For he was no longer a humble, otherworldly ascetic, but the *guru* of a prince, and the spokesman of a nation.

In July this son of India arrived in Chicago just in time to enjoy the World's Columbian Exposition with its masterful monuments of Western science and industry, and by the end of twelve days he had spent most of his money. Ramakrishna the master would not touch money; Vivekananda the disciple could not keep it. He was robbed and cheated at every step. His hotel was one of the best. Moreover, he discovered to his dismay that the World's Parliament of Religions would not open until September. To cap the climax, he learned that he was not registered as a delegate, and that the time for registration was past! He wondered why he had been foolish enough to listen to those sentimental schoolboys of Madras who fondly imagined that their swami had only to appear in America to be given his chance. So in despair, he turned to Boston, a less expensive place, to Boston the Athens of America.

On the train he met a delightful lady who welcomed him to her home in Boston. In this city of tolerance and culture he was befriended by J. H. Wright, Professor of Greek in Harvard University, who sent him back to Chicago with money and influence. To his friend the chairman of the delegate committee he wrote, "Here is a man who is more learned than all of our learned professors put together."[14] Alas, our learned world teacher had little business about him! He lost his instructions, and had to spend his night of arrival in a big box in the railroad yard. But luck was with him, for at daybreak he began to beg along "millionaire's row" on Lake Shore Drive. Again he met a delightful lady, and all was well. American ladies and American reporters, each in their own way, made the handsome oriental famous.

4. THE ORIENTAL ORATOR

And now the great Parliament of Religions is holding its first meeting. A new era has dawned. For the first time in the history of the world, the various faiths meet on a public platform on equal footing and in a friendly atmosphere to discuss what service each can render, what contribution each can make. Our hero is seated on the platform (at last!) with learned celebrities from far and near. The chairman, Rev. John Henry Barrows, D.D., the organizer of the congress, asks him to speak.

"No, no, not now!" whispers the young man, abashed, "Let some one else speak." He has no notes or prepared address, and his Mother has given him no command. So the son sits dumb. Again and again he puts off his time to speak until at last, at five o'clock in the afternoon, the chairman rises and openly names Vivekananda as the next speaker. Mother or no Mother, he must speak now! In the magnificent hall he faces a yawning audience, worn out by masses of manuscripts. Confused hesitation. Then a beginning: "Sisters and Brothers of America. . . ."

At once the house shakes with deafening applause as in a political convention. The splendid oriental has spoken in such sweet friendship! Encouraged, the son of India goes on: "It fills my heart with joy unspeakable to rise in response to the warm and cordial welcome which you have given us. I thank you in the name of the most ancient order of monks in the world. I thank you in the name of the mother of religions, and I thank you in the name of the millions and millions of Hindu people of all classes and sects."[15]

In this first address, our speaker pleads for a tolerance that will accept all religions as true. "I belong to a religion," he cries, "into whose sacred language, the Sanskrit, the word exclusion is untranslatable. I am proud to belong to a nation which has sheltered the persecuted and the refugees of all religions and all nations of the earth." At a later meeting, in violation of the rules of the congress that no speaker should in any way reflect on others, he sneered at Christian missionaries for wanting to help Hindus by spiritual teaching. "If they want to help our people," he shouted, "why don't they send them something to save their starving bodies?"[16] Like his master,

Vivekananda was not a man of science, but a man of emotion.[17]

5. THE SOCIAL LION

Immense crowds flocked to hear the son of India, and the chairman wisely put him last on the program to hold the audience through the weary round of manuscript reading. Said an American newspaper, "This man, with his handsome face, magnificent personality and wonderful oratory, is the most prominent figure in the Parliament."[18] Everytime he was to speak, "ladies, ladies everywhere filled the great auditorium."[19] Before and after his appearance on the platform he was beset by hundreds of these charming persons who almost fought with each other as at a bargain counter, to get a chance to be near him and shake his hand.

Now why was he so popular, especially with the ladies? First, because of his superb bearing and attire. The princely raiment his rich friends lavished on him in India did not fail in its mission. We read in a newspaper of that time, "His finely poised head is crowned with either a lemon-colored or a red turban, and his cassock . . . belted in at the waist, and falling below the knees, alternates in a bright orange and rich crimson."[20] The social lion judiciously varied his costume. At another date, "he was attired in Oriental garb, consisting of a scarlet robe of soft cloth, which reached below the knees, bound round the waist with a crimson girdle. On his head was a turban of white silk which set off to advantage the swarthy complexion of his cleanly shaven face."[21]

Besides his dress, several causes contributed to our hero's popularity in America: his winsome personality, his Bengali fluency as a speaker, his command of English, his wise silence on some points, and his sincere reverence for Christ. Moreover, as a striking oriental, he excited curiosity, of which Americans have such an abundant supply. Any great novelty attracts attention. Crowds would flock to see a tatooed savage, stone hatchet in hand, going through a war dance. The princely swami—if we can still call him a swami—was the first real Hindu many Americans had seen, and the first missionary from the East to the West. About him spread the fascinating aroma of oriental mystery. He appealed also to cranks and charlatans who supposed they had found in him a proper tool to forward their interests.[22]

Yet the basis of his popularity was deeper than all this. Here was a man with a great heart who opened up new vistas of expanding life and religion to thousands. In him they saw a symbol of international fellowship, especially with the lovely and loving land of India, and felt a release from the stuffy chambers of familiar dogma. They thrilled to discover a new and exhaustless spiritual treasure which would ennoble their own religious life. Here was something savoring of ancient oriental wisdom, yet refreshingly new!

So doors swung wide open to him wherever he chose to go. Finally, in response to an insistent demand for his message, he went on a special tour from coast to coast, lecturing and teaching, a strenuous work that lasted two years after the close of the parliament. He met with friendliness everywhere he appeared—even among the orthodox clergy. His musical voice, boyish frankness, surprising generosity and simple genius made him at home with all. Like his master, he could mingle with women as one of them, for he was himself too feminine to regard them otherwise than as sisters and mothers.[23] And his rapturous addresses held ever a charm for the ladies.

Wherever he went, he went as a guest. In Detroit for about four weeks he was the guest of Mrs. John J. Bagley, the cultured widow of the ex-Governor of Michigan. Then he spent two weeks as the guest of the Hon. Thomas W. Palmer, president of the World's Fair Commission, formerly a senator, and also minister to Spain. When not traveling in answer to invitations from far and near, he was often in the home of Mr. George W. Hale of Chicago. After giving a series of lectures in the Unitarian Church at Detroit in February, 1894, he visited Chicago, New York and Boston.

During the midsummer months he spoke at the "Greenacre Conferences." Sarah J. Farmer, a New England spinster, spent a fortune organizing an institution at Greenacre Inn, Eliot, Maine, that would continue the study of faiths inaugurated by the great Parliament of Religions. There the swami exponded Vedanta philosophy to a group of earnest students sitting on the ground in oriental fashion under a venerable tree known as "The Swami's Pine." Miss Farmer's conferences became famous through the School of Comparative Religions conducted there by the late Dr. Lewis G. Janes, who was long the gifted and liberal president of the Brooklyn Ethical Society.[24]

6.   THE CULT FOUNDER

After lecturing in Brooklyn at the Ethical Society, the swami established himself in New York in rooms of his own, and started his regular work. Thus was the Vedanta Society in America "founded in 1894." He announced classes and lectures free of charge, supporting himself and his work by the money he had gained in lecturing. Miss S. E. Waldo of Brooklyn, who was later initiated into the order as Sister Haridasi, describes his first classes as follows:

It was just an ordinary room on the second floor of a lodging house. The classes grew with astonishing rapidity and as the little room filled to overflowing it became very picturesque. The Swami himself sat on the floor and most of his audience likewise. The marble-topped dresser, the arms of the sofa and even the corner washstand helped to furnish seats for the constantly increasing numbers. The door was left open and the overflow filled the hall and sat on the stairs. And those first classes! How intensely interesting they were![25]

And what did the swami teach? Just the old fashioned "knowledge" and "meditation" of India, the *jnana-yoga* and the *raja-yoga*, aiming at the suppression of the body and the exaltation of the "spirit."[26]

By June 1895 the swami had placed his work on a solid foundation. He had constant support from wealthy and influential followers, whose gifts went into the work. Thus encouraged, our preacher dreamed of further conquest, and "decided that the whole Western world should hear the Light of Asia and the glory of the Indian *Dharma*." [27] So he pondered a trip to England. Said he, "Organization has its faults, no doubt, but without that nothing can be done."[28] Yet he often felt worried and exhausted. "I long, oh I long for my rags, my shaven head, my sleep under the trees, and my food from begging."[29] It *is* hard to be a genuine swami in America!

To get some help and relief, our novice at toil planned to initiate some of his followers into *"sannyasa,"* and let them carry on the work. He already had good material in Madame Marie Louise and Herr Leon Landsberg, and soon they became renouncers of the world. Said the *New York Herald*:

The Swami Abhayananda is a Frenchwoman, but naturalised and twenty-five years a resident of New York. She has a curious history. For a quarter of a century she has been known to liberal circles as a materialist, socialist. . . . Twelve months ago she was a prominent member of the Manhattan Liberal Club. Then she was known in the press and on the platform as Mme. Marie Louise, a fearless, progressive, advanced woman, whose boast it was that she was always in the forefront of the battle and ahead of her times. The second disciple is also an enthusiast. With that skill which Vivekananda shows in all his dealings with men, the Hindu has chosen his first disciples well. The Swami Kripananda, before he was taken into the circle, and took the vows of poverty and chastity, was a newspaper man, employed on the staff of one of the most prominent New York papers. By birth he is a Russian Jew, named Leon Landsberg, and, if it were known, his life history is probably as interesting as that of Swami Abhayananda.[30]

From what I have discovered of the Vedanta Society today, I conclude that it still deals in "interesting" personalities, mostly of foreign extraction, men and women —mostly women—that have done rebellious thinking in youth. Among others devoted to the oriental teachings were Mrs. Ole Bull[31] (wife of the celebrated violinist and Norwegian nationalist), Dr. Allan Day, Professors Wyman and Wright, Dr. Street, and many clergymen and laymen of note. Sarah Bernhardt, the famous French actress, and Madame Calvé, the celebrated singer, became the swami's ardent admirers. Mr. and Mrs. Francis Leggett and Miss J. MacLeod, New York society leaders, became his most intimate friends and helped him in many ways. Members of the Dixon Society became his champions, and Nicolas Tesla declared the Sankhya cosmogony had something to offer modern science. Dr. Paul Carus had been the swami's companion in lectures for the Parliament of Religion's Extension.

Almost exhausted on account of his work of organization, our hero accepted a friendly invitation, and went to Percy, New Hampshire, for a period of rest in the silence of the pine woods. But his eager disciples prevailed on him to teach them at Thousand Lake Park, on the largest island in the St. Lawrence River. There the swami with his inspired talks fulfilled and surpassed the hopes of his rapturous feminine devotees. But this sort of thing was not restful enough, so he took to the ocean, sailing for Europe in the middle of August, 1895. He travelled on the Continent, and in England was the guest of Miss Henrietta Müller and of Mr. E. T. Sturdy, both lovers of Hindu lore. There he met an Englishwoman by the name of Miss Margaret Noble, who later became the famous Sister Nivedita. While he was doing popular speaking in London, a cry for help came from his American disciples, and he returned.

After three months' absence, Vivekananda arrived in New York in December, 1895, in excellent spirits. With Swami Kripananda, the former Mr. Landsberg, he now opened a center in Thirty-ninth Street. They occupied two spacious rooms which could accommodate as many as one hundred and fifty persons. The lady who had promised him help was hindered in giving it, but the Hindu leader was not discouraged. He now began to preach work and devotion, the *karma-yoga* and *bhakti-yoga*. When he first came to America as a raw ascetic, he preached intuition and meditation, the *jnana* and *raja yogas*. Now that he had gained some experience as a Western minister, he exalted the notion of work. In New York he lectured in Hardeman Hall, Madison Square Garden, and the auditorium of the People's Church. The Metaphysical Society in Brooklyn and in Hartford, Connecticut, gave him an eager hearing, while Ella Wheeler Wilcox kept sweet during bank failures by gazing on the Hindu "jewels of truth." Dr. Street became Swami Yogananda.[32]

In Detroit our hero started a successful class which he turned over to Swami Kripananda while he went and harangued the Harvard Athenians on the Unknown God. The professors liked his stress on unity, but thought he served them more emotion than intellect. We are told he rejected a chair of Eastern philosophy at that celebrated university because he was a *sannyasi*. Perhaps there were other reasons. He consolidated his work and prepared

to return home to India.   First he issued his teachings
in book form.   Then he named his original class, The
Vedanta Society of New York.   And finally he decided
to bring Swami Saradananda from India to America, writing him to come to London at once as the guest of Mr.
E. T. Sturdy.

Exhausted once more, partly by hard and unusual work
and partly by the fair and unfair criticism of Christian
missionaries and ministers, the son of India set off for his
motherland, on April 15, 1896.   He stopped in England
to strengthen the work, and remained till the end of the
year.   He was overjoyed to find there his *gurubhai*, or
brother monk, Saradananda, and sent him to New York
in June.   While in Europe, Vivekananda had a "beautiful
time" hobnobbing with Paul Deussen and Max Müller.
He sent to India for Swami Abhedananda, who came and
took charge of the London center.   Then bidding his
friends a fond farewell, he steamed away, and arrived at
Ceylon January 15, 1897.

7. THE CONQUERING HERO

The swami had felt "the overwhelming difficulties he
had met with in presenting Hinduism to an aggressively
self-conscious Christian public,"[33] but he consoled himself
by crying aloud, India will hear me!   What are the Western nations!   My own India will receive me in triumph!
So he was quite ready for the exuberant celebration that
actually occurred on his arrival, but he may have been a
bit surprised to learn from the chairman of the reception
committee that his three years' work had laid all humanity
under obligation to India.   This was only the beginning.
The ovations accorded him along his triumphal march
from Ceylon's palms to Himalaya's pines were tremendous.
Bands, flowers, garlands, arches, flags, cheers, processions
and receptions sang his praise.   At a Columbo temple,

the returning conqueror was received with shouts of "Jai, Maha Dev!" or "Victory, great god!" The notion was abroad among the people that their spokesman had demonstrated to the West the superiority of Hinduism over Christianity.

Soon the swami came to believe it himself, as far as we can judge from his speeches. With all its boasted civilization, he declared, Christianity is only a collection of scraps from the Indian mind—a very patchy imitation.

Today, when religion in the West is only in the hands of the ignorant, and the knowing ones look down with scorn upon anything belonging to religion, here comes the philosophy of India . . . where the grandest philosophical facts have been the practical spirituality of the people.

The eyes of the whole world are now turned towards this land of India for spiritual food, and India has to work for all the races. Here alone is the best ideal for mankind, and western scholars are now struggling to understand this ideal. . . .

This is the land from whence, like tidal waves, spirituality and philosophy have again and again marched out and deluged the world, and this is the land from whence once more such tides must proceed in order to bring life and vigor into the decaying races of mankind.

Before ten years elapse a vast majority of the English people will be Vedantic.

I helped on the tide of Vedanta which is flooding the world.[84]

Truth is stranger than fiction, and if the truth must be told, our hero's work in India produced far greater results than his work in America, for in 1897 he established in India that splendid and far-reaching institution of service known as the Ramakrishna Mission. Like a Buddhist that believes in both renunciation and service, he combined otherworldliness and constructive power; and if he was a Hindu to America, he was a Christian to India. Coming back to his own people as a veteran Westerner, he at once set about organizing regular work. The original monastery was moved to Alambazar, and Swami

Brahmananda was appointed president of the order. Then the monastery was moved again in 1899 and permanently located near Calcutta at Belur,[35] on the right bank of Mother Ganges—the river so sacred to the heart of Sri Ramakrishna—in the beautiful and spacious premises that Swami Vivekananda secured for his fellow monks as their own abode and the final resting place of the master's relics.

Another monastery was opened at Mayavati on the Himalayas, near Almora. Others came later, but the one at Belur remained the center of all the work. In these abodes the young students, or *brahmacaris,* and the older monks, or *sannyasis,* are trained in renunciation and service. The very year Vivekananda arrived home, there was widespread famine in India. With courage and resolution, he managed to collect funds for relief, and organize a number of enthusiastic followers at several centers to save the famine-stricken people from an untimely death. Mass education, especially the novel education of girls and women, was also dear to his heart, and he made great strides in this line.[36]

When he had left England for India, there was an understanding between Sister Nivedita and Miss Henrietta Müller her friend, that they would soon help the swami in educational work for India's women. A year later, the sister followed him to India as Miss Müller's guest, and having made a tour with Vivekananda and some of his brother monks, she settled in Calcutta and began her work, adopting the customs of the most rigid Hindu life. She soon found a place in the public thought of her adopted land, and made a name for herself in the world at large both as an author and as a public-spirited Indian. She is immortalized by her picturesque books, *The Web of Indian Life, The Master as I Saw Him, Cradle Tales of Hinduism,* and *Kali the Mother.*

In less than two years Vivekananda's health again gave way. In July, 1898, he wrote from Almora, "The way is long, the time is short, evening is approaching. I have to go home soon. . . . I feel my task is done."[37] He was advised to go to Britain and America for a change. He went, and the faithful Sister Nivedita went with him. He took along, also, Swami Turiyananda to assist him in the work. In England he stopped only a fortnight, and pushed on to America, reaching New York on August 26, 1899. On that very afternoon, the two swamis went to stay with Mr. and Mrs. Leggett in their beautiful country home in the Catskill Mountains. The sister joined them later.

While Vivekananda was in India, Saradananda had been working in America, making his chief center New York, but lecturing also in Montclair, Boston, Cambridge, Memphis and other cities. In 1897 Swami Abhedananda had come from England to help him, finding the new world richer soil for the Hindu seed, and together they incorporated the Vedanta Society at New York in 1898.[38] But Saradananda returned to India when Vivekananda came over to America this second time. After a fortnight's stay in New York and its environs, the leader, leaving Turiyananda to hold the fort, set out for Southern California, that Mecca of strange cults, and remained there for over six months. In Los Angeles he was soon pressed into work, and delivered a series of lectures in Blanchard Hall, at the Amity Church, and in ordinary public halls. He also went into Pasadena as the guest of the Universalist Church and the Shakespeare Club, lecturing on "Christ, The Messenger," and "The Way to the Realization of a Universal Religion." In Los Angeles he spent nearly a month at the chief center of the "Home of Truth." He discovered that, of all Americans, Californians are specially fit to understand the *raja-yoga* of intuitive meditation, which he labelled "Applied Psychology." In the north, several Vedanta centers were formed in San Francisco, Oakland and Alameda, with Mr. C. F. Patterson as president.

Since the work was prospering so rapidly, the leader wrote for Turiyananda to come out to California after Abhedananda had returned from his own preaching tour to relieve Turiyananda at New York. Before he left California, Vivekananda received through the generosity of Miss Minnie C. Boock the munificent gift of a large tract of land, 160 acres in extent, as a place of retreat for Vedanta students. It was a charming place, surrounded by forests and hills, and only twelve miles from the famous Lick Observatory. To this *Santi Asrama,* or "Peace Retreat," came Swami Turiyananda with twelve students, whom he trained in meditation and the austere monastic life of India. After sweet communion with his California disciples, and a stay in Detroit at the home of Mrs. Greenstidel, whose daughter, as Sister Christine, later helped Sister Nivedita in India, the tired leader returned to New York, and departed from America forever on July 20, 1900.

After passing through Paris, he returned to his beloved India almost used up. Like his master, he had little sense of limitation; he could not say "No" to an appeal. So he kept on working. A third monastery was founded, in Madras, and service centers were formed in Madras, Benares and the Murshidabad district of Bengal. He was deeply impressed with the need for work and self-sacrifice. He would not lecture, but did all he could to set men to the labor of love. Yet in the midst of it all, the swami would seek his times of quiet freedom. At such a time, in the Belur *Matha,* or Monastery, he entertained his friend Jules-Bois, a young French poet. Says the poet:

From a small skiff on the Ganges, Calcutta receded into the

distance, and finally the Math [or Matha] came into sight, all white in the midst of a grove of palm trees, the trident of its pagoda rising high above the pleasant terraces.

Vivekananda stood on the threshold. His first words were: "I am free, my friend, free again. I have given away everything. In the poorest country of the world, I am the poorest man. But the house of Ramakrishna is rebuilt, and his spiritual family there finds shelter." [41]

The poet looked about him and saw the beauty of India, with its fresh green fields under a burning sun, ponds like mirrors which a goddess might have dropped in her flight, and the arms of the Ganges embracing the earth. He went inside and saw the hermit's simple cell, and was surprised to find that the poorest man on earth yet retained some American furniture including rocking chairs, and a library in which Herbert Spencer and Ralph Waldo Emerson were prominent. Said the swami unasked:

What you others call a dream is for us the only reality. Cities, luxuries, the marvels of material science,—we have awakened from that brutal dream by which you are still enthralled. We close our eyes, we hold our breath, we sit under the kindly shade of a tree before the primitive fire, and the Infinite opens its doors to us and we enter into the inner world which is the real one.[39]

A bell sounded, and they leaned out of the cell window. Under a big tree the monks sat in a circle round their fire and the trident of Siva decked with garlands, and swung their bodies in monotonous rhythm while one of their number pierced the silence with a strident, quavering song that soared like a joyful lamentation. Behind, in the sacred stables, the cows lifted their venerable heads.

In 1902, on the Fourth of July, the missionary to America breathed his last, and his weary body was consumed in the sacred fire.

8. THE WORLD TEACHER

What we want is action, not speech, said Vivekananda,

and spoke seven volumes full. What is their gist? Our Hindu's first conviction is that all religions are true.

Be brave and sincere, then follow any path with devotion, and you must reach the Whole.[40]

Each religion is a narrow path leading to the open meadow of the undifferentiated Absolute. So it is futile to force a fellow-man into *your* particular path. Reduced to clear outline, the argument runs as follows. God is the only reality. The world is quite separate from God. Hence the world is unreal. Now the function of religion is to give men true happiness. But if the world is unreal, true happiness can only mean escape from the world into God. Hence every religion must somehow provide a path from the world to God. Hence any religion is ultimately as true as any other religion.

Such is the old Hindu dogma which is being preached with increasing conviction as Hinduism seeks to defend itself against the doctrines of Muslim or Christian supremacy. If all religions are equally true, then all the evangelical preaching of dogmatic Christian missionaries is both futile and false, and Hinduism, which proclaims the equality of *all* religions, is on that very account, the only true religion! So says the Vedantist in America. But as a chain is no stronger than its weakest link, this argument is no stronger than the premise that God is quite separate from the world. This premise, it seems, is a dogma arising from certain circumstances in Indian life and civilization that made the world appear burdensome, undesirable and futile. If we glory in the world as a field for creative endeavor, we shall not be likely to accept the dogma that the world is futile and hence quite separate from God. But if not separate, then just how is the world related to God?

Taking Sankara's monism rather than his dualism, we

may call God the substance whose modes comprise the world. Here we find no separation between God and the world, but a practical unity. On this basis, the relation of one religion to another would appear quite different. God is the only reality. The world is a system of practical distinctions in God. Hence the world is real. Now the function of religion is to give men true happiness. And if the world is real, true happiness can only mean a certain control of practical distinction. Hence the truth of any religion is measured by the extent to which it enables its followers to enjoy true happiness in the control of the world. Accordingly, while all religions may spring from God, and thus have a common foundation or fundamental unity, they are not therefore equally true, for they obviously differ in the measure of control they afford.

Our Hindu's next conviction is the divinity of man.

> Know you are the Infinite, then fear must die. Say ever "I and the Father are one."[41]

This identity of man with God can be interpreted in two different ways according to the relation conceived between God and the world. If the world is conceived monistically as a system of practical distinctions in God, then man is already one with God even while living in the world of practical distinctions, in the world of good and evil, of righteousness and sin. When he hears religion telling him he is one with God, he will then regard sin not from the point of view of the finite brute, as an unexplainable state of misery, but from the point of view of the infinite God, as God's judgment on certain kinds of acts for the sake of improving action in general. Thus *sin*, like *evil*, is a valuable and universal tool of criticism, an instrumental concept that distinguishes between good and better in conduct, and bids us choose the better. Clearly, the proper use of the concept of sin is necessary for human progress or creative achievement.

But if the world be conceived dualistically as a system of practical distinctions that are unreal, or irrelevant to God, then, as Sankara says, man is one with God only when he somehow rids himself of all practical distinctions, such as good and evil, righteousness and sin. As a child of both West and East, Vivekananda seems to waver somewhere between these two views. In monistic mood he exclaims:

Ye are the Children of God, the sharers of immortal bliss, holy and perfect beings. Ye divinities on earth,—sinners? It is a sin to call man so; it is a standing libel on human nature.[42]

Here the swami administers a just rebuke to those who claim to be children of God and yet sinners. If man is *essentially* a child of God, that is, of the nature of God, he cannot be *essentially* a sinner. He must be "made in the image of God." Some of his *acts* may be reckoned sinful, but these are opposed to acts that are righteous. Man himself, then, is neither a saint nor a sinner, but a "child of God" doing both good and evil according to the accepted standard of judgment.[43] The swami's dominant mood, however, is not monistic but dualistic, a mood in which he holds that man is one with God only when he is oblivious to all distinctions, including those of morality.

The rest of Vivekananda's teachings stick together in a common historical culture, for which they serve as apologies. Hinduism, he says, is true in every detail. The reformers are mistaken. In trying to uproot the weeds of pernicious custom, they are also tearing up the precious wheat of culture. Hindu civilization, he points out, is the flower of Hindu religion, and so must be true and spiritual, beautiful and good in every fiber of its being. Since Western scholars altogether fail to understand it, their criticism is utterly worthless. As for the comments of Christian missionaries, they are wickedly slanderous.

This spiritual nation must teach the world in the present as in the past. To this end it must shake itself free from the degrading dominion of Western nations, with their gross materialism and selfish sensuality. Every Hindu must awake and do all in his power to defend his religion and civilization from the poison of Western influence. Yet the Hindu, he concedes, will find Western methods and education most useful. He must even give up his horror of meat and become a beef eater if necessary in order to grow strong enough to build up once more a flourishing civilization on the soil of India.

In this willful logic of emotion, renunciation of the world works out into nationalism and political rebellion.[44] The exaggerated praise of India and condemnation of the West coming from Swami Vivekananda, Sister Nivedita and others was an important influence leading to the anarchist movement in Bengal, and the more recent drives for "Civil Disobedience" which Manmohandas Karamchand Gandhi, the saintly politician, has been organizing on a nation-wide scale. Of course, Swami Vivekananda was no politician. All he did was to arouse his countrymen to toil for India. But his religious doctrine of wholesale condemnation for the West was to the ordinary Hindu a sacred sanction that smoothed the way for anarchy and "non-coöperation."

Vivekananda's exposition of Hinduism is fourfold. All the cults of the world, he says, are only different examples of the four paths prominent in the history of Hindu doctrine. To each path, or way of restraint, he devotes a book, compiled from shorthand notes taken of his speeches. His chief books are thus *Jnana Yoga, Raja Yoga, Bhakti Yoga,* and *Karma Yoga.* These works are perhaps more widely read among the students of India, especially of Bengal, than any other religious books.[45] In his *Jnana Yoga* he aggravates the illusionism of Sankara with a Buddhistic and even a Schopenhauerian pessimism. In view of our many desires and few satisfactions, he calls the world hideous.

At best it is the hell of Tantalus, and nothing else. Here we are with strong impulses and stronger ideas for sense enjoyments, and nothing outside to fill them. . . . Unhappiness is the fate of those who are content to live in this world, born as they are. A thousandfold unhappiness is the fate of those who dare to stand forth for truth and for higher things and dare to ask for something higher than mere enjoyable brutish existence here.[46]

For this world there can be no explanation, says the teacher, but "the Vedanta can show a *way out.*" All our troubles come from the craving for individuality. But let us rather be indifferent to the pain and sorrow of ourself and others. "Millions come and go every minute. Who cares? Why care for the joys and vicissitudes of this little world?"[47] Let us rather enjoy the bliss of the solitary Self.

His *Raja Yoga* simply points the "way out." All the orthodox systems of Hindu philosophy have one goal in view, the liberation of the soul. The *raja-yoga* is the most elaborate and refined classic method of reaching this goal.

According to the *Raja-Yogi,* the external world is but the gross form of the internal, or subtle. The finer is always the cause, the grosser the effect. So the external world is the effect, the internal the cause. In the same way external forces are simply the grosser parts, of which the internal forces are the finer. The man who has discovered and learned how to manipulate the internal forces will get the whole of nature under his control. The *Yogi* proposes to himself no less a task than to master the whole universe, to control the whole of nature. He wants to arrive at the point where what we call "nature's laws" will have no influence over him, where he will be able to get beyond them all. He will be master of the whole of nature, internal and external. The progress and civilization of the human race simply means controlling this nature.[48]

In his *Bhakti Yoga* our thinker attempts to reconcile to the divine abstract unity those who are emotionally inclined. "He wishes to direct the love which normally expends itself on particular objects towards the supreme objects, or God, and so to increase the intensity of devotion that the Object remains no longer an Object, but becomes a Subject—the Universal Subject, one with, or absorbent of, all particular subjects. An intense wave of feeling may be able to reach what reason or even intellectual intuition may not be able to secure."[49] At the very beginning of the book he says:

Bhakti-Yoga is a genuine real search after the Lord, a search beginning, continuing and ending in Love. One single moment of the madness of extreme love to God brings us eternal freedom.[50]

Bhakti is the smoothest and easiest path of all. We begin where we are. We are not called on to renounce anything at first. But as our love to God becomes more and more intense, we gladly give up all objects for the love of the one Subject, so that in the end, the bliss of *bhakti* is the same as the knowledge of *jnana*. "There is really no difference," he says, "between the higher knowledge and the higher bliss."[51]

Thus the *jnana, raja* and *bhakti yogas* are all practically the same. Vivekananda himself sees the need of reconciling this renunciation with ordinary human life with its pressing duties and social affairs, but in spite of his contact with Christianity and his knowledge of Buddhism, he does nothing more than hark back to the *Bhagavad Gita* for the material of his *Karma Yoga*. He preaches service as a part of *karma,* or work, but not Christian or Buddhist service, not service with the motive of love. We must work for work's sake, without any motive, ideal or reward. We may call this "work for God," but must remember that God himself has no motive but idle play, and is unattached to the world.   In short, we work because we have no capacity to renounce the world.   There are two ways to obtain release, says the teacher, the negative way of "meditation," and the positive way of "work."

The negative way is the most difficult.   It is only possible to the men of the very highest exceptional minds and gigantic wills. . . . But such people are very rare; the vast majority of mankind chooses the positive way, making use of all the bondages to break through these bondages.   This is also a kind of giving up, only it is done slowly and gradually, by knowing things, enjoying things, and thus obtaining experiences, and knowing the nature of things until the mind lets them all go at last and becomes unattached.[52]

This is the *Gita* with a dose of the *Tantras*.   By blowing the bubble bigger and bigger, we shall soon burst it, and realize it is only a bubble.   Service is not for the world, but for ourselves.   We must not try to patch up the world, but get beyond it.   Social reform is mere "social scavenging."

Our world teacher is patently Hindu, and his philosophy is Hindu dogma in Western dress.   If we would know how Hinduism develops when it really takes root beyond India, we must pass beyond the conservative Vivekananda.

CHAPTER V

VEDANTA CENTERS, THE RAMAKRISHNA
MOVEMENT IN AMERICA

The following notice appeared in the *New York Times* announcement of Religious Services for Sunday, September 23, 1928:

VEDANTA SOCIETY

Founded by Swami Vivekananda, 34 W. 71st.
11 A. M.—"The Existence of Soul."
    Speaker, Swami Bodhananda.
3 P. M.—"Vedanta in Everyday Life."
    Speaker, Swami Gnaneshwarananda.

The name of the afternoon speaker, meaning "Bliss of the Lord of Knowledge," is spelled Jnanesvarananda in the normal English transliteration of the Sanskrit, and should be pronounced Gyaneshwar-ananda. Eager to learn what practical message a preacher of the generation-old movement of Vivekananda wished to deliver to America in 1928, I went to hear about "Vedanta in Everyday Life." The Society's place of worship is a brown stone and red brick house of four stories and basement, situated just west of Central Park, in a region notable as a home for various cults, such as Christian Science and Theosophy.

As I drew near I noticed a bronze tablet near the door:

VEDANTA SOCIETY
FOUNDED BY
SWAMI VIVEKANANDA
1894

95

Above it was a painted wooden sign:
SERVICES
11 A. M. SUNDAYS 3 P. M.
ALL ARE WELCOME

I ran up the steps and rang the bell. The door opened
at once. I walked in, and met the Dutch superintendent,
who told me that the main floor of the Vedanta house is
devoted to public meetings, while the two swamis live
elsewhere in the building.

I entered the long parlor to the right, and met Swami
Bodhananda, dressed in neat black clericals. As I turned
to take my seat, I noticed that the glass doors of the square
back parlor were open, so that the two rooms together
made a small public hall. Since the pulpit stood at the
far end of the back room, the audience faced the rear.
About twenty-five worshipers were present, mostly
women. Sitting down in the dead stillness, I noticed a
sign with the single word, SILENCE. The rooms were
dark and handsome, tastefully furnished, and dimly
lighted.

On the wall behind the pulpit hung a painting of
Swami Vivekananda. To the left was a large French window covered over with heavy curtains of golden cloth.
To the left of the window, in the corner, stood a kind of
altar bearing a small framed photograph which I rightly
judged to be of Ramakrishna, the master of Vivekananda.
His likeness was honored with vases of flowers, burning
candles, and fuming incense. Looking around to the left,
I saw in the long parlor a large bookcase containing about
a thousand books, which I later discovered to be mostly
the works of Western Idealists.

Just then Swami Jnanesvarananda entered and mounted
the one-step platform supporting the pulpit. A young
man, rather short, with a pleasant face. He wore a shin-

ing golden robe. With folded hands he spoke in solemn tones.

"Let us all try to meditate on our inner divine nature."

Silence. Broken by the swami's resonant voice in a quaintly appealing Sanskrit chant. Then a prayer in English:

"May that One who is called Siva by the Shivaites, Visnu by the Visnuites, Brahman by the Vedantins, Allah by the Muslims and God the Heavenly Father by the Christians, inspire our hearts with love for all mankind. Peace! Peace! Peace!"

The swami then announced his subject and began to preach with lucid statements and apt illustrations. The substance of his sermon may be presented as follows:

What is Vedanta? It can be set forth in three propositions:

1. Reality is universal Love, the underlying unity manifested in all variety. To realize this Love within the heart is literally Veda-anta, the goal of knowledge. If you know the One, you know the many. Brahman alone is. This is a rational, philosophic creed.

2. The world is illusion. All the variety of manifestation is nothing but appearance. Only the Cause exists. In themselves effects are unreal. In reality they are identical with the Cause.

3. The individual "I," or ego, that we feel within us is always identical with the ultimate principle. The self is the same as Reality.

Now success in life, or the practical application of Vedanta, consists in living in accordance with this intellectual conviction. Your lives will then realize the ideal. *Siddhi*, or practical success, comes from *Sadhana*, or instrumental theory. Convinced of the truth of Vedanta, you must enter the conflict of daily life, fighting without misgiving, struggling with assurance of victory.

In realizing Vedanta there are three levels of conduct. The first and highest is *pure passivity*. When convinced you are Brahman, the nameless, birthless, qualityless, sexless principle, you feel the conflicts of daily life utterly vanish. You do not harmonize these conflicts, for to you they simply do not exist. If you don't do anything at all, how can you harmonize?

The second level is *desireless activity*. If you cannot maintain the first level, then try the second. At the first level, you believe reality is one without difference. This is "non-dualism." At the second level, you belive reality is One *with* difference. This is "modified non-dualism." In your daily behavior according to this conviction you must try to realize you are a part of the big mechanism of the entire world, and accept all actions in yourself and others as the will of the Lord.

The third level is *obedient activity*. If you cannot maintain the second level, try the third, in which you accept the "dualistic" belief that you are separate from the Lord. You will then try to do what the Lord tells you, even though your nature may be quite unsteady and frivolous. But the devotee that is perfectly steady can attain the highest level of pure passivity wherein the world becomes illusion.

After the sermon, one of the members took up the offering. The coin I dropped into the basket compared unfavorably with its burden of paper money. The swami then gave his announcements:

"After the political elections, three classes will be formed this year as usual, each to meet once a week at eight o'clock in the evening: on Tuesday, the class on the *Bhagavad Gita;* on Thursday, the class in meditation; and on Friday, the class for the study of Sanskrit. Only the class on the *Gita* is open to the public; the others are for members only. On the table near the door are various books for sale in which you may study Vedanta more deeply. You may see either of the swamis at any time by making an appointment beforehand."

The meeting closed with another period of silence, Sanskrit chant and English prayer. I then sought the book table. Most of the books were by Swami Viveka-vanda and Sister Nivedita. A few were by swamis who continued Vivekananda's work in America, the present Swami Bodhananda among them. As I left the place of meeting no one rushed over to shake my hand, tell me he was glad to see me, offer me literature, or ask for a subscription. Not the busy cordiality of an American Protestant Church, but the quiet air of an Indian retreat prevailed. I introduced myself to the preacher of the afternoon, and made an appointment, remembering to pronounce his name Gyaneshwar-ananda.

The appointed day found us sitting together in the bare front parlor. The swami looked and acted like a gentleman, and was dressed in the conventional American way.

"Swamiji," I began (*ji* is the usual term of respect), "when you chant in Sanskrit, what do you say?"

"The English prayer that follows is a free translation of the chant. I use Sanskrit because it *is* the sacred language."

"Another question. Vivekananda and Tagore and others repeatedly speak of *realizing* God. But how can we real-ize or make real what is Reality itself?"

"Oh, the trouble is in the translation. Perhaps *experience* is a better word. We realize an *idea* about God, but God Himself we experience."

"Very good. Tell me now why you call your religion rational. Is it not based absolutely on the authority of scripture, namely the *Upanishads*?"

"Yes, but it's rational in the sense that the authority

of scripture is verified by the intellectual intuition of each individual worshiper. The scripture only points out the way to God. You yourself find it true or rational when you experience it."

"That's a curious use of the word rational," was my reply, "and moreover, I can't see that it's scientifically rational to believe the world is illusion. And yet you consider this the highest level, don't you?"

"Well—yes, but it may not be the highest level for *you*. It doesn't matter which level you choose and practice, if only you do it sincerely."

"Then how can you say one level is higher than another?"

"Theoretically it may be higher, but practically all levels are equally good. You see philosophy is theoretical and hence universal, but religion is practical and hence individual. Since individuals differ in native capacity, certain individuals need one kind of religion, while others need another kind."

"But if you don't regard one religion as better than another why do you come over to America to preach?"

"Merely to show the eternal principles underlying *all* religions. As Swami Vivekananda declared in his famous address at the World's Parliament of Religions at Chicago in 1893, we want to make Hindus better Hindus, Muslims better Muslims and Christians better Christians."

"Your society, then, helps Christians to do better work in their churches?"

"As a matter of fact, very few of our members come from the churches. They are usually dissatisfied with Christianity when they come. We present their own religion in a new way that appeals to them. They seldom join up with the churches, because they get so much help here. But they may be Christians without going to church. I myself claim to be a Christian."

"Then in America you are actually making Christians by means of the Vedanta Society! Is this your missionary goal?"

"Our goal is simply to fill all America with the spirit of Vedanta, which is the spirit of the eternal, universal religion of understanding and tolerance."

"How do you propose to infuse this spirit of tolerance among us?"

"By disclosing the four *yogas*, or methods of each and every religion: (1) *jnana*, or knowledge, (2) *raja*, or the best kind of meditation, (3) *bhakti*, or loving devotion, and (4) *karma*, or work. Swami Vivekananda has written a book on each *yoga*."

"Yes, so I noticed when I glanced at your book table. And I suppose you stress the method of meditation above all others as the most suitable cure for the complexity, hurry and tension of our American life. I notice you have a whole class devoted to this method alone."

"Yes, and besides, we want to rid Americans of the idea that Hindu meditation is something hypnotic, occult or magical, full of visions and trances. But we stress meditation mainly because it provides the key for the other methods. The knowledge that this world is illusion, the devotion to God for His own sake, and the ability to work without any interest in the fruits of your work are all developed by the practice of meditation, which brings the peace of *samadhi*, or union with God. We should enjoy this *samadhi* in the workaday world, but we can cultivate it best in private, just as we should go off to a place where the water is smooth and shallow when we want to learn to swim."

I left Swami Jnanesvarananda feeling that I understood at least this much about the Vedanta Society. It was here in America to make us peaceful and tolerant Christians by means of a meditation free from magic. Imagine my surprise when I attended a meeting of the meditation class at a later date, and overheard the following remark from one of the members as we all were leaving:

"These swamis are wonderful! They have more knowledge in a little finger than we have in a whole hatful! Just think! Every letter means something by itself—by knowing them all we could control the elements of the universe! Where is Jesus Christ now? Dead already—gone to nothing. These Hindus have the only true religion in the world!"

All this with a German accent. Is this effusion a result of the tolerant, non-magical teaching of the swamis? After all, does Vedanta supply the universal principles of *all* religions? Or does it merely supply the underlying principles of *Hinduism*, which does indeed *presume* to regard other religions as various practical cult-forms of itself? The latter is the clear impression we get from Ramakrishna, ensconced in his native India. But does Hinduism presume as much in America? A careful study of the Vedanta movement in its actual practice and teaching will help us to answer this and other perplexing questions.

1. THE GROWTH

American Vedantism is a tree of which the seed was Vivekananda. The seed was planted in American soil by the Parliament of Religions, and the sprouting plant cultivated by wealthy Americans, especially women of leisure, as in the case of many other cults. Whereas Christian missions to India are inspired and supported mainly from the home base, this Hindu mission to America was originally inspired and is now supported by the field in which it operates.

How has the tree developed? How has the American soil and gardening directed the Hindu plant? How far has the growth adapted itself to American ideals and methods? Does Vedanta entice people away from the churches or dampen missionary ardor? Is it widening or narrowing the gap between East and West?

When Vivekananda sailed away from America for the last time in 1900, he left Swami Turiyananda at San Francisco on the western seaboard, and Swami Abhedananda balancing him at New York.[1] But just two years later, in the same year that Vivekananda fell to earth like a spent rocket, Turiyananda returned to India weak and nervous. Apparently these two men were exhausted by preaching the *raja-yoga* of perfect peace and control. Perhaps this yoga cannot bring lasting peace in the midst of toil. Perhaps the *karma-yoga* of incessant, impersonal toil fails to suit the man of high hopes and keen sensibilities, the man of charming personality. Or perhaps American life is a bit too varied and strenuous for the old Hindu methods in general.

In any case, a fresh worker was sent out from the East to preach in the West: Swami Trigunatita, who took the place of Turiyananda in Los Angeles, San Francisco and the nearby Santi Asrama. Soon the centers grew and asked for another swami, so in 1904 Saccidananda (bliss of reality and knowledge) came over and took charge of the Los Angeles Center. Meanwhile, Swami Nirmalananda arrived in 1903 at New York to help Abhedananda. But he lasted just three years in America, going back to his motherland after a siege of pneumonia in the winter of 1906. Abhedananda, however, not only held his ground in New York but also opened up a center in Pittsburgh. Since Trigunatita in San Francisco was likewise expanding his work, three swamis sailed in 1906 from Belur to America, Prakashananda (bliss of radiance) to San Francisco, Paramananda (bliss of the highest) to New York, and Bodhananda (bliss of intelligence) to take charge of the new center in Pittsburgh.

In 1909 Paramananda[2] set forth from New York and
established a center in Boston, where the valiant leader
Vivekananda had won his first triumph in 1893, and during the summer he gave his first course of lectures at the
Greenacre Summer Conference, where both the leader and
Swami Saradananda had delivered addresses. Then he
formed a branch in Washington, placing it in charge of
an American convert called Sister Devamata (holy
mother). Taking advantage of this new source of help,
the swami set out for India in 1911, lecturing on the way
in Germany and at Stratford-on-Avon during the Shakespeare festival there. By Christmas he was back in Boston.
Then for three successive summers he toured Europe, holding classes in Germany, France, Switzerland and Italy, and
starting a branch in Geneva.

In the meantime, Abhedananda also left New York,
retiring in 1912 to an *asrama* of 370 acres at West Corn-
wall, Connecticut, in the foothills of the Berkshires; and
Bodhananda was called from Pittsburgh to take his place.
Nine years later, Abhedananda went back to his native
land after a long and fruitful period of service in America, pleasantly interrupted by about ten visits to Europe
during the summer vacations.

We turn now to the western seaboard just in time to
see Saccidananda sail for home in 1913, and Trigunatita
pass away from this life a year later. To replace these
losses, Prakashananda set out for India and returned with
two more swamis, Prabhavananda (bliss of lordship) to
share his work in San Francisco, and Raghavananda (bliss
of Rama) to help Bodhananda in New York. Thus Los
Angeles was left without a swami, but not for long, because in 1915 the enterprising Paramananda, hindered by
the War from making his usual summer visit to Europe,
journeyed westward in America, lecturing by invitation at
Minneapolis and San Francisco, and in 1916 reëstablished

the work in Los Angeles by forming a permanent center there, with radiations in Santa Barbara, San Diego, Long Branch, Pasadena and other points in southern California. In the spring of 1918 he met with surprising success in Seattle, and lectured in Tacoma and Portland as well. In the spring of 1919, visits to Louisville, Cincinnati and Gallup, New Mexico, added fresh centers in interest.

Six years later, in 1925, some of those who heard him in Portland asked for a permanent swami to guide them, and received Prabhavananda from San Francisco. So the next year, in 1926, Paramananda went to India and brought back two more swamis, Dayananda (bliss of pity) for San Francisco, and Akhilananda (bliss of the whole) to help in the Boston center. The next year, in 1927, a veteran named Madhavananda, who had edited the English *Life of Sri Ramakrishna* and published the *Complete Works of Swami Vivekananda,* came to replace Prakashananda, who had passed on to the next life. In the same year Raghavananda in New York suffered a nervous breakdown and was replaced by Jnanesvarananda (bliss of the lord of knowledge), who spells his name Gnaneshwarananda. In July 1929 Prabhavananda went from Portland, Oregon, to Hollywood, California, the capital of the cinema world, and Vividishananda was called from India to take his place in Portland. Just after Christmas in 1929, Jnanesvarananda was sent from New York to open up a center in Chicago, the city of Vivekananda's great triumph in 1893. In the near future another swami may be summoned from India to shepherd a group in St. Louis aroused by the lectures of Prabhavananda.

In all, there have been seventeen Ramakrishna swamis in America, but never more than eight at a time, the number reached in 1929.[3] Their movement is not one big society with an all-American organization and central office, but just a number of centers operated by local American officers and funds. Unlike Christian missionaries in India, the swamis do not control their centers, but are really Hindu guests who have gladly accepted the invitations of their American hosts. Guests do not control their hosts. The relation is simply one of friendship. So too the centers do not control their swamis, but the leading swami of each center is directly responsible to the Ramakrishna *Matha,* or Monastic Order, at Belur near Calcutta.

This *matha,* we know, was founded in 1886[4] and incorporated in 1899[5] as a dual order of renunciation and service. But the service side was soon embodied in the Ramakrishna *Mission,* founded in 1897[6] and incorporated in 1909[7] as a separate organization responsible to the *Matha,* which then specialized in renunciation. Although Vedanta centers have appeared from time to time in Western countries such as Switzerland, Argentina and Australia, the Ramakrishna movement is now flourishing in only two countries, India and the United States of America.[8] And whereas most of the Indian centers are now specializing in social service, such as relief work, mass education and village organization, all of the American centers, responsible as they are to the *Matha* and not to the Mission,[9] have confined themselves to the teaching of conservative Hindu doctrines. While India is getting more of the Christian-like side of Vivekananda's dual religion of renunciation and service, America is getting only the strictly Hindu side.[10]

What does this mean? It means that of all the countries of the world including India itself, the United States offers the most fertile soil for the growth of conservative Hindu ideals. Why? In the first place, these ideals are more novel to America than to India and many other countries, and so more appealing. England, again, is not so willing to listen to India, because of their master-and-servant relation. On the European continent looms the language barrier, for most educated Indians speak only English besides their native tongues. Moreover, these continental countries, unlike rich America, cannot provide the funds required to bring the swamis all the way from India. Finally, America is not only the land of religious freedom, but also the land of religious seeking, for its background is Protestant and pioneer.

Moreover, since the Ramakrishna movement is in many ways more conservative than other Hindu movements, such as the Arya Samaj and Brahma Samaj, the Americans that accept its ideals become, curiously enough, more strictly Hindu in their beliefs than many Hindus in India. And this tendency is increased by the fact that Americans are generally aggressive, single-minded and wholehearted in whatever they do, so that when they join a Hindu movement, they often want to be more specifically Hindu than the swamis themselves, and whereas the swamis are tolerant of Christianity, their converts often despise the pit from which they were digged, and become violently anti-Christian. Partly because of this disposition of many American converts, Hindu beliefs have not adapted themselves very much to the dominant beliefs of America. But of course there has been some adaptation. How much, let us now seek to discover.

2. THE MESSAGE

In New York today Swami Bodhananda delivers substantially the same message that Swami Vivekananda delivered in the same city over a generation ago. And his censure of popular Christianity is even keener. The doctrine of original sin, he declares, is a lie, and the worst sin in the world. Why do Christians allow their ministers to insult them by calling them sinners? Perhaps because the biggest sinners are supposed to have the best chance for salvation! But we are really gods, not sinners. We must not beg for salvation, but demand it as our spiritual birthright, and then proceed to remove the darkness of ignorance. Whatever we think, that shall we become. So if we think we are sinners, we will indeed become sinners, but if we think we are divine, we shall really become divine.

Salvation, moreover, comes not by vicarious atonement but by individual realization. Each soul itself must pay the price for its salvation, and work out its destiny alone. Gautama Buddha, says the swami, had knowledge of at least five hundred past lives, yet he did not presume to come from God to save men. In his great pity for humanity, he saw not sin but misery. Hence the claim that Jesus Christ is the only begotten Son of God who saves all men is simply a conceit. In short, salvation is not an involution from without, but an evolution from within, an individual, spiritual evolution.

The West, continues the swami, is torn between two extremes, the Christian dogma of creation out of nothing, and the scientific dogma of evolution out of matter. But Vedanta chooses the golden mean by teaching a *spiritual* evolution, in which the same soul gradually purifies itself by successive reincarnations. If we have only one birth and one death, how can God be at once wise and benevolent and just? Would such a good God create men with unequal opportunities and endowments, if they had only one chance in the world? Would He send men to eternal punishment for temporal sins? And why should the Christian believe in eternal life after death if he does not believe in eternal life before birth? This conception of immortality, as Schopenhauer says, is an infinite stick with only one end! The ordinary Christian says, "I have a soul to be saved in Heaven bye and bye," but the Hindu says, "I *am* a soul, and Heaven is here and now within me." Yet in spite of all his fallacies, the Christian wants to force his views on others. But the Hindu knows that as every individual must have his own kind of food, so too he must have his own kind of religion, or *svadharma.* Accordingly, he is broad and tolerant.

But how can you attack another religion, Swamiji, and yet claim to be tolerant?

I am tolerant,[11] replies the swami, in allowing everybody freedom to follow his own religion, but I am intolerant when I find insincerity and hypocrisy in the name of religion, when I find a gap between profession and practice, and in this I follow all the divine masters, including Jesus who condemned the Pharisees.[12]

Swami Jnanesvarananda, a younger monk, is less polemic and more illustrative. While he holds to all the conservative Vedanta doctrines, he dresses them up to appeal to an American audience. Here are a few examples. Religion, he says, is a response of the soul to the stimulus of God. The soul is the motor-car driver whose car is the body. Vedanta brings success in everyday life. It is a rational religion, because based on experience.[13] The world is a vast mechanism controlled by God. All the world is God, just as all the images on the motion picture screen are light.

The young swami even uses ideas that if carried out to their logical conclusion would revolutionize the Hindu position. The Bliss of Brahma he calls the Love of the Heavenly Father. Is our preacher aware of the road he travels? It is a road that leads from ascetic, individualistic renunciation to harmonious, socially-minded creation. Again, he says that God creates the world as an obstacle for His struggle and delight. Play may be struggle, to be sure, and the Hindu holds that God creates in play or *lila,* but there is considerable difference between the purposeful play, or joyous work, of Christian romanticism, and the purposeless play, or idle magic-making, of classical Hinduism. Which does the swami mean? Finally, he tells us that life's highest good is not desirelessness, but absolute control over *selfish* desires. If such preaching should be fully developed, it might make the Vedanta movement as much Christian as Hindu.

Is it likely, however, that such preaching *will* be developed? Will Vedanta ever adjust itself to American life? Let us consider this possibility on the basis of a survey of adjustments of Hindu convictions to Western culture made successively by the three most influential swamis of the movement: Vivekananda, Abhedananda, and Paramananda.

3.   THE ADJUSTMENTS

Vivekananda went so far as to accept Western values, but he interpreted them according to Vedanta. For example, the West values science. So the swami says in effect, "Religion must submit to scientific investigation. What can judge between the claims of holy books and codes? Only the light of reason." Then comes the interpretation. "Vedanta, with its utmost generalization, is the completely rational religion."[14] Again, Western idealism values democracy, and fights against privilege. So the bold Hindu joins the fray. "Break down privilege!" he cries, then adds a few words for Vedanta.

> Once a gigantic attempt was made to preach Vedanta ethics, . . . and . . . those years were the best times for that nation. I mean, the Buddhistic attempt to break down privilege. Some of the most beautiful epithets addressed to Buddha that I remember are, "Thou the breaker of castes, destroyer of privilege, preacher of equality to all beings."[15]

Finally, the West values Christianity. So what does the swami do here? He attempts to show that as an oriental religion, Christianity is only a form of Hinduism.

> The Vedas are . . . the oldest sacred books in the world. Nobody knows anything about the time they were written or by whom. The religion of the Vedas is the religion of the Hindus and the foundation of all oriental religions.[16]

Since the keystone of Christianity is Christ, the swami must give him a special interpretation.

"The foxes have holes, the birds of the air have nests, but the Son of Man hath not where to lay his head." That is what Christ says is the only way to salvation; he lays down no other way. . . . He had no family ties . . . no sex ideas . . . no other thought except that one, that he was a Spirit, a disembodied, unfettered, unbounded spirit.[17]

Such was Vivekananda's way of preaching, which must have given him a feeling of solid satisfaction, for in his naïve freedom from historical detail, he was not much bothered by the fact that the classic Vedanta goal is not rational but mystically non-rational, that the Buddhistic attempt to break down privilege was at first aimed precisely at such cults as Vedanta, that Christianity is not simply a form of Hinduism, and that Christ never said the only way to get saved is to wander poor and homeless. The first swami to visit America was a bold, well-meaning, lovable impressionist.

Paying more attention to history and his field of operation, Swami Abhedananda did more than his leader to adjust Vedanta to Western culture. Rather than overpower by flashing oratory, he seeks to convince by sweet reasonableness and a vast array of new and picturesque facts. His case for vegetarianism, for example, makes a strong appeal on its own merits. Again, he argues with a show of reason, that if we accept the Christian Bible as revealed of God we must then accept *all* bibles. Unlike Vivekananda,[18] he does not scorn spiritualism as a cheap American product competing with the measureless penetration of the Hindus, but simply states that for all his conversation with spirits through Western mediums, he has learned nothing, and so regards them as earth-bound and ignorant.

He even reinterprets his message to suit Western demands. Whereas his master Ramakrishna scorned the body and works of healing, this swami sympathizes with Christian Science, and encourages the study of healing power. What this American cult is striving to do, he says, Vedanta has already mastered.[19] Moreover, in his treatment of the doctrine of reincarnation, he is very theosophic and modern, rejecting the notion of the god-man-beast-plant wheel of life from which escape is desirable, and stressing the creative, evolutionary, purposeful aspects of the soul's cosmic peregrinations. Finally, his handling of the doctrine of "work" is quite Western. Like Ramanuja, combining the *Gita* rule of unselfish devotion with the early Vedic idea of purposeful work for reward, he takes the "duties and work of our daily life as a means to a higher end," and declares that "all good or unselfish works bring as their results peace, good health, prosperity and happiness in the end."[20] This kind of work is a far cry from the utterly disinterested and result-despising duty proclaimed as the highest path in the *Bhagavad Gita* and in the *Karma Yoga* of Vivekananda.

In Swami Paramananda, however, we see a return to conservatism. Instead of sweeping history, science and Western religion like Abhedananda to find illumination and expansion for his Hindu convictions, he dwells forever on the cultivation of the "inner," or "spiritual," life by the methods taught in the *Gita*. In his magazine *Message of the East,* his associate, Sister Devamata, speaks of escape from the wheel of life; the Brahman Saradananda now back in India praises work done without any desire for name, fame, material benefit or future reward; and the veteran Ramakrishnananda, also in India, maintains that life is the struggle of spirit against matter.

Thus the historical development of Vedanta teaching in America does not show any one steady trend of adjustment towards American culture. In Abhedananda and

Jnanesvarananda we notice considerable adaptation, but in Paramananda and Bodhananda not so much. To be sure, Paramananda teaches the congenial *devotion* and *work* rather than *knowledge* and *meditation,* but here he stops. It is not easy to tell what the future may bring, but unless the basis of propaganda be definitely shifted from Hindu *Dharma*[21] to individual reason or life's present needs, we are not justified in predicting much more adjustment. And as for the past, we must still maintain that apart from social customs, certain Americans have proved themselves good old-fashioned Hindus.

The contrast between the Hindu conservatism of the Ramakrishna *Matha* in America, and the Hindu liberalism of the Ramakrishna Mission in India appears even more striking when we note the remarkable adjustment of Hindu ideals to Western culture now taking place in the work of the Mission in India. Dr. S. L. Sarkar, for example, in addressing the great Ramakrishna Convention at Belur in 1926 embraces not only the Buddhist and Christian ideal of *service motivated by love,* but also the Christian and Ramanuja conception of *God's joy in purposeful creation.*

In studying the subject of organization we get many a valuable suggestion from the creation of the world and evolution of mankind. In creating the world God has given Himself up and His joy lies in it. This joy in creation, through sacrifice, He has imparted to all those who want to build or create. The painter, the sculptor, the poet, the philosopher, the scientist, the monk and the householder—all find delight in their respective creations, and creations connote sacrifice on the part of the person concerned. The more rigorous the sacrifice, the happier the result. Thus self-sacrifice must be the basis on which the real work of village organization should rest.

We find there are two types of work; work impelled by a mere sense of obligation and work inspired by love. Of the two the latter is more effective, and produces real joy. The Ramakrishna Mission has shown good example of the latter kind, inspired as it is by its noble motto "For the liberation of the self and for the good of the many." Here "the service to others" becomes identified with "service to one's own self." . . . In doing an act of service, one must not be actuated by a sense of obligation alone, but one should be stimulated by a spirit of love and self-sacrifice. "Moksha" is the experience of joy derived from the hardship of sacrifice. What else can be the meaning of Moksha?[22] I have given . . . the philosophy of service. It is the idea of Ananda (joy) which impels a man to sacrifice all his comforts for the sake of others.[23]

4.   THE METHODS

Turning back to America, let us now attempt to discover whether the monks of the *Matha* have adjusted their methods to American culture any more than their message. The old-fashioned Indian methods employed by the teaching friars, such as personal instruction, private classes, and birthday celebrations with an offering and distribution of *prasada,* or blessed flowers, fruits and sweetmeats, are carried over to America, and Western methods also adopted, such as Sunday preaching services and newspaper notices, public classes and paid membership, reading rooms and circulating libraries, the sale of books and magazines, and the distribution of bulletins and magazines to libraries, colleges and universities.

In several ways, however, the American advance of the movement is limited. In the first place, the training of the monks at Belur as *brahmacaris* and *sannyasis* fits them more for meditation than organization, and while most of the swamis that come to America are graduates of Indian universities, especially the University of Calcutta, they do not care enough for American life to adopt its ways. In the second place, following Vivekananda, the monks come only as guests, having no funds[24] of their order for the work, and so can advance no faster than the demand for their services stimulated by literature or friendly contact. In the third place, the supply is not even as great as the modest demand. In St. Louis, for example, an interested group has the desire and the funds for a swami, but the swami in question is unwilling to come out from India because of his interest in training *genuine* monks. In the fourth place, finally, the swamis fail to use either of the two methods necessary for spreading any religious work in America, (1) prominent advertising or (2) community cultivation.

In view of the conservatism of both message and method, we are not surprised to discover that the influence of the Ramakrishna movement in America, outside its membership and local following, is scarcely perceptible, and its membership is generally on the decline. In 1906 there were 340 members in the whole country, but in 1916 only 190. And membership does not necessarily mean conversion. By 1926[25] ten members had been added, owing perhaps to the increase of swamis and new centers. But on the whole, from its inception until the present, the movement shows a marked decline in local interest, and after 1906 a decline in membership levelling into stagnation. The failure to expand is probably due first to the wearing off of novelty, and second to the retirement of Swami Abhedananda, who was willing to adjust himself to American institutions in both message and method. His *Vedanta Bulletin,* for example, had a circulation of over 3000 copies, 300 of which were sent free to libraries and student organizations.

However, the principle cause of Vedanta stagnation in America is the master Ramakrishna himself. Scorning the body, he put his stamp of disapproval on mental healing, and so prevented the movement from developing in a popular way along the line of such cults as Christian Science. Shunning wealth, he made the order minimize the value of great funds of its own. And with his old-fashioned Hindu conviction that the disciple will always come to the master, so that the master need not go out and preach, he limited aggressive propaganda. It was really not so much the Hindu Ramakrishna that sent Vivekananda to America, as English education, Indian nationalism and liberal Christianity. For Swami Jnanesvarananda says today, "I will sing my song here whether crowds listen or no," and Swami Bodhananda feels that as far as membership goes, the Vedanta movement in America is never likely to prosper. In the spirit of the ancient *Upanishads,* he says, "Vedanta does not appeal to the masses. And as for me, I shall never compromise its truth to make it popular. Even if the masses flocked to my door, I would still continue the intensive cultivation of the individual."

5. The Members

If Vedanta does not appeal to the masses, then to what kind of people does it appeal? Swami Vivekananda, we remember, was supported by men and women of wealth and influence; but according to his biographers, he preached to rich and poor alike, and the accounts of contemporary newspapers,[26] as well as the judgments of contemporary leaders of American opinion,[27] indicate that his followers can best be classified, not by financial income, but by mental disposition. They were intellectual, odd, and venturesome; religious liberals, social rebels and cultural faddists. But that was over a generation ago. What kind of people are Vedanta members at present?

I have attempted to answer this question by means of personal acquaintance and questionnaire letters,[28] and now set down the results of my study. Since I cannot claim information from more than one fifth of the members, my observations will apply only to this limited group comprising probably the most devoted members. In just this

group, then, most of the members are native Americans,
with a sprinkling of English, Germans, Swedes and Jews.
Their ages run from 35 to 70, with an average of 48.
Two-fifths are unmarried, and more than three-fourths
of the group are women. Most of the women are occupied at home, but some of the single women have high
clerical positions. No one occupation is dominant among
the men, their work ranging from "manual" to "mental."
More than half of the group come from Protestant homes,
while the rest, half come from parents who confess no
religion, and almost half from Catholic parents. Several
inherit the Christian Science tradition. So far the group
seems fairly normal. There are very few men and young
people to be sure, but perhaps men and young people
are not apt to volunteer to fill out questionnaires. The
census shows in the whole movement no more than twice
as many women as men.

Now, however, we come to some eccentricities. Of
those who came from religious homes, about two-thirds
strayed away from the church of their parents into other
cults even before they had heard of Vedanta, and of these,
many changed their connection several times. For example, one Unitarian became an Episcopalian, then
dropped out of the Church altogether, then took up in
turn New Thought, Christian Science and Theosophy before coming to rest in Vedanta. If we add to this number those who had no church to begin with, we find that
almost all of the group were religious wanderers, restless souls who passed through many "borderland" cults
till they found Vedanta. And half of the few church
members who joined the Hindu cult without wandering,
have now left their churches, in spite of the fact that
Vedanta demands no severing of former church connection, and even claims to support all cults and sects. It
seems that the estimate of the character of Vedanta ad-

herents in the time of Vivekananda still holds today in the main.

Now what do our pilgrims find in Vedanta that they missed in former churches and cults? In other words, what are the causes of their conversion? Half of them find a broadening of outlook that brings sweet tolerance and appreciation of all religions. A few find for the first time a personal religion of experience and practice, a few enjoy its otherworldly emphasis, while the rest feel relief in giving up their old, perplexing doctrines such as the sinfulness of man, the necessity of faith, the vicarious atonement, an extra-cosmic God, Christ the only incarnation, the need for conversion, Bible "myths" and the exclusive claims of Christianity.

Then after devoting themselves to this Hindu cult, what do our pilgrims come to? Do they worship Christ and read the Bible with a Vedanta interpretation, or do they find other leaders and books to guide them? In other words, what are the effects of their conversion? Only a few give first place in their estimation to Christ and the Bible. The vast majority prefer Hindu books and leaders although the names of Emerson and Lincoln are prominent, and the *Imitation of Christ* is a favorable book. One-third look to Ramakrishna or Vivekananda as the supreme human model, while not a few love their own swami the best.

Thus the Ramakrishna cult in America performs a dual function. In a few cases it takes nominal Christians and enlarges their views, and Swami Jnanesvarananda is right when he says that his cult presents Christianity to Christians—at least to *some* Christians—in a new and appealing way.[29] But in most cases, it takes stray seekers for truth without any definite tradition, and leads them into Hinduism as their first vital religion. While Vedanta is indeed not a sect, with hard and fast lines of distinction, it cannot, on the other hand, be called an impartial, universal religion that keeps everyone in his own tradition of worship. It is just one cult among others—more tolerant and broad than many, it is true—but still a particular cult, a magnetic center of influence that slowly but surely draws some kinds of people from indifference and nominal Christianity into Hinduism. In this way, the protestation that all cults are equally true, made by Hinduism in India as a defence against the conversion of nominal Hindus to Christianity, becomes in America a subtle instrument for the conversion of nominal Christians to Hinduism, for it is precisely the Hindu method of broad generalization that entices certain doubting and creed-bound Christian rebels into the capacious Hindu fold.

As a bit of tangible evidence that American Vedanta is not merely a kind of Christian interpretation but a special Hindu cult, stands the San Francisco Vedanta Society's Hindu Temple[30] on the southwest corner of Webster and Filbert Streets, erected as "the first Hindu temple in the whole Western world" August 21, 1905, under the auspices of the Ramakrishna *Matha* in India. It is a splendid three-storied structure in Hindu style adapted to American building material. In the beautiful auditorium appears a large picture of Christ sitting in the *yoga* posture. Above the main roof of the building rise several picturesque Hindu cupolas, one serving as a small conservatory and another as a special temple to the god Siva. Inside this little temple are displayed a number of Hindu utensils and religious symbols in brass and wood and stone.

6. The Critics

Alarmed at this "Hindu Invasion of America," Mrs. Mabel Potter Daggett, among others,[31] sounded a vibrant note of warning to Christian men and women in the

Hampton Columbian Magazine issue of October, 1911, which found an echo in *Current Literature, The Missionary Review,* and *The Literary Digest.* This Christian defender of the faith sees American Vedantism as just a part of a great oriental invasion, and points to the Buddhist temple at Seattle, the Krishna temple at Los Angeles,[32] the Zoroastrian temples at Chicago and Lowell (Massachusetts) as startling evidence. And what is the result of it all, she asks. Futility at best, but here and there—insanity!

Miss Sarah J. Farmer,[33] you remember, who gave a fortune for the study of oriental religions at Greenacre Inn—what became of her? She is in the insane asylum at Waverly, Massachusettes, says Mrs. Daggett. And Mrs. Ole Bull,[34] who died in 1911, bequeathing several hundred thousand dollars to the Vedanta Centre—her will was set aside by the courts on the ground of mental incapacity and undue influence. Then the wife of a college president renounced her home with the words, "My husband and children are no more to me than any others equally deserving of regard. My religion teaches me that I am free to seek the perfect life alone."[35] And finally, a club woman of national repute is said to be a physical wreck through the practice of *yoga* and the study of occultism.[36] The danger to American women, says Mrs. Daggett, lies not so much in the worship of images such as little brown Buddhas and little jade Krishnas—although this is bad enough—but in the worship of men, their Hindu *gurus,* or swamis. After a certain swami has finished his devotions, his female devotees bow eagerly to kiss his sandalled feet.

What shall we say of these strictures? Is Hinduism really dangerous for America? First of all, we must remember that women have been known to go insane over other creeds than Hinduism, and perhaps men also!

So even if these reports are true, it is hard to tell just what they indicate with regard to the relative risks and dangers involved in Hinduism. I have heard Hindu rites in America called "awful mysteries," but I have also read that the Christian rites of the Lord's Supper in the Roman Empire were supposed to be loathsome by those who knew them not. Having myself partaken of the Lord's Supper, a communion restricted to Christians, I report nothing harmful therein; and having also attended a Hindu meditation class, confined to members of the society, I report that I escaped unharmed, and even benefited by the period of relaxation. But whether the *yoga* practice of the Ramakrishna movement contains subtle dangers or not can best be discovered by a faithful study of the *yoga* presented by Vivekananda in his book *Raja Yoga*, and taught by his present day followers in their meditation classes.

7. GROUP PRACTICE

"Each soul," says Vivekananda, "is potentially divine. The goal is to manifest this divine within, by controlling nature, external and internal.[37] Do this by work, or worship, or psychic control or philosophy, by one, or more, or all of these—and be free."[38] Thus the goal of life is the liberation of the soul. As for the methods of this attainment, "work" is *karma-yoga*, "worship" is *bhakti-yoga*, "psychic control" is *raja-yoga*, while "philosophy" is *jnana-yoga*. It is the *raja-yoga* of phychic control that is studied and practiced in the meditation classes of the various Vedanta centers as the key to the other *yogas*, says Vivekananda:

Raja-Yoga is divided into eight steps. The first is *Yama*—non-killing, truthfulness, non-stealing, continence, and non-receiving of any gifts. Next is *Niyama*—cleanliness, contentment, austerity, study, and self-surrender to God. Then comes *Asana*, or posture; *Pranayama*, or control of *Prana*; *Pratyahara*, or restraint of the senses from their objects; *Dharana,* or fixing the mind on a spot; *Dhyana,* or meditation; and *Samadhi,* or super-consciousness.[39]

In the weekly class of about fifteen members in the New York Society, we are first told to relax the body and empty the mind completely. Each worshiper is to imagine he is the absolute passive witness of the world of action, including his body, quite apart from himself. Then follow six "Steps in Meditation."[40]

(1) *Guru-pranama,* or Salutation to the Masters. Here each one may invoke the blessing of his special savior, or all the saviors at once. The swami chants a Sanskrit *mantra,* or holy affirmation, and then tells us to imagine we are charging the machinery of the body with electricity. We may think of this electricity as a spiritual energy emanating from the divine masters.

(2) *Asana-suddhi,* or Purification of Posture. Here we are told to sit at ease, but quite erect, with the spine, neck and head in one straight line. We breathe deeply with a slow and measured rhythm. The swami chants again, and then tells us to imagine a holy circle, a protecting wall[41] of divine elements surrounding and keeping us from all harm.

(3) *Bhuta-suddhi,* or Purification of the Subtle Body Elements. This is accomplished by meditation on the astral upward progress of the *Kundalini,*[42] or serpent-power, from the fire at the bottom of the spine through the six successive lotus flowers of the *Susumna,* or spinal canal, until it merges in the "Infinite Divine Consciousness" of the *sahasrara,* or thousand-petalled lotus, of the brain. All of these elements, of course, are not physical, but "astral." As the swami gives us the cues, we imagine the serpent power mounting, lotus after lotus, supposedly feeling an exaltation and sublimation of our now stimulated animal nature.

(4) *Ista-dhyana* and *Manas-puja,* or Meditation on the Ideal Person and Worship with the Mind. Now I am supposed to call up in my mind an image of the god or ideal person I most revere, the most lovely figure I know—it may be Siva, Kali, Rama, Krishna, Ramakrishna, Vivekananda, Jesus, Spinoza, my mother, wife or sweetheart—and mentally exchange loving offerings as if my beloved were actually present in form. Again the Sanskrit chant, and again the silent worship.

(5) *Asirvad,* or Blessing. Now that we have reached the peak of spiritual joy and love, let us not be selfish, but send out to all beings, whether plant, animal or human, spiritual blessings, or vibrations of love and best wishes. Again the chant and the worship.

(6) *Atma-samarpana,* or Self Dedication. To escape all trace of selfishness, we now dedicate the fruit of our holy exercises to the deity.

These devotions are intended to occupy one third of the hour. During the next third the swami lectures on Vivekananda's *Raja Yoga,* and the final third is reserved for questions and answers. The group meditation practised in class is of course sketchy and incomplete. It contains only two of the eight steps mentioned by Vivekananda, and deals with the *Kundalini* only in rapid outline. In the privacy of the home, especially in a small sacred room, or domestic temple, reserved for the purpose, one is supposed to practice with greater persistence and in greater detail. This greater detail, especially in regard to the control of the breath, and meditation on the *Kundalini,* is elaborated in Vivekananda's book, and explained by the local swamis.

8. INDIVIDUAL PRACTICE

Breath control is not an end in itself, but the means of rousing the *Kundalini* to begin its upward progress.

But what is the *Kundalini,* and why should it go up? In the first place, you will never discover its path by dissecting the human corpse, as Swami Dayananda Sarasvati, the founder of the Arya Samaj, once tried to do. It is purely astral, that is, psychic, occult, mystic, imaginary, autosuggestive, we are told. I suppose if everyone imagines it in the same way, it may be called a real, or public, object like a mermaid, a nightmare, or a volt.

The *Kundalini,* then, is astral fire, or lurid light, in the form of a serpent. It is perhaps what Freud would call the *libido,* the surplus animal energy of man. Unless it be aroused, man is dull and apathetic, but once aroused it makes him fiery and passionate until it can be controlled and directed into the higher, more intellectual centers of human activity. In other words, man's infinite potential power must be made first kinetic and then sublime. The *jiva,* or individual life, must unite with the *Siva,* or universal life. Man must rise to God in the exalted intuition of "That art thou," (God art thou), the consciousness of Buddhahood or Christhood, the "realization" of absolute existence, knowledge and bliss, in short, *samadhi.* So speaks the swami, but confesses he has never attained *samadhi.*

You feel tired and listless because your *Kundalini,* or "coiled one," is coiled up true to its name in a tight little spring down below. If you are a disciple of Ramakrishna, what do you do? First you sit down in proper form to meditate. Early evening, like early morning, is auspicious. Then you rouse your serpent-power by breathing.

Why breathing? The connection is this. The fiery serpent lies coiled at the base of a *nadi,* or tube, of light called the *susumna,* running vertically through the center of the spinal cord. In this cord on each side of the *susumna* is another tube, the *ida* on the left, and the *pingala* on the right. These three tubes are openly connected at their base, but the *susumna* is temporarily closed near the bottom by the dormant *Kundalini*, which prevents the *Prana*, the cosmic breath, or *élan vital*, from rising in it. By breathing, you force the breath against the *Kundalini* from below, and rouse it to ascend. As it ascends it not only sublimates the personality, but also makes way for the *Prana* to come up after, causing an inflow of universal power.[43]

First you close the right nostril, and breathe in through the *ida* (or left tube) up to capacity in four seconds, counting mentally with the sacred sound *"Om."* Then you close both nostrils, and hold your breath for sixteen seconds, allowing it to press on the *Kundalini* from below. Then you close the left nostril, and breathe out through the *pingala* in eight seconds. Then you repeat the whole process over and over again, breathing deeply with equal periods according to the rhythm 1:4:2 as, for example, in 4:16:8 seconds. When you become adept, you can increase the duration of each count, holding the breath four minutes, let us say. Concentration of attention aids the power of breath. After enduring repeated stresses, the channel of *susumna* finally opens, and the *Kundalini* begins to rise.

Now before it reaches the top, it must shoot through six astral nerve centers conceived as lotus flowers hanging at intervals from the inner side of the spinal channel. This main process is called the *sat-cakra-bheda,* or literally, "six-circle-shooting." As you meditate on the soft pale light of the *Kundalini,* it rushes up the *susumna,* striking in turn each hanging lotus bud, tossing it into an erect, full blown flower, and passing on upward through its center.[44] By this time you are feeling fit and spry, entirely rid of your bodily and mental fatigue.

Do not presume, however, that you have reached the goal, for the goal is nothing less than "superconscious" bliss. If you practice long enough with sufficient intense persistence, they say, you may at certain levels experience wonderful visions, and gain control over a variety of occult powers, but unless you continue to meditate stead-fastly until the *Kundalini* strikes the blissful *sahasrara,* or thousand-petalled lotus in the brain, your devotion will not be crowned with spiritual success.

The normal person who has his brute nature of eating, drinking and reproducing fairly well under control can imagine that the *Kundalini* when aroused rises without delay through the three baser lotuses of animal nature, and pierces the fourth lotus opposite the heart in the plane of fiery ambition. Then if the mind be filled with the ideal of truth and peace and control over emotions, this uncoiled serpent may shoot up and pierce the fifth lotus opposite the *medulla oblongata.* An expansion of peaceful sentiment will raise it to the sixth lotus in the pineal gland opposite the eyebrows, and in rare cases persistent meditation will cause it to strike the *sahasrara,* and fuse the individual with the universal in the blissful state of *samadhi,* or waking sleep. Even after the state has passed away its effects will persist in everyday life as a sense of peace and power.[45]

I have met no one who says his *Kundalini* has ever struck the *sahasrara.* The swamis of the New York Vedanta Society make no such claim. However, one of the faithful members, by driving his *Kundalini* up through the first lotus has gained relief from the temptation of "women," and now feels the peace and joy of private sex-sensation that seems not to drain but enhance his vitality. But this "wonderful" realization only spurs him to greater efforts to raise the serpent above sex altogether into the realms of finer, more spiritual delight. This novice in *raja-yoga* is the odd one of his family, away from his home and country, unmarried, and compelled to drudge for his daily bread. His main relief and enjoyment comes from this practice of *yoga* before the peaceful idol and amid the fragrant incense of the temple of his neat little bedroom.

Another Vedanta adherent, also away from home and country, is a somewhat younger man of more reflective type who takes truth wherever he can get it, and who prefers study to marriage on a small salary. He finds that *raja-yoga* enables him to control his stray thoughts and fiery temper, and helps him secure peace, and efficiency in his business life. He has no desire to renounce the world, but would like to attain perfection in self-control in the six months mentioned by Vivekananda. Still another wanderer from abroad, a successful business man whose race suffered religious persecution in the "old country" when he was a child, finds in the mystic vision and practice of Hinduism such freedom, health and joy that the world seems ever like springtime. His insight "makes all things new." In spite of his prematurely stooped shoulders and white hair, he is happy with his wife and children, and although he smokes over a hundred cigarettes a day, he feels healthy, wears light clothes in cold weather, works hard, and devotes much time to the study of books on mysticism.

One member confessed he suffered a heart attack while spurring on his *Kundalini,* but this was due to his failure to consult his swami. Vivekananda expressly states that students who wish to practice the *raja-yoga* "are especially and earnestly reminded that, with few exceptions, *Yoga* can only be safely learned by direct contact with a teacher."[46] This however leads us to inquire whether the implicit obedience to the teacher demanded by Hinduism from the days of the *Upanishads* is not in itself a danger. In so far as the devotee is immature such practice cannot be justly condemned if the character of the teacher is above reproach. But who can judge the character of the teacher? He may be a saint with very eccentric ideas. In fairness to the swamis, however, it must be said that the members seem to be more responsible than they are for retaining this ancient custom.

The *yoga* practice as it now stands is opposed to the spirit of modern science, for its whole ancient background of theory is magical and ascetic. A practice is magical (1) when it seeks to work in a realm above nature, or (2) when it is secret or limited to a select few. Now on the basis of classic Hindu philosophy, Vivekananda[47] posits two realms, one of which is psychical, inner and subtle, while the other is physical, outer and gross. The subtle, he says, is the controlling cause of the gross. The yogi seeks to control nature, or the gross realm, by working in the subtle realm of the mind above nature. Moreover, he tells us that "*Yoga* fell into the hands of a few persons who made it a secret, instead of letting the full blaze of daylight and reason fall upon it. They did so that they might have the power to themselves."[48] Thus the classic *yoga* practice is magical according to both parts of the definition.

With his admiration for modern science, Swami Jnanesvarananda would *like* to "rid America of the idea that Hindu meditation is something hypnotic, occult or magical,"[49] but he will have a hard time doing it unless he changes his view of reality as sharply divided into "outer" and "inner." According to this teaching, the inner, or subtle, realm is the *Prana,* or cosmic energy, which manifests itself inside the body as the power of breathing. By controlling our breathing, says the Hindu leader, we may learn to control the cosmic breathing, or *Prana,* and thus come to master all nature. Says Vivekananda:

The knowledge and control of this *Prana* is really what is meant by *Pranayama.* This opens to us the door to almost unlimited power. Suppose, for instance, a man understood the *Prana* perfectly, and could control it, what power on earth would not be his? He would be able to move the sun and stars out of their places, to control everything in the universe, from the atoms to the biggest suns, because he would control the *Prana*. This is the end and aim of *Pranayama*. When the *Yogi* becomes perfect there will be nothing in nature not under his control. If he orders the gods or the souls of the departed to come, they will come at his bidding. All the forces of nature will obey him like slaves. When the ignorant see these powers of the *Yogi* they call them miracles.

The *Yogis* say that behind this particular manifestation there is a generalization. Behind all particular ideas stands a generalized, an abstract principle; grasp it, and you have grasped everything. Just as this whole universe has been generalized, in the Vedas, into that One Absolute Existence, and he who has grasped that Existence has grasped the whole universe, so all forces have been generalized into this *Prana*, and he who has grasped the *Prana* has grasped all the forces of the universe, mental or physical. He who has controlled the *Prana* has controlled his own mind, and all the minds that exist. He who has controlled the *Prana* has controlled his body, and all the bodies that exist, because the *Prana* is the generalized manifestation of force.

We see sects in every country who have attempted the control of *Prana*. In this country there are Mind-healers, Faith-healers, Spiritualists, Christian Scientists, Hypnotists, etc., and if we examine these different bodies, we shall find at the back of each this control of the *Prana*, whether they know it or not. If you boil all their theories down, the residuum will be that. It is the one and the same force they are manipulating, only unknowingly. They have stumbled on the discovery of a force and are using it unconsciously without knowing its nature, but it is the same as the *Yogi* uses, and which comes from the *Prana*.[50]

I confess I have never had the privilege of attending any of these exhibits of mental power, nor can I testify to the exercise of the various powers mentioned specifically in Patanjali's *Raja Yoga*, on which Vivekananda bases his amazing statements: clairvoyance, the understanding of animal speech, mind reading, invisibility, supernormal strength, television, telescience, walking on water or thorns, illumination, telaudition, levitation, alternation of size, extreme endurance, control of involuntary organs, surpassing speed, broad intuition, fine discrimination, imperturbability, personal isolation, and others.

Here we have an enormous mass of enormous claims. What shall we say about them? Shall we throw them all overboard as so much obsolete fiction? Such procedure would accord nicely with a certain modern temper, but would it be scientific? On account of the dualism and secrecy of the old-fashioned *yoga,* these astounding assertions have persisted up till now in all their bold entirety. When they meet the monism and publicity of modern science, they will be welcomed, tested, criticized and appraised. How much of their substance will remain?

Just now it is hard to tell, for modern scientific investigation of mental capacity is still in its infancy. Perhaps group hypnotism is one of the chief explanations of the yogi's wonders. No doubt many beliefs are based on nothing more substantial than clever frauds. Again, the very concentration employed by the yogi produces a simple uncritical state of mind in which any bit of imagination is felt with the force of the utmost truth and reality. Certainly I shall believe I can touch the moon with the tip of my finger if for a long while I persist in thinking nothing else, just as when I am on the operating table and almost overcome with anaesthetic I may be convinced that the whole universe is pervaded by the odor of ether. Any event will seem true if unchecked by any other. All of science and philosophy is just the criticism of events originally taken as self-evident truths.

Yet for all our hard-headed slashing at reported wonders, there will most likely remain a solid core of significant and unusual powers that can be developed by anyone who has a certain capacity, knows the method, and is willing to take the time. One of the chief obstacles in the way of sifting the *yoga* practice for genuine achieve-

ment is that those who know most about it are the most
reluctant to divulge their knowledge, perhaps on account
of pride, bashfulness, exclusiveness, or the justifiable desire to prevent the spread of half-knowledge and mis-
guided popular enthusiasm which would foster all degrees
of trickery and deception. Moreover, the true yogi is not
supposed to use his powers. Another difficulty in learning about *yoga* at first hand is the excessive amount of
time, patience, self-discipline and strenuous practice it
requires. To practice *yoga* in addition to regular work
is to burn life's candle at both ends.

For example, the celebrated Hindu inventor, Shunkar
A. Bisey, D. Sc., Ph. D. (whose first name in classic transliteration is Sankara), tells me that he used to practice
yoga in youth, and gained the power to read the mind in
a very simple, mechanical way, but only after a severe
course of diet, fasting and mental training. Consequently,
in the words of a friend writing in the *East-West* magazine,[51] "he found it impracticable to carry out such *Yoga*
practices any further while giving his attention to government service." With his Hindu lore, his knowledge of
magician's tricks, his long residence in the West, and his
scientific habit of mind, Dr. Bisey is eminently fitted to
conduct research into *yoga* in coöperation with Western
scientists for the benefit of the modern man, and we may
hope that some day he will find leisure enough to turn
his attention to this fascinating problem.

Now the *raja-yoga* as presented to us by Vivekananda
is not only magical but also ascetic. Above the two
realms of this world is a third—the absolute, potential
realm of *akasa*.[52] Here we have a double dualism—a
dualism between mind and body, and a dualism between
the world of mind and body and the posited reality of the
passive and solitary self.

Beyond the vibrations of matter in its gross and subtle

aspects, beyond motion there is but One. . . . Modern physics
. . . has demonstrated that the sum-total of the energies in the
universe is the same throughout. It has also been proven that
this sum-total of energy exists in two forms. It becomes potential, toned down, and calmed, and next it comes out manifested
as all these various forces; again it goes back to the quiet state,
and again it manifests. Thus it goes on evolving and involving
through eternity.[53]

Here we see an attempt to identify "kinetic energy"
with the cosmic *Prana*, the goddess Kali and the "lower"
Brahman; and "potential energy" with the infinite *akasa*,
the god Siva and the "higher" Brahman. This combination
of Herbert Spencer and Hindu cosmology reminds us of
Zeno and Plotinus. How much science is there in this
persistent view?

As we look back over the spread of the Ramakrishna
movement, what difference can we note between its Indian and American development? In the first place, as
we have already seen,[54] the social service of the Ramakrishna Mission is not carried on in America, while the
preaching of the Ramakrishna *Matha* is kept up in both
countries. In India, the swamis of the *Matha* may either
wander alone or share the work of the monastery, but in
America they never lose touch with society. In their
native land all the monks are garbed in the saffron robes
of renunciation, but in the West, except when preaching,
they dress even as you or I. These are matters of land and
custom. But has there been any adjustment of message
and method?

We know that Swami Abhedananda made a few ac-
commodations to American institutions, and Swami Jnanesvarananda adapted his preaching to American ideas—
mostly in form, but somewhat in substance also. However, no radical adjustment has taken place. The methods
are still based on the notion that the pupil will seek out
the teacher, and the message still includes the idea that

the world *is* illusion. As in India, so in America, the function of the *Matha* is (1) to harmonize religious tradition and (2) to preach the peaceful old Hindu *Dharma*. We notice two kinds of people among the converts to Vedanta of the Ramakrishna type: the few who remain in their original churches with broader and more tolerant views, and the many who plunge into Vedanta to find peace for their restless souls.

If we stop here, however, we miss the most important point of all, for in the Ramakrishna movement the influence of East on West is not so great as the influence of West on East. The work of the Ramakrishna Mission in India is far more extensive, and certainly more fruitful in its practical results than the work of the Ramakrishna *Matha* in both India and America. And the Mission, as we have seen, is a growth of the Christian spirit and American methods grafted on to Hindu stock. Getting his Christian spirit from his Alma Mater and the Brahma Samaj, and his training in organization from America, Vivekananda went back to India and started a movement that has won universal esteem for its unusually devoted and effective service.

CHAPTER VI

THE YOGODA SAT-SANGA SOCIETY, YOGANANDA'S PRACTICAL CULT

One day a friend gave me a pamphlet bearing this title:

Descriptive Outline of
YOGODA
or
A system for Harmonious and Full Development
of Body, Mind and Soul
A Practical, Scientific Technique of Concentration
and Meditation Leading to Conscious Contact
with Inner Divine Forces
A Method of Recharging the Body, Mind and Soul
Batteries from Inner Cosmic Energy
as Taught by
SWAMI YOGANANDA, A.B.
of India
Swami Dhirananda, M.A., Associate
Ninth Edition
Published by
YOGODA SAT-SANGA SOCIETY
Los Angeles

On the inside of the front cover is this advertisement:

BOOKS BY SWAMI YOGANANDA, A. B.

Scientific Healing Affirmations. This book has become a world-wide inspiration. These affirmations have been used at Swami's Healing Meetings and thousands have been healed and liberated from body, mind and soul inharmonies. Scientific Explanation and Unique Methods of Healing for different types of mind. 50c.

Psychological Chart. 9th Edition. A practical and helpful chart for Analyzing Human Nature and Conduct. A Psychological Mirror. Highly recommended by many University Professors. 50c.

Songs of the Soul. Intuitional Poems, inspired thru spiritual realization. Includes "Vision of Visions" from the Bhagavad Gita. For Chanting, Meditation, and Soul Revelation. "We mark in some poems the power of Milton, in others the imagery of Keats, and in all the philosophic depth of the Oriental Sages." $1.50.

Science of Religion. Douglas Grant Duff Ainslee writes: "This small book is the clue to the universe. Its value is beyond estimation in words, since between these narrow covers is to be found the flower of the Vedas and Upanishads, the essence of Patanjali (foremost exponent of the Yoga philosophy and method), and the thought of Sankara (greatest mind that ever dwelt in mortal body!), placed for the first time within reach of the multitude." $1.50.

SET OF ABOVE FIVE BOOKS, $3.75.

Philosophic Insight, by Swami Dhirananda. Unique philosophical exposition of the ideal and real in life. It embodies in essay form the deepest Oriental thought. Its elevating message presented in a strictly psychological way is intensely gripping. $1.25.

Sheet Music (for Piano). "Songs of Brahma," 35c. "My Soul is Marching On," 20c.

Pasted on the blank page opposite this list of books are a couple of dull yellow slips bearing the following suggestion:

Enclosed please find my personal check (or money order) for $25.00, for which please send me the twelve Lessons of the Yogoda Correspondence Course. With these I will receive free a set of five books by Swami Yogananda, and also one year's subscription to the East-West Magazine.

In enrolling myself as a student, I declare on my honor that:

(1) I will practice the Yogoda lessons to the best of my ability, and

(2) I will keep the Yogoda lessons for my own personal use and knowledge unless otherwise permitted.

On the inside of the back cover is pasted and folded a light-green four-page leaflet containing testimonials to Swami Yogananda given by certain members of his Yogoda classes in several large cities of the United States. Finally, on the outside of the back cover, the following advertisement may be seen:

A Unique Magazine
Published by Swami Yogananda
EAST-WEST
Beautiful—Inspiring

A New Illustrated Non-Sectarian Magazine devoted to the Spiritual, Psychological, Artistic and Cultural aspects of all Civilizations, especially the Oriental, with special reference to their bearing on Present-Day, Practical Life. Articles dealing with Spiritual Realization, Hindu Psychology, Practical Metaphysics and the Truth-Offerings of East and West.

25c a Copy

509 Fifth Avenue   New York, N. Y.

About one-half of the 80 page pamphlet is devoted to photographs and descriptions of Swami Yogananda and his work, including many glowing testimonials of newspaper writers, physicians and famous Yogoda students, Luther Burbank and Madame Galli-Curci among them. The other half is devoted to an explanation of his system tending to arouse a keen desire to take his Correspondence Course.

Yogoda, says the swami on page 18, is the method of giving harmony to the individual. "The word *Yogoda* is derived from *Yoga,* meaning harmony or equilibrium, and *da,* that which imparts. Hence *Yogoda* means that particular system whose proper use can impart harmony and equilibrium, to all the forces and faculties that operate for the perfection of body, mind and soul." Here the swami is reinterpreting the classic *yoga,* which teaches the *annihilation of mental activity. Sat-sanga* is the society that practices the method of Yogoda. Since *sat* means truth, and *sanga* fellowship or society, the word *Sat-sanga* means fellowship with truth, or The Truth Society.

The swami's explanation of his method abounds in such terms as electricity, vibration and evolution; will, concentration and meditation; consciousness, subconsciousness and superconsciousness; immanence, divinity and revelation. He is American in both the terseness of his style and the exuberance of his claims. He speaks in words of popular science, and supports his statements by Hindu lore and verses taken from the Bible. All his teachings in the course described imply the notion that each human body is connected by *will* with a divine cosmic consciousness, or infinite energy.

In *concentration,* or the focussing of attention on various parts of the body during exercise, the will can infuse them with the healthful energy it draws from the cosmic source of supply. The first part of the course deals with this concentration, which the swami claims is his own invention. In *meditation,* or the focussing of attention on the cosmic energy itself, the will can merge itself with the divine. This second part is said to be adapted from the ancient Hindu *yoga* for the use of the modern West. The third and final part is devoted to various practical suggestions culled from East and West for the improvement of personality. The swami scorns neither medicine nor exercise; he simply wishes to supplement and direct these aids to health by force of will.

Aroused by these rich promises and two urgent follow-up letters, I managed to obtain the Correspondence Course and complete set of books, as well as all the copies of the *East-West* magazine. The *Psychological Chart* is published in the form of a pamphlet with a pale-green cover, while all the other bits of literature are small books that shine forth in covers of brilliant orange or saffron, the same color as the *sannyasi's* robe. The magazine is of ordinary size, with an attractive cover showing the two hemispheres and the lotus-and-eye symbol of Yogoda. The paper is excellent, and the thirty odd pages profusely illustrated with photographs. Soon after, I received a little folder with the swami's picture and this announcement:

Fellowship of Faiths
in cooperation with
DHARMA MANDAL
(The Hindu Religious Association)
Three Lectures
by Swami Yogananda
Preceded by Music
Interpretative Plays or Pictures
AT THE UNION AUDITORIUM
229 West 48th Street, West of Broadway
On January 14, 21, 28 at 8:15.

I attended the first lecture, which was on The Metaphysical Unity of Hinduism and Christianity. The "Union Auditorium" I discovered to be the Union Methodist Episcopal Church. This small church was comfortably filled—at least the main floor—with women and a sprinkling of men, some of whom were Hindus. After a brief organ recital, the chairman, the Reverend Eliot White, a certain Episcopal rector, offered a prayer for the sense of unity among men, and then introduced Mr. Kedar Nath Das Gupta of the Fellowship of Faiths, who read a short drama of love and faith called *Savitri*. Then the chairman urged the formation of a group sufficiently interested in the play to provide an audience and cast for its actual performance. He also advertised Yogananda's books and the *Calamus*, a London quarterly of the Threefold Movement. He held in his hand the first number, from which he read an editorial by the Reverend Will Hayes.

Calamus, says the editor, is the name for the common pond-weed chosen by Walt Whitman as the symbol of comradeship. It also means pen, the pen of mutual appreciation more powerful than the sword. Out of the calamus, finally, is made the calumet or peace pipe of the American Indian. Thus the *Calamus* magazine shall promote the unity of mankind. The Threefold Movement works for *human* unity through the League of Neighbors, for *cultural* unity through the Union of East and West, and for *spiritual* unity through the Fellowship of Faiths.

Then Swami Yogananda was introduced as an Indian lecturer, writer and philosopher. As he rose from his seat in the audience to mount the platform, several persons in the audience rose also, perhaps out of gratitude for some benefit conferred by Yogoda, perhaps in honor of the spirituality of the East, perhaps in accord with the Indian pupil's respect for his master. The swami is short and plump, with a striking face. His raven hair hung over his shoulders in wavy locks—even longer than usual among Bengalis—and he wore the vivid orange robe over his Western attire. His first act was to read one of his own poems, which he called "The Royal Sly Eluder," a record of his personal search for God in ocean, tree and sky, a search which ended in hearing God's voice within the soul, calling out "Hello, playmate, here am I!" The swami's voice was loud and clear, his pronunciation good. He then began his demonstration of the "metaphysical unity of Hinduism and Christianity." Out of the playful popular presentation, I derived the following argument:

There are two methods of understanding the sacred scriptures of any religion. The one is *inference* based on *sense-perception*, the other is *intuition*. The method of sense breeds conflict and misunderstanding among different religions, while the method of intuition brings appreciation and unity. Intuition means experience, "realization," simple feeling. For example, let us take first the doctrine of God. Intuition reveals that both Hinduism and Christianity worship one God only, conceived variously as Father, Mother, Friend, Lover and so on. Of course, Hinduism often worships God by the use of idols. But does not Christianity have its "flagolatry"? If Hinduism has its castes, does not Christianity have its denominations? Will the Pope and the Archbishop of Canterbury exchange pulpits?

Or take the doctrine of creation, continued the lecturer. By intuition we can find Hindu teaching in the book of *Genesis*. If we use the method of sense and inference, we notice a contradiction between the first and second verses of the first chapter of *Genesis*. "In the beginning God created the heaven and the earth," says verse one; but verse two says, "The earth was without form and void . . . and the spirit of God moved upon the face of the waters." That is, the earth was *not* yet created. But by the method of intuition, we understand clearly that verse one refers to God's creation of the world in *idea,* whereas verse two refers to God's creation in gross *matter.*

In like manner, the Eastern philosopher declared that the Christian scriptures teach the Hindu doctrines of *karma* and reincarnation. The doctrine of the Trinity too, he said, is fundamentally the same in both scriptures. According to Hinduism, God was at first a great Spirit living all alone. Bored with this monotony, he then projected from Himself a vast ball of vibration. He then penetrated the ball, filling every particle with His presence. This is the Christian doctrine of the Trinity. Only the terms are different. The original great Spirit is God the Father, the ball of vibration is the Holy Ghost, while the spirit in the ball is the "Christ-Consciousness."

It seems that the swami is seeking to explain Christianity in the light of the supposedly deeper knowledge of Hinduism. Like Ramakrishna and his followers he is using Hinduism as a basis for the reconciliation of all faiths. Like the Theosophical Society, he regards Hindu lore as the source of the esoteric, or essential, truths that underlie the exoteric, or literal, truths of Christianity. The preacher of the evening surely had his audience with him

—at least its audible members. Clearly they felt in him a source of truth and comfort, inspiration and stimulation. They nodded assent to his pronouncements and laughed heartily at his jokes, especially when he called Christian preachers "spiritual victrolas" and proclaimed that Christianity was suffering from "theological indigestion."

Yogananda closed his address with the famous Hindu stress on the "inner" life. At a certain time of year, he told us, the little musk deer goes mad after a certain fragrance wafted to its nostrils. It rushes hither and yon to find the source of it, and often perishes from over-exertion, never knowing that the odor delectable came from its own navel. Likewise, we in the West frantically look for God *outside,* but fail to look *within,* where He really can be found.

1. OUT OF INDIA INTO AMERICA

Swami Yogananda (bliss of yoga), like Swami Vivekananda (bliss of discrimination), was drawn to America by a Christian congress. Like his forerunner also, he received his Bachelor of Arts degree from the University of Calcutta. He is likewise a Vedantist, but not a follower of Ramakrishna, and not a member of the *Puri* group of Sankara's monastic order. He claims to belong to the *Giri* group, and considers a Bengali yogi called *Babaji,* or "Great Father," the "Supreme Master of the Yogoda Sat-sanga movement in America and India."[1] Although this master is Swami Yogananda's spiritual great-grandfather, he is still living, and his disciples claim he is several hundred years old.

But Babaji's disciple *Sri Syama* Charan Lahiri *Mahasaya* did not wish to live so long, and although apparently in good health he deliberately took leave of his body forever, while his circle of pupils were pleading with him to remain on earth. Anniversary celebrations are now conducted. This Lahiri *Maharaja,* as he is called, was known in India as a great yogi[2] who developed that part of Patanjali's *Raja Yoga* known as the *kriya-yoga,*[3] which means the strict control of the body, mind and soul, the study of ways of liberation, and the surrender of "fruits of works" to God. Its plan of salvation is very much like that of the *Bhagavad Gita,* teaching one to be "calmly active and actively calm." Yogananda's parents were Lahiri's disciples. Lahiri was not a swami or celibate, but a married saint and *yogi,* who "found God in the jungle of city life and taught others how to find God there." Outward renunciation with inward craving, he declared, is as bad as indulgence. What the world needs is moderation. Whereas the West suffers from too much materialism, the East suffers from too much spirituality. The golden mean is best, the practice of balance by meditation.

Srimath Swami Sri Yuktesvara *Giriji,* initiated as a *sannyasi* by Babaji and as a yogi by Lahiri, was likewise a man of power, influence and balance, and the *guru,* or master, of Yogananda. As his title indicates, he is a member of the *Giri* group of the monastic order founded by Sankara. From this Yuktesvara came the inspiration and command for the spread of Yogoda Sat-sanga in America. Even as Vivekananda in his university days neglected his classes and books to be with Ramakrishna, his master, so did Yogananda before his initiation slip away from study to enjoy the fascinating personality of his master Yuktesvara. Says Swami Yogananda today:

It took me a long time to understand my master and his miraculous power, though I had close contact with him. I have seen miracles, and of all the wonderful things witnessed, I shall declare to the world that I secured my A.B. degree through his miraculous power. I used to always visit and stay with him, and neglected my college work so much that I hardly knew where my college books were. Two days before the university examination, I told my master I wasn't going to appear at the examination. He just changed suddenly and said, "Then all my rela-tions with you cease this instant." He insisted and said, "All I ask of you is to *appear* at the examination." He declared I would pass even though I had not studied. I agreed reluctantly, thinking I would write about his teachings in the answer paper to questions on the writings to Shakespeare. I just agreed literally to carry out his behest.

Next day he asked me, at first gently, then vehemently, to go to a certain friend of mine and ask certain questions of him every morning of all those days that my A.B. examination lasted. This Calcutta University A.B. degree, in some respects, is more diffi-cult to obtain than a Harvard A.B. degree. There is so much injustice and difficulty set in the path of those being examined. I did as my master told me; and strange to say, whatever questions this friend of mine unconsciously told me to prepare for, I found those very questions in my examinations.

After the first day I declared to the world that I was going to pass, and when I received the A.B. degree, my parents and friends, who had given up all hopes about the success of my college life, told me I had performed a miracle. That is why I am fond of putting the A.B. after my name in all my books and articles. The A.B. title reminds me of this singular experi-ence. When I questioned my master, Sri Yukteshwar Giriji, he just replied that faith, works, and knowledge of supermental law can work miracles, where physical efforts of man fail.

. . . .

My master is still living in flesh and blood in India, and i dare not tell all the wonderful things I have seen. This much I can say: throughout the whole western world I have not found a single one like him. . . . Americans who are good listeners and love real progress now ought to go deeper than mere listening to the philosophical message of India's spiritual science. They should learn the technique by which the super-miracles of the mind can be understood, and the higher laws applied to make life not only financially successful, but blissful in every way.[4]

Yoga technique, financial success and all-around bliss is the swami's message in a nutshell, which was fairly well outlined before he ever came to America. And in India a university degree means financial success much more than in America. Whereas Vivekananda's life was a series of fitful turns, Yogananda's has been a steady development.

While still in India, the swami was impressed by the ideal of popular education along the lines laid down centuries ago by Hindu saints and *risis,* or wise men.

In 1917 he made an impassioned appeal for establishing a Residential School in India for boys where they could receive not only the ordinary intellectual training but also the knowledge of leading the practical spiritual life and unfolding their own inner powers for lasting happiness and success in life. One of the noble princes of India, the Honorable Maharaja Sir Manindra Chandra Nundy Bahadur, of Kasimbazar, Member of the Imperial Council, Government of India, responded to the Swami's appeal by offering one of his palaces and other surrounding buildings, situated at Ranchi, in Bengal, and possessing spacious grounds and suitable country environment, for use in establishing such a school. The Maharaja . . . also offered to finance the institution until . . . it could be self-supporting.

Accordingly, on March 22, 1917, the Brahmacarya Vidyalaya . . . opened its doors with a modest enrollment of seven pupils. At the end of the first year the repute of the school had spread so far that there were hundreds of applicants for admission. . . . Only 300 were accepted. . . . Much of the class work is done out of doors. An agricultural course is given and gardening is one of the occupations of the boys. . . . Industrial and commercial training is given in tailoring, spinning, book-binding, cane-work, modelling, typing, bookkeeping, etc. The boys are taught hygiene, nursing, and first aid work. The regular school subjects are taught. . . . There are story classes . . . for the younger children, and dramatic and debating societies for the older boys. Excursion outings to distant places form part of the regular routine, to encourage love for natural beauty and to accustom the body to bear exertion and fatigue.

But the chief distinguishing feature of the school is individual attention received by each student and the close study made of his nature and possibilities by his trained teachers, who record the general character and psychological development and learning of each child in a chart originated by Swami Yogananda for that purpose. The students are divided in groups not according to age and intellectual progress, but according to individual moral and spiritual growth. . . . They are made to avoid all luxuries and wrongly conceived ideas of happiness. Each student keeps a record of his own changing tendencies, and is taught to make it his own business to be better. . . . The atmosphere of harmony, service and happiness is remarked by all visitors to the Institution, which is being conducted during Swami Yogananda's absense by the capable Swami Satyananda. . . . Two other smaller Schools similar to the one at Ranchi have been opened at Puri and Bankura in Bengal.[5]

The swami's method in America is just an outgrowth and adaptation of this enterprising, all-round method of education. Unlike Vivekananda, he seeks to meet a need rather than preach a dogma.

In 1920 Yogananda came to America as the delegate from India to the Pilgrim Tercentenary Anniversary International Congress of Religious Liberals in Boston, Massachusetts, held under the auspices of the Unitarian Church.[6] Thinking this Congress wanted something theoretical and profoundly Hindu, the swami did not explain his educational methods or *yoga* technique, but spoke on "The Science of Religion," a work which had already been published in India, and was later elaborated and printed in book form in America. While in Boston, however, he learned something very practical. Coming into contact with various American cults such as Christian Science and New Thought, he began to admire their efficient methods of propaganda. At the same time, he was convinced that they were teaching only smatterings of the truth that Hinduism possessed as a whole. So he conceived the idea of combining his genuine Hindu message with American methods, and stayed in the new land to teach. Before he had departed from India, his father, who had undertaken the expenses of the long journey, had said to him, "When do you expect to return?" The son had replied, "In about four months—if the Americans don't need me." But as events turned out, many Americans did seem to need his message, as in the case of Vivekananda, and so he stayed.

Through the financial assistance of his father and the enthusiasm of a few devout students, the Swami started a small Sat-Sanga (fellowship of truth) Center in Boston. He lectured before many clubs, colleges and associations. A small summer-school was established near Waltham for students, mainly through the cooperation of Sister Yogamata. The work grew and Swami sent for his beloved associate, Swami Dhirananda, to come to America. . . . Swami came to New York in 1923, aided by Dr. M. W. Lewis of Boston, and in one lecture at the New York Town Hall sowed the seed of interest in his work. He was invited by the management of the Pennsylvania Hotel to become their guest, and he gave lectures and weekly classes there.

Swami marvelled to find a great hunger for spiritual knowledge among the New Yorkers, who are considered to live under a very material environment. He had many distinguished students, including Mr. Alvin Hunsicker, President of the Standard Textile Products Company of New York, and employer of 15,000 men, and Mr. J. W. Mott of the Traymore Hotel, Atlantic City, both of whom have helped the Swami in his work. Mrs. G. F. Harriman, Mrs. E. Klotz, and Mr. E. C. Crowley were also instrumental in spreading the mesage of Yogoda.

In early 1924 Swami visited Philadelphia and spoke there in the Public Library to a capacity house, from which several hundred were turned away. He left a large and enthusiastic class in Philadelphia, including Mr. Leopold Stowkowski, the internationally known conductor of the Philadelphia Orchestra. He received great cooperation from Mrs. E. Richdale (a friend of India), Dr. Wilson, Mr. and Mrs. Eynon, and others. Swami felt every city to be like a big human mind that vibrated differently. New York said, "How much have you got?" Boston said, "How much do you know?" Philadelphia said, "Who are you?" One Philadelphian did actually ask this question of Swami and he replied: "I come from a very high family headed by the Almighty Father."[7]

In connection with this work, and in pursuance of his plan to adopt American methods, Yogananda published his captivating promotion booklet *Yogoda*, which gave the prospectus of his class and correspondence courses.

About this time he was fortunate enough to secure the services of a devoted and effective American secretary, and he felt an inner call to extend the work further. In his mind's eye he saw the West, and especially Los Angeles, swept by his teachings.

Accordingly, he started out to cross the continent in a Maxwell automobile, accompanied by Mr. Rashid and two students. . . . By leisurely travelling and camping, the Swami managed to see and study America and Americans very closely, and enjoyed each moment of the trip. . . . Swami spoke to a cultured audience of 3,000 people in the Denver City Auditorium, where the city organist played "The Song of India" when the Swami entered for the lecture. A large class of Yogoda students was formed with the helpful cooperation of Mrs. F. Simmons, Mrs. Tedrow and Mr. and Mrs. Smith. The city of Denver vibrated to Swami the love for Nature, health-giving life, and the great personality of Judge Ben Lindsey. Swami met Judge and Mrs. Lindsey, and they became good friends and studied Swami's Yogoda System.

After traveling through Colorado Springs and Yellowstone Park, he sailed to Alaska and then returned to Seattle where he spoke to large audiences. Mrs. C. W. Wiley and Mr. and Mrs. A. Willatsen helped to arrange for a large and enthusiastic Yogoda class.

Proceeding to Portland, Swami lectured to huge crowds at the Multnomah Hotel and had a large class of students. Mrs. Kloh of the Portland Metaphysical Library and Mr. and Mrs. C. P. Scott were among those who aided materially in helping Swami to spread his message. In Portland for the first time Swami gave his public divine healing meeting and prayer affirmations which have proved so popular everywhere.

In connection with these meetings he wrote and published his booklet *Scientific Healing Affirmations.*

In late October, 1924, Swami and his staff of three young men reached San Francisco, and lectures were given to packed houses in the Scottish Rite Auditorium. Classes of several hundred students were given in San Francisco and Oakland. Finally, in

January, 1925, Swami arrived at his goal and final destination of Los Angeles. The Great Divine Power seemed to have aroused the whole city to receive the message of Yogoda, for truly Los Angeles gave Swami a royal and hearty welcome. Clubs, colleges, societies, educational centers, churches and newspapers extended to him every courtesy and Swami's days were filled to overflowing with engagements to speak, write, and be interviewed everywhere. Then, when the free lectures began at the Philharmonic Auditorium . . . thousands were turned away each night. Swami gave several classes and had about 1,500 students, who are among the most loyal followers of the Yogoda Course and also of a Special Advanced Course which the Swami gave in Los Angeles for the first time in America.

One day during his Los Angeles stay, one of his students casually mentioned Mount Washington. Swami's soul was strangely stirred at the mention of this place and suggested that they drive up there on the following day. When he entered the grounds of the Mount Washington Hotel site, he strolled about, and then touching the bars surrounding the tennis court, he exclaimed to his companions, "This place feels like *ours!*" . . . Through the kind and willing cooperation and donations of his thousands of students throughout America, this property was purchased for the American Headquarters of Sat-Sanga and Yogoda. The Hon. James McLachlan, Mr. W. C. Bramham and Mr. P. Rogers helped greatly in the detailed legal end of acquiring the property. On Easter Morning, Swami gave a beautiful and impressive Sunrise Easter Service on Mount Washington. After Los Angeles, Swami took a short vacation to view the unrivalled grandeur of the Grand Canyon of the Colorado, and then proceeded to Long Beach and San Diego where he met with great response, then on to Fresno, and then a second series of lectures and classes in San Francisco, Portland and Seattle. He spent September, 1925, in Spokane, Washington. . . . Everywhere the message of Yogoda has aroused . . . attention and has been supported by leading citizens of each city where the Swami has lectured.

With Swami Dhirananda holding down the main center of Yogoda at Mount Washington, Swami Yogananda felt free to tour the country from coast to coast with his message of the balanced life, and during the next three years he visited in turn Chicago, Rochester, Cleveland,

Pittsburgh, New York, Detroit, Cincinnati, Washington, Buffalo, Minneapolis and St. Paul, and then Philadelphia, Boston and New York again. He was not able to start classes in New York, he says, on account of the high cost of halls and advertising. Before he would enter any city, a small staff of devoted voluntary workers, headed by his secretary, would go before him and prepare the way by advertising in papers and on billboards, and arranging for meetings in clubs, liberal churches and similar institutions. Then the swami himself would arrive—a distinguished metaphysician, educator, lecturer and poet from India—and give a series of free lectures on India, religion or the art of living. For example, in Buffalo he lectured to the Rotary Club on "How to Recharge Your Business Battery Out of the Cosmos."

After the lectures would come free healing meetings. Men and women of wealth would become interested and help to organize classes in private homes, hotels or halls, as in the case of Vivekananda. In spite of the fee of twenty-five dollars—or perhaps because of it—many of the classes were large, but the contagious personality of the swami would effectively dominate the group and put it through the Yogoda system of physical, mental and spiritual development. In the midst of the enthusiasm and gratitude aroused by the success of the classes, the swami would appoint a local committee to carry on the work under a more or less gifted local leader who would be instructed by the swami personally, and later directed and encouraged by letter. Some leaders would give their services free. Others would be supported by the group. If in a year's time everything went well, the swami would allow a Yogoda Sat-sanga Center to be established with more or less permanent officers, rules, and places of meeting.

In addition to this "Traveling University" of Yogananda and his disciples, there has been developed at Los Angeles the "Correspondence University" of the Yogoda Course, which is announced by the ten cent booklet *Yogoda,* sold with the aid of several high-pressure follow-up letters on ochre, or "sannyasa-colored," paper for twenty-five dollars or less,[8] and presented in three parts: the "Tissue-Will System of Physical Perfection," the "Scientific Technique of Concentration and Meditation," and the "Art of Material and Spiritual Success." In enrolling himself as a student, the novice pledges himself to earnest practice and obedient secrecy. This injunction of secrecy is to prevent an unqualified or commercial teacher stealing the system. The student understands that he may write to the Yogoda Main Center for further instruction of personal guidance.

The beautiful magazine *East-West,* published under Yogananda's ownership and control, supplies the binding twine of information and inspiration that holds together the twenty-five thousand Yogodans scattered over the United States in groups and as individuals. True to its name, this magazine culls its literary gems from both East and West, in striking contrast to Paramananda's Vedanta monthly, the *Message of the East,* which is also true to its name in propagating only Eastern culture. Whereas the *Message of the East* abounds in Hindu stories, quotations from the mystics of various lands and ages, Bengali hymns, Krishna tales and commentaries on the *Upanishads,* the colorful and copiously illustrated *East-West* tells you what Mussolini says about science and religion, how an American student held his breath for fourteen minutes, why a certain Silesian miner can run needles through his flesh without injury, and that Zaro Aga of Constantinople, who has been married ten times, has just celebrated his one hundred and forty-sixth birthday. It publishes editorials by Yogananda, and concerns itself with American problems such as yellow journalism and the crime wave. It delves into the borderland between science and the occult, reviews "inspiring new books," and offers poems and pictures from East and West. And revelling in a little multitude of "Yogoda Notices and Announcements," it keeps alive the apostolic zeal of this new American cult.

Literary contributions by members are encouraged as a testimony to the place Yogoda is making for itself in the hearts of the American people. One student offers this fruit of his inspiration:

I am a Yogodan—
I believe in a god of the medulla oblongata—
I seek to unite East and West—
I would recharge the batteries of my life,
Bathing my soul's beauty beneath cosmic rays.[9]

And another bursts into song with a hymn to the tune of "Oh Paradise":

Yogoda! Yogoda!
Thou art my joy, my stay,
Thou cheerest me, thou leadest me
Through every joyous day![10]

2. THE MESSAGE

In his address before the Unitarian Congress of Religious Liberals at Boston in 1920, Swami Yogananda delivered a pure Hindu message based on a work published in India, and later published in America in amplified form as *The Science of Religion*, inscribed to his great Hindu patron, the Maharaja of Kasimbazar. The final end of all beings, says the swami in pure Vedanta style, is *bliss*, or the negation of pain. Through a great blunder, however, we confuse bliss with happiness, and so in our ignorance desire happiness with its pain rather than absolute bliss without pain. The *intellect* will not rid us of this fatal mistake, but in the *intuition* of "all in One and One in all" a glorious vision of light appears, and we know by inner feeling that the bliss of the self is God, the goal of life. There is no value in the finite, in life itself: it is only a means to the infinite.

Now there are four fundamental methods, continues our Vedantist, "that will free the Ever-Blissful, Spiritual self from its baneful connection and identification with the transitory body and mind, thus causing it to permanently avoid pain and attain Bliss, which constitutes Religion."[11] The Meditation Method is better than the Intellectual and Devotional Methods, he says, but not so good as the final "Organic, Scientific Method."[12] The Meditation Method, to be sure, induces a state of "conscious sleep" in which we are free from the disturbance of the voluntary organs, but it fails to free us from the disturbance of the organs that are "involuntary and internal."

This complete freedom can be accomplished only by the "Organic, Scientific Method," says Yogananda. "I set it down here from my own experience. I can say it will be found to be universally true. *The practice of it is far more purely blissful than the greatest enjoyment that any of our five senses or the mind can afford us.* I do not wish to give any one any other proof of its truth *than is afforded by his own experience.* The more one practices it with *patience* and devotion, the more one feels intensely and *durably fixed in Bliss.* Owing to the . . . bondage of the body for how many ages we know not . . . it will require *patient* practice for a *long, long* time."[13]

Our swami and yogi then explains the conditions of practice. "The brain is the supreme electrical Power House" of the body. Out of this brain supply is discharged the "Pranic Current," or "Life-Electricity," through the six main centers of the nervous system: the medulla, and then the cervical, the dorsal, the lumbar, the sacral and the coccygeal centers. These centers, in turn, "discharge electricity to the different efferent and afferent nerves." Now if the Self wishes to shut out the disturbing reports of bodily sensation, it need only draw back the electric flow "from the nervous system as a whole to the seven main centers" where it is "experienced in the form of light." This can be accomplished by "magnetizing the spinal column" by the concentration of *attention,* "the great director and distributor of energy." When the attention has succeeded in withdrawing the energy, the Self, or Spirit, is freed from its contact with the body and mind. "Death will then be under our control; for when we think this bodily house is unfit and broken, we shall be able to leave it of our own accord."[14]

Since the attainment of painless bliss is the universal goal, says the swami, and magnetizing the spinal column is the best way to reach this goal, the problem of comparative religion is solved. "If to abolish the sense of want and attain Bliss is Religion, . . . everyone in the world is trying to be religious, and can seek to be more completely so by adopting the proper means. There is no distinction here of caste or creed, sect or faith, dress or clime, age or sex, profession or position. For this Religion is Universal. If you said that all the people of the world ought to accept the Lord Krishna as their God, would all the Christians and the Mahomedans accept that? . . . But if you say, 'Oh, my Christian, Mahomedan and Hindu Brethren, your Lord God is Ever-Blissful Conscious Existence,' will they accept this? Can they possibly reject it? Will they not demand Him as the only One who can put an end to all their miseries?"[15]

Let us ask the swami one question. If you admit that as a matter of fact most people seek happiness and not bliss, on what ground, Swamiji, do you claim that everyone *really* seeks bliss and not happiness?

On the ground, replies the swami, that bliss *is* a kind of

happiness. It is *unceasing* happiness, whereas ordinary happiness is fitful. Surely if a person wants happiness at all, he will want unceasing happiness even more. Happiness is the absence of pain. It is present when desire is satisfied, to be sure, but only because the desire has been removed, not because it has been fulfilled. It is present twice as strong when there is no desire at all. Bliss, or unceasing happiness, is the native state of the soul. When desire comes, it disturbs this state and causes misery. When the desire is removed, the misery is relieved, and we have a state called happiness, but since the pain of former desire still lingers, it is only half-happiness. Complete happiness, or bliss, comes only when there is no desire at all.

Thus we are asked to believe that happiness is the absence of pain, and desirelessness the native state of the soul. This is the fundamental creed of the "Universal Religion" offered by the swami. If we doubt this creed, we are asked to put it to the test of experience. Do not doubt whether sugar is sweet, says the swami. Taste it.

But here lies the difficulty. The test will require *"patient* practice for a *long, long* time." A life might be consumed—perhaps several lives—just in making the test. Furthermore, suppose the test is successful, and bliss be attained. How can we tell this bliss is God? How do we know there is not a better experience to be discovered by another test? The swami does not condemn action—only desire. Perhaps we could all agree that peaceful action is true happiness. But would this mean absence of desire?

Now the belief that God is painless bliss is a Hindu dogma or principle. Holding this dogma to be actually universal, the swami therefore believes that every sacred scripture must teach it. The Christian Bible, then, as one of the world's sacred scriptures, must have a fundamental Hindu meaning. Since the literal meaning is obviously not Hindu, there must be another and deeper meaning that *is* Hindu. Its real meaning must be hidden, esoteric, allegoric, intuitive. Thus Swami Yogananda, like Dr. Annie Besant and others, proceeds to deal freely with Christian scripture according to his own rules of interpretation or exegesis. Every passage, he says, has three meanings: the physical, the moral and the spiritual. The spiritual, of course, is final. Let us see how the swami uses his method.

"Unless ye have lifted up the Son of man, ye cannot enter into the kingdom of God."[16] This saying the swami attributes to Christ. "The Son of man," he says, means the *body,* and the saying as a whole means that "unless we can *transcend* the body and realize ourselves as spirit, we cannot enter into the kingdom or state of that Universal Spirit."[16] Again, when Saint Paul said, "I die daily," he meant that he knew "the process of controlling the internal organs and could voluntarily free his Spiritual self from the body and mind."[17] And finally, "the mystery of the seven stars of Revelation" means "the seven star-like centers" of the cranium and spine.[18]

The source of Yogananda's view of Reality lies in the *Upanishads,* while the source of his "Organic, Scientific Method" of attaining Reality lies in the *Raja Yoga* of Patanjali, especially in its *kriya-yoga* as developed by his master's master, Lahiri *Mahasaya.* He differs from Vivekananda in not mentioning the *karma-yoga* in *The Science of Religion,* in dividing the *raja-yoga* into the "Meditation Method" and the "Scientific, Organic Method," and in declaring that one method is the best. This best or "Scientific, Organic Method" with its "seven main centers" of "nervous electricity" is based on our old friend the *Kundalini,* with its seven "lotuses," or astral nerve centers, which was added to the *raja-yoga* in India some time after the seventh century.[19] Yogananda, unlike Jnanesvarananda, does not insist that the nerve centers are astral. Indeed, we get the impression they are physical. The *Ojas,* or infinite power in the brain, mentioned by Vivekananda in his *Raja Yoga*[20] is conceived by Yogananda in modern terms as "the supreme electrical Power House."

Such was his message to America when he arrived fresh from India. To this message he still clings, but his emphasis has shifted. Owing partly to his shift of function from delegate to preacher, and partly to the influence of busy American life, he no longer stresses the "baneful connection" of the Spirit with the "transitory body and mind," but insists on the *karma-yoga* of the *Gita,* which is active calm and calm activity. And owing to his admiration for the practical methods of Christian Science and New Thought, especially in the work of healing, he has adapted his own system of "bodily, mental and spiritual development" to the art of healing as practiced in his "healing meetings" and presented in his booklet *Scientific Healing Affirmations.* Here he seeks to show that "Life Electricity" (*Prana*), or "Omnipresent Cosmic Vibratory Intelligent Energy," or simply God, is the only real source of health.

Drugs, medicine, massage, spinal adjustment or electrical treatment all help to bring back the lost harmonious condition of the cells by chemicalization of the blood or stimulation of certain tissues. These are external methods that sometimes assist the life energy to effect a cure. But they have not the power to act on a dead body, whence the life energy has vanished, for there is nothing in a dead man that can utilize the properties of medicine or electrical currents. Without the life energy, medicines, etc., cannot have any healing effect on the human body. Hence it can be seen that it is the life energy alone that can effect a cure; all external methods of stimulation can only co-operate with the life energy and are powerless without it.[21]

The Power of Cosmic Consciousness is greater than the power of your mind or the mind of others. Thus you should seek its aid alone. But this does not mean you should make yourself passive, inert or credulous, or that you should minimize the power of your mind. Remember God helps those that help themselves. He gave you will power, concentration, faith, reason and common sense to help yourself in your bodily or mental affections. You must use them all as you seek the Divine help. . . . Always during affirmations or prayer vibrations feel that you are using *your own* but *God-given* power to heal yourself or others. Always believe that it is not God only but yourself also who, as His beloved child, tries to employ His-given will, reason, etc., to react on the difficult problems of life. A balance must be struck between the old idea of wholly depending on God, and the modern way of sole dependence on the ego.[22]

During the different affirmations, notice should be taken of the physiological centers where the attention should be directed— *i. e.,* the heart is the center where feeling is concerned, the medulla is the source of energy, and the will proceeds from the spot in the center of the forehead. Attention is unconsciously directed to those centers, *e. g.,* when we feel, the attention is centered in the heart and we feel it to the exclusion of all other parts of our bodies. We want to cultivate a conscious power over the direction of attention to the centers of thought, will and feeling.[23]

Before starting to affirm, always free the mind of all worries and restlessness. Choose your affirmation and repeat it first loudly, then softer and more slowly, until your voice becomes a whisper. Then gradually affirm it mentally only, without moving even the tongue or the lips. Affirm mentally until you feel that you have merged into deep unbroken concentration, not unconsciousness, but conscious continuity of uninterrupted thought.

GENERAL HEALING AFFIRMATION

Make us little children, O Father
Even as Thy Kingdom contains such.
Thy love in us is perfection
Even as Thou art whole, so are we holy.
In body and mind we are healthy
Even as Thou art, even as Thou art.
Thou art perfect,
We are Thy children. . . .

Thou art everywhere,

In my heart, in my brain
In my eyes, in my face
In my limbs and all.
Thou dost move my feet
They are whole, they are whole.
My calves and thighs
They are whole, for Thou art there.
My thighs are held by Thee
Lest I fall, lest I fall.
They are whole, for Thou art there,
They are whole, for Thou art there. . . .

Let me feel
Thy loving thrill, Thy loving thrill.
Thou art my Father
I am Thy child.
Good or naughty
I am Thy child.
Let me feel Thy healthy thrill,
Let me feel Thy wisdom's will
Let me feel Thy wisdom's will.

MATERIAL SUCCESS AFFIRMATION

Thou art my Father
Success and joy
I am Thy child
Success and joy
All the wealth of this earth,
All the riches of the universe
Belong to Thee, belong to Thee.
I am Thy child
The wealth of earth and universe
Belongs to me, belongs to me. . . .

I have everything, I have everything
I am wealthy, I am rich
I have everything, I have everything
I possess all and everything
Even as Thou dost, even as Thou dost,
I possess everything, I possess everything.
Thou art my wealth,
I have everything.[24]

The swami's harmony of Hindu and Western notions appears also in his Correspondence Course in practical concentration and meditation, which is his most important contribution to American life. First let us consider the Hindu notions. In the "Scientific Technique of Concentration and Meditation," the "concentration" may be traced to the *raja-yoga's dharana,* or the fixation of the mind on one thing at a time in order to free it from distraction, while the "meditation" may be traced to its *dhyana,* or the fixation of the mind on some divine manifestation. His favorite word "contacting," as in the slogan "contacting Cosmic Consciousness," comes from the phrase "making *samgama* on," which means combining concentration, meditation and trance to penetrate any given object. This is how "wonderful powers" arise.[25] And when he tells us to charge the body with *Prana,* or "Inner Cosmic Energy," he is taking over the vitalistic dualism of the *Upanishads.*

The aim of the old-fashioned yogi is to devote all his energy to the practice of withdrawing from the body and mind into a transcendent realm of visions and motionless bliss. In like manner, the swami advises his pupils to eat meat substitutes, to eat only twice a day if sedentary, and to fast one day a week. Since matter is only illusion, he says, eventually we shall learn to live without food, like a certain Indian woman near Ranchi, Bengal, who has not eaten anything for forty years, so he claims. The sex life also should be sublimated, he urges, even between man and wife, until the spiritual union in love becomes a substitute for the sex union. The pledge of secrecy exacted from each student goes back to the pre-Buddhistic times of "secret sessions," or "upanishads," between master and disciple, while his use of mystic identifications as in the statement that the "sound of many waters" of Revelation is the same as the "rolling, roaring Om" also goes back

to the *Upanishads*. In addition to the primary Yogoda
Course, there is the "Advanced Course," which deals with
comparative religion by the "spiritual" allegorical method,
and the still higher "Initiation Course" called the "Auxili-
ator," which deals with the *Kundalini*.

At the same time, the course shows many Western attitudes. The original strenuous practice of *yoga* was intended to free the soul from the body and mind, and
Vivekananda only followed an old-fashioned rule when
he cautioned his students, "Do not practice when the body
feels lazy or ill, or when the mind is very miserable and
sorrowful."[26] But since Yogananda has adopted the modern aim of *healing* the body and mind, and not *escaping*
them, he especially prescribes his system for all kinds of
illness and depression, and personally conducts healing
meetings. Like many other religious leaders today, the
swami wants to be scientific and philosophic. So he says
he agrees with Professor Millikan that all reality is vibration, spirit differing from matter only in its higher rate.
Although he tells us to "contact" Life-Energy in the old-
fashioned way, he also tells us to turn in the opposite
direction, and charge the body with Life-Energy. And
after we have become filled with God, we should go about
helping others to overcome their troubles. Without serving God in this way, he says, we will never know Him.[27]

The Yogoda Course, then, is not merely a *yoga* practice,
but a special combination more or less applicable to East
and West. As Yogananda says, it is unique in its combination of breathing, muscular tension and attention. He
might also have added, "suggestion" and advice. He
hopes to introduce this course into churches and schools
all over the world, to increase the power of attention in
the rational control of life. On this point of control the
East and West can agree, but seem to differ with respect
to the *end* of control, the West stressing creation, the old
East renunciation.[28]

The swami does not stop with teaching autosuggestion. Combining East and West again, he uses suggestion on his disciples in the form of a spiritual radio. In the *East-West* Magazine we find this Yogoda announcement:

DIVINE PRAYER HEALING SERVICE FOR ALL

Every morning at seven o'clock Swami Yogananda sends a Divine Healing Prayer Vibration to his students and all who ask his help in healing and liberating themselves from physical or mental disease or the spiritual suffering of ignorance. Anyone who wishes to avail himself of this help, which the Swami is happy to extend to all, may write to the Los Angeles headquarters, briefly stating the nature of his or her trouble.[29]

The result in one case is a poem by a grateful and rapturous devotee:

AT SEVEN

With hands elate,
My heart was lifted up
In prayer to the Great Spirit,
That I might receive
The blessing of my Master,
Garnered in the treasurehouse
Of cosmic Love

. . . .

Then, like a stream of molten gold,
    There flowed to me such treasure,
As ne'er in fabled tales was told
    Of riches without measure.

. . . .

And still it flowed, until at last
    My heart o'erflowed with gratitude
To God, and to His Servant Blest,
    Who sent me this Beatitude.[30]

Wondering whether seven o'clock referred to the swami's time or to the devotee's time, I asked for official information, and received the reply that the healing message starts by the swami's time, but remains vibrating permanently in the atmosphere, so that the devotee can be sure of results whenever he or she tunes in.[81] The message must be repeated daily to keep the vibrations strong, fresh and adaptable.

In every way possible Yogananda makes a combination of East and West. In addition to morning meditation, he recommends the devotional study of the Bible. But his followers are urged to read other bibles besides the Christian, such as the *Bhagavad Gita,* the *Imitation of Christ,* Shakespeare, Emerson, Walt Whitman, Francis Thompson, or Tagore. In the Bible, he says, read just one verse a day—and try to *feel* it. We need less study and more meditation. But the Bible is not above other books, and Jesus, of course, is just one savior among many. "Spiritual truth is one: interpreted by Christians it is called Christianity; by Hindus, Hinduism; and so forth."[32]

In all his work the swami is careful to announce that his movement is East-West and universal, and does not interfere with anyone's traditional religion. The ideal of the Society, he says, is only "universal scientific propaganda." Whoever becomes a true Yogodan need not renounce his church, but may simply call himself a Methodist Yogi or a Unitarian Yogi or a Roman Catholic Yogi or a Christian Science Yogi or a Jewish Yogi or a Muslim Yogi or some similar name. The truth of Yogoda, he continues, lies not in any special creed, but in the common intuitive, ineffable experience of its devotees, just as blindfolded people can unite in enjoying the taste of an orange.

Our swami has even dabbled in the "social gospel," although it cannot be said that he connects it with his teaching on meditation or devotion, or puts it at the heart of his message. Indeed, every literary attempt at social reform seems to be inspired by some special interest. Judging from his own statements in print,[33] his worthy editorials "Yellow Journalism versus Truth" and "Spiritualizing the Newspapers" were stimulated by newspaper misrepresentations of himself and his India. His concern with immigration reform was apparently due to the fact that the United States laws worked against the individual plans and national pride of his countrymen. Naturally, he wanted a test based on quality, not race. Even Jesus Christ, he said, would have been excluded as an Oriental. His attention to the crime wave in America not only suggests measures of control but also operates as a counterblast to an American woman's exposure of the worst side of India, while his interest in American educational progress affords a nice opportunity for such a defense of Hinduism as this:

> In India the ideal of continence and self-control is taught in every house down to the lowest and most illiterate. There is more immorality in any large American city than in the whole length of India today.[34]

Yogananda's eclectic spirit shines best in the realm of general religious culture. He learns as he teaches, he practices give and take. The celebration of Easter, Thanksgiving and Christmas is not neglected at the Mount Washington main-center, nor is the Western Santa Claus omitted from Christmas. Lincoln's birthday is utilized as "Gardening Day," and the Center itself has its birthday party with cake and candles. Our swami even welcomes American missionaries to India, especially those like Henry Ford! On the other hand, he often regales his admirers with Indian music which he plays on four different Indian instruments, and publishes many oriental gleanings in his magazine. When Walter Hampden's presentation of *The Light of Asia* failed, he wrote an editorial in defence of this drama, and he likewise advertised the reincarnation-teaching play called *The Ladder* produced for about two years at a loss of millions of dollars by Mr. Edward B. Davis, a Texas oil magnate.

The universality of the swami's selections can be clearly seen in his treatment of immortality. His first solution of the problem, of course, is the doctrine of reincarnation, to which every orthodox Hindu clings as a description of his *Dharma*, or eternal cosmic duty. In spite of his many Western beliefs, our Hindu teacher is willing to defend this doctrine in what he admits is its most fatalistic form.

Even though we are tied to this wheel of cosmic birth and death, even though no end is in sight, yet there is a way of escape for us. All religions point the path. Through knowledge, through non-attachment, through selflessness, through the fire of meditation on spiritual reality, the seeds of all karma may be roasted, may be reduced to ashes, and thus the soul may be liberated from the otherwise eternal Wheel of Necessity.[35]

To demonstrate the universality of this "cosmic truth," the swami tells us it is potent in the heritage of the West. In trying to make all *scriptures* teach Hinduism he relies, as we have seen, on the allegorical method of exegesis. In trying to make all *philosophy* teach Hinduism he interprets history as follows:

Aristotle and Plato, both of whom have contributed very largely to Western thought, very decidedly believed in Reincarnation, and so did Socrates. The Jewish faith thoroughly approved this belief. The early Gnostics and practically all the Christian fathers, up to the fifth century, accepted it and wrote elaborately about it. The doctrine slipped out of the European mind during the Dark Ages.[36]

Not content with this attempt at historical proof, the swami claims that reincarnation has actually been verified by ecstatic yogis whose cosmic memories have recalled definite events of their past lives. Suppose I am a genuine yogi. Suppose also I happen to know nothing about Abraham Lincoln in this life. But after a trance I reveal certain facts to my friends, who are then convinced on historical evidence that these facts belong only to the life of Lincoln. According to the swami, this would prove that in one of my past lives I was Abraham Lincoln.[87]

Verification aside, the Hindu claims for the doctrine of reincarnation many virtues. These claims may be combined into three main arguments. The *moral* argument deals with justice. If according to *karma,* or the law of cause and effect in moral acts, the individual soul is responsible for the deeds done in its past reincarnation, then it is responsible for its present condition, and so God is relieved of all injustice due to present inequality of individuals in rank and circumstance.[88]

The *religious* argument deals with immortality. If we believe in necessary immortality, we must logically admit not only a never-ending individual life after death, but also a never-beginning individual life before birth. If the soul is eternal, it cannot possibly begin at one point of time, such as the birthday of the body.[39]

The *scientific* argument deals with individual indifferences. Take the case of genuine twins growing up together under the same circumstances. What can explain the striking difference in their character? Only the theory that the soul of the one is eternally distinct from the soul of the other, says the Hindu. And this means reincarnation.[40]

Hence Swami Yogananda's first solution of the problem of immortality is the doctrine of reincarnation, a solution that must be expected from any Hindu. But when he wants to comfort his beloved flock with regard to the "Mystery of Life and Death," he uses quite novel notions gathered from Professors J. C. Bose, Millikan and Lovett Evans, and then paints a picture of Heaven—a social Heaven, mind you—that might possibly be conceived by Saint Ramanuja, Emanuel Swedenborg and Sir Oliver Lodge working together as a committee on the after-life.

Nothing is said about returning to an earthly body in the next life.

Death above all else is a transition to a better land—a change of residence. The wise man who has opened his spiritual eye finds that the death of the earthly life gives him a new beginning in another supernal life. On this earth seeing we see not—a fluoroscope can show the bones of the fingers which the eye cannot see. We do not see the cords of light—blue, violet, aquamarine, orange, yellow, white, which bind the atoms and the earth together. We hear the gross noise of the world and a few sweet melodies and nothing more. . . .

In the mellow light of the other world, the wise perceive the inner sides of stars, stones, living beings, corpses, dust, iron, gold, earth, planets, dazzling with Infinite brilliancy. Every object which we perceive has two sides—the gross ugly outer side present before the physical eyes, and the inner, most beautiful side revealed to the eye of wisdom. The crude brick revealed by the physical eyes appears to be like a garden of electrons, when viewed through the spiritual eye. Human beings with skeletons, ugly sinews and red blood appear as beautiful many-hued living beings made of visible mellow materialized love. . . .

Everything talks there silently. The roses talk to the souls with the language of spirit. . . . The gentlest earthly flower—the lily, violet, drunk with gross sunlight—is not allowed to tread the sanctity of that fair garden of the gods. The mortal, enslaved by oxygen and sunlight, gorged with material food, faints at the delicate airless atmosphere of that divine supernal region. . . . Souls in that region do not encase themselves in bundles of bones with fleshly covers. They carry no frail, heavy frames to collide and break with other crude solids. . . . No bacteria, no thirst, no selfish desires, no heartaches, no lust, no pain or sorrow, nor boisterous fleeting joy, no accidents, shattering bones and skulls, and no excruciating pain of parting, can ever visit there. . . . Why pity the dead? In wisdom—they pity us.[41]

Thus Swami Yogananda is all-embracing in his tolerance and desire to harmonize. In this he is not heretical, but typically Hindu; for the Hindu theologian, as we have seen in the case of Sankara, wants to take in everything and drop out nothing. When Yogananda first came to America he stressed the way of "knowledge" like Vivekananda, but after staying a while he began to stress the way of "work." As a yogi he still insists on the *raja-yoga,* but in his preaching he relies less on Sankara and more on the *Bhagavad Gita.* He has shifted from renunciation to resignation. It seems that in Yogananda a portion of ancient Indian history is being enacted again before our eyes, only on a world-wide scale. He is the reincarnation, as it were, of the author of the *Bhagavad Gita.* He takes his *Upanishad* heritage and adapts it not to the hardworking people of India, this time, but to the hardworking people of America. He preaches sweet resignation not to caste duties this time, but to modern business methods and financial ambition for success. As Vivekananda, figuratively speaking, was a Buddhist, Yogananda is a Stoic of the more joyous and progressive kind,[42] a Stoic saturated with Hindu bliss and American optimism.

With his genius for organization, Swami Yogananda has put his message into systematic form, which I now present as the last word on the subject.

AIMS AND TENETS OF THE YOGODA SAT-SANGA MOVEMENT

1. Universal all-round education, and establishment of educational institutions for the development of man's physical, mental and spiritual natures.

2. Contacting Cosmic Consciousness—the ever-new, ever-existing, ever-conscious Bliss-God—through the scientific technique of concentration and mediation taught by the Masters of all ages.

3. Attaining bodily health through the "Yogoda" technique of recharging the body-battery from inner life-energy.

4. Intelligently maintaining the physical body on unadulterated foods, including a large percentage of raw fruits, vegetables and nuts.

5. Physical, mental and spiritual healing.

6. Establishing, by a scientific system of realization, the absolute basic harmony and oneness of Christianity, Hindu Yoga teachings, and all true religions.

7. Serving all mankind as one's larger Self.

8. Demonstrating the superiority of mind over body, and of soul over mind.

9. Fighting the Satan of Ignorance—man's common enemy.

10. Establishing a spiritual unity between all nations.

11. Overcoming evil by good; overcoming sorrow by joy; overcoming cruelty by kindness.

12. Realization of the purpose of life as being the evolution from human consciousness into divine consciousness, through individual struggle.

13. Realization of the truth that human life is given to man to afford him opportunity to manifest his inner divine qualities, and not for physical pleasure nor selfish gratifications.

14. Furthering the cultural and spiritual understanding between East and West, and the constructive exchange of the distinctive features of their civilizations.

15. Uniting science and religion through the study and practical realization of the unity of their underlying principles.[43]

3. THE METHODS

Aside from the saffron robe, worn only on ceremonial occasions, the dim lighting, soft music and incense of his meetings for worship, and his tours of personal instruction, the swami has only himself to show that he is a Hindu teacher, as far as methods are concerned. Unlike the Vedanta Centers, his movement is centered not in India, but in a well-knit, nation-wide organization called the Yogoda Sat-sanga Society of America, of which he is the president.[44] It is governed by a national committee which includes Mr. J. Harold MacDowell, a Cleveland architect who built the Cleveland Auditorium, and Mr. Alvin Hunsicker of New York, prominent in the textile industry. The attorney is Judge John F. Hylan, former Mayor of New York. Since the Society is incorporated under the laws of Jersey City, New Jersey, the swami is responsible to his master in India only spiritually, not legally.

The main center of the Society is at Mount Washington, Los Angeles, formerly in charge of Swami Dhirananda, but now in charge of Swami Yogananda himself.[45] Each of the twelve centers in America[46] is well organized with a governing body and a religious leader who has been personally trained by the master, and has signed a pledge of loyalty. He is not considered an independent Yogoda teacher, but just a teaching disciple. Three of these local leaders are Hindus: *Brahmacari* (or Student) Nerod at Los Angeles, *Brahmacari* Jotin at Washington, both Bengalis, and Pandit (or Sanskritist) Upadeshak at Cleveland, a Panjabi. These Hindus and some other local leaders are supported by the local centers, while other leaders give their services free. Some of the centers are incorporated. Unlike the Vedanta societies, each center is not independent, but a local branch closely connected with the main center through legal responsibility, correspondence, and the travels of master, secretary and staff.

We have noticed that the Vedanta centers have done neither intensive community cultivation nor extensive advertising. The Yogoda Society does both. The main center at Mount Washington is very much like an American church in its methods. The Free Lectures on Sunday are the preaching services, and a Sunday School is added. The Wednesday Class is the prayer meeting. The Helpers Association is the Ladies' Aid. There is also a Candy Department that specializes in cactus candy, no doubt inspired by Luther Burbank, one of the staunch Yogodans. Plans for the enrollment and training of more teachers have been announced.

The Society is supported by fees from the Yogoda Classes and Corespondence Courses, by voluntary monthly payments on pledges to the main center, and by free gifts. The institution of a two dollar national membership fee is being considered. From time to time the swami receives personal gifts, such as a typewriter. He maintains himself partly by money sent from India by his parents and partly by one-quarter of the total income from the classes and courses, giving three-quarters to the Society. The members are encouraged to give towards the support of the swamis' schools in India.

In order to release the swami from all commercial work so that he can devote more time to "spiritual" meditation and the propagation of the Correspondence Course, the "Yogoda Publishing Company" has been organized by Mr. Harry F. Sieber, a Yogodan and former bank president. The company is incorporated in Pennsylvania, the original ten thousand dollars in cash having been supplied by the Philadelphia Yogoda members. It plans to distribute its stock of two kinds among Yogoda members broadly, and to have the stockholders of each center appoint their own representative as a director. While the company is to acquire by purchase from Yogananda all his writings and publishings, the control of the voting stock is to be held by the swami himself.

Extensive advertising is carried on by the swami's repeated city visits and lectures previously announced in every feasible way by his staff, by the Yogoda booklet, classes and courses, by letters, by the *East-West* magazine, for which a special binder is sold, by books and three pieces of sheet music for the piano, *Song of Brahma, My Soul is Marching On,* and *Om Song.* The American love of insignia is not overlooked. The main center puts out Christmas cards decked with Yogoda symbols, sentiments and mottoes. For one dollar a member may purchase the gold-plated, orange-and-blue-enamelled Yogoda pin with the Yogoda emblem. This emblem appears also on the front cover of the magazine. It signifies "the single spiritual eye of meditation, the pranic star door through which we must enter to find Cosmic Consciousness, taught by the Yogoda method of meditation."

Swami Yogananda himself is the biggest advertisement for the Society, in spite of a newspaper announcement that "Swami Yogananda keeps himself in the background." His face appears in newspapers and on billboards, in some of his books, and several times in his magazine. Every Yogoda class has its photograph; the class-members are seated while the swami stands well in the foreground. On one Fourth of July a large notice board at the entrance of the Mount Washington grounds displayed a life sized picture of the swami beside his message to America. The organization arranges for photographs of the swami playing one of his four musical instruments or conversing with some American notable such as Governor Fuller of Massachusetts or President Coolidge. The swami attracted notice when he prescribed a meatless diet for Coolidge to keep him cool! For two dollars any member may purchase a beautiful framed photograph of his or her beloved master. It is clear that Swami Yogananda is even more American in method than in message.

The greatest difference between Vedanta and Yogoda lies in method. The Vedanta swamis are still Hindus, while Swami Yogananda, as it were, is a naturalized American. The Vedanta swamis had to use American methods to some extent in order to endure at all, but Yogananda plunged into them completely. Both movements are confined to the cities—even the "peace retreats" are for city dwellers—but Yogananda has learned how to work the cities. How can this striking difference best be explained?

(1) Yogananda's master Yuktesvara was not as ascetic as Vivekananda's master Ramakrishna. From his married and city-dwelling master Lahiri he had learned the life of balance, the Stoic rule of the *Bhagavad Gita,* and this he passed on to his disciple, who was thus prepared to accept the world, to do in Rome as the Romans do.

(2) Yogananda himself has a different personality from Vivekananda. Not only is he less ascetic—he is also less impetuous and moody. He felt no great frustration, crisis and sudden conversion, but developed his religious life slowly and steadily from early youth. He was thus more fit for the grind and responsibility of organization work.

(3) Yogananda arrived in America a generation after Vivekananda, and thus found a more tolerant and liberal nation which had learned something of India and had accustomed itself to support a considerable number of unorthodox cults.

(4) Yogananda attended a religious congress that was more congenial than the one attended by Vivekananda. He was not forced to defend his message against a host of world-wide religions, but simply encouraged to explain it before a group of appreciative liberals. He felt the spirit of coöperation, and learned the methods of successful American cults.

(5) Yogananda was fortunate in securing the services of an efficient American secretary soon after the beginning of his work, and he came on the scene after Los Angeles, the hotbed of novelty, had grown tremendously. He did not bother about Europe or India, but settled down to "conquer" America.

(6) Yogananda, unlike Vivekananda, was a yogi by nurture as well as nature when he arrived in America, and thus met its shocks and strains with the methodical technique of relaxation drilled into him by his master. He keeps his health even when deprived of sleep, and so can stand the strain of nation-wide organization. He has now developed the movement so that he can give more time to writing and spiritual training. He expects soon to publish a work which will serve as the Yogoda textbook, and a new book on prayer according to a modified *yoga*

method has just appeared (1930), entitled *Whispers From Eternity,* and proclaimed as "a completely fresh analysis of the bewilderment in which multitudes of the present generation find themselves . . . a gateway to the art of consciously contacting God."

All these factors enabled Yogananda to adapt his work to American conditions more closely than Vivekananda.

4. THE MEMBERS

To Yogoda students as well as to members of the Ramakrishna movement I sent out questionnaire letters. But on account of the larger numbers of Yogodans, the reports are much less reliable statistically, covering only about two per cent of the entire membership.[47] Yet they can show which way the wind blows, and provide some comparison between the Vedanta centers and the Yogoda Society. If we omit the New York Vedanta Society, and the Buffalo and Minneapolis Yogoda centers, where natives of other lands are to be expected, both movements appeal chiefly to ordinary white Americans of Anglo-Saxon tradition, some of them descendents of original settlers. The average age of the members responding is practically the same in both movements, although several of the Yogodans are under thirty-five, the lowest age of the Vedanta group. Indeed, the more American methods and breezy personality of Yogananda would be apt to draw youth as well as age.

As in the Vedanta group, the women of the Yogoda group outnumber the men three to one, but in the Yogoda Society as a whole, judging from the faces in the numerous clear photographs of the large Yogoda classes, the proportion is only two to one, the same as in the Vedanta movement according to the Census. Thus both Hindu movements show an unusually large, though not alarming, percentage of women. This is to be expected in most

religious bodies. The occupations of both men and women
show nothing unusual—professional service, housekeep-
ing, clerical work and small business bulking more largely
than manual labor. Perhaps Yogoda attracts more teachers, lawyers and medical men than Vedanta. Both movements clearly operate in the great middle class, as do the
Protestant churches.

In the Vedanta group about three-fourths of the members had orthodox parents, but in the Yogoda group,
nearly all. And while with Vedanta only a few of these
have remained in the churches, with Yogoda at least one-
third of them have done so. Moreover, in the Yogoda
group the percentage of religious wanderings or chronic
"seekers," is lower. Yet in both groups those who have
been wandering truth-seekers outnumber those who have
dropped into Hinduism by chance. It seems that on the
whole, Yogoda is much closer to the traditional Christian
Church than Vedanta, a point which is not surprising, in
view of the deliberate effort of Yogananda to adapt his
Hindu teaching to American methods and sentiment.

In many respects the reasons for conversion are the
same in both groups—with some, a progressive broadening of outlook; with others, a solution of perplexing problems of creed. Many in the Yogoda group claim that the
swami's teaching makes them better church members.
Many delight in Yogoda's universal tolerance and love,
and its teaching of optimism and divine immanence. But
the vast majority become earnest Yogodans because of the
"wonderful" bodily, mental and spiritual benefits they
gain from its practice of concentration and meditation.
In Yogoda much more than in Vedanta it is the clean-cut,
definite and systematic *practice* that converts people and
absorbs their leisure time and energy. Only two of the
fifty-one Yogodans reported less than a half-hour daily
practice, while many practice two hours a day and attend

several meetings a week. Some devote all their spare time to Yogoda, which in a few cases amounts to three hours a day. It is not hard to see where Yogoda makes its strongest appeal.

The testimonials of those healed in the swami's meetings, classes or courses compare favorably with those of Unity or the work of the Angelus Temple.[48] Every issue of the *East-West* rings with the witness of fresh grateful devotees. Suffering humanity is cured of eyestrain, nervousness, stomach trouble, tobacco, fear, stiffness, and many other ailments due to strain, worry, doubt, distraction or lack of exercise. One person says the swami has removed the cork from the bottle of life to let in God's truth. Another says the Bible is now understood as never before. A third exclaims that Yogananda has done as much good as Jesus, a fourth that he must be a reincarnation of Jesus. And so on. Says Luigi von Kunits, Conductor of the New Symphony Orchestra of Toronto, "Yogoda has done and is still doing for me all that is claimed for it; youthful energy that spurns fatigue, an almost complete immunity from sickness and disease, intellectual alertness, steady firmness and decision in willing and acting, a truly remarkable quickening of . . . memory, and a constantly progressing calmness and mental tranquillity." [49]

So much for the causes of conversion. Now for some of its effects. In the minds of one-fourth of the group, Swami Yogananda fills the place of the ideal person, while Jesus Christ remains the supreme savior of a bit larger number. This comparative loyalty to Jesus makes a sharp contrast with the indifference shown by Vedanta adherents. However, a plurality of the Yogoda group worship no one savior above another, but have many favorites such as Luther Burbank, Albert Einstein, Thomas Edison, Henry Ford, Bernard Shaw, Abraham Lincoln, Manmohandas Karamchand Gandhi, Rabindra Nath Tagore, Charles Fillmore, Stanley Jones, Walt Whitman, Dhan Gopal Mukerji, L. Adams Beck, Ralph Waldo Trine, Ralph Waldo Emerson, Marie Corelli, Helen Petrovna Blavatsky, and Annie Besant. Many Yogodans delight in works that are oriental and occult.

In the Vedanta group two kinds of people are prominent: those who have just broadened their views, and those who have adopted the Vedanta cult as their very own. We meet with the same two kinds in Yogoda, with the addition of a third, which is still actively Christian. Thus in the Yogoda Sat-sanga Society of America we have three classes: orthodox Christians, pure Yogodans, and spiritual pilgrims who have wandered through the "borderland" cults, such as Theosophy, Christian Science, New Thought and Unity. Both Vedanta and Yogoda have much in common with these American cults, but Vedanta harks back to conservative Hinduism, while Yogoda leans forward toward liberal Christianity.

CHAPTER VII

HINDUISM IN VARIOUS MOVEMENTS, A SIGN OF EASTERN POWER

The position of the Vedanta and Yogoda cults in American Hinduism, and the importance of this Hinduism for American religion in general is not fully evident from the intensive study of these two cults alone. Hence a wider observation is necessary. While I do not claim to know the number and extent of Hindu movements in this country, and have neither the time nor the money to make a systematic study of them all, I shall now set down briefly what I know about all the movements that have come to my notice, according to the ninefold classification presented in Chapter I. This will make nine sections. The tenth and final section of this chapter will be devoted to the world-wide cultural background of the advance of Hinduism towards the United States.

1. ADDITIONAL HINDU CULTS

Baba Bharati's Krishna cult, which in America is now either defunct or very quiet, seems to be the oldest in America after Vedanta. In 1904 a book called *Shree Krishna, the Lord of Love,* written by Baba Premananda (bliss of love) Bharati, was published by the Krishna Samaj at New York. It seems that the Baba, or great father, as he is called, stayed in America for about five years, perhaps from 1904 until 1909. According to Dr. Robert E. Speer, he was formerly a hill hermit in Tibet. Coming to Los Angeles, he established a Radha-Krishna temple there, and later claimed over five thousand fol-

lowers. He declared that he preached the eternal Hinduism unadulterated by the West. Yet strange to say, this
pure orientalism, in his opinion, is just the principle that
makes intelligible the dominant religion of the West. At
a farewell meeting presided over by a former minister of
the Gospel, he declared:

It has been my privilege these five years to preach to you your
own Christ, even as much as my god Krishna. I came not here
to thrust my religion upon you, but to help you to understand
your own God and your own religion. If I have talked of
Krishna and of the Vedas and Hindu philosophy it was only to
illuminate the teachings of your own Christ, to present him
before you in the limelight of the Vedas, and the X-ray of our
own scientific philosophies.[1]

Here we have the familiar Hindu endeavor to accept
Christ, but only according to Hindu standards; and the
usual Hindu claim that Hindu philosophy is scientific,
although it was systematized before the age of modern
science.

* * *

Yogi Hari Rama is another religious teacher who visited America for only a brief period, and then went back
to India never to return. He began his work here in 1925
and departed forever on September 1st, 1928, leaving his
Benares League, which embraces several centers in the
big cities, with national headquarters at 133 West 42nd
Place, Los Angeles, California. Like Yogananda, he combined some harmless social and theological sentiment with
his *yoga* teaching, for his professed aims were to further
communal and international brotherhood, and to build up
in our hearts "Christ's love for all and everything in the
universe."[2] He stressed everything "spiritual"—nothing
"material."

His lectures dealt with the control of the *Prana*, or *élan vital*, by the "science" of breathing in order to master disease; with concentration and meditation for vitalizing any part of the body; and with the mystic and occult powers of the "Great Masters" of India. Like Yogananda again, he gave more than one course, in ascending levels. The Beginners Course taught the healing of self and others by the control of food, and the awakening of the "Christ-consciousness" by the control of the optic nerves. The Advanced Course taught how to awaken the *Kundalini*. It referred to the Mosaic law and other tenets familiar to the West. These courses were printed in outline form. He also published a book containing a list of food combinations useful for "spiritual" development, recipes for bodily ailments, and exercises for bodily defects.

In this way Yogi Hari Rama, more or less like every other swami and yogi in the United States, sought to mingle with Western tradition the Eastern lore of the *Tantra* manual and the *raja* and *hatha* disciplines.

*   *   *

Very similar is the teaching of Deva Ram of 232 East Erie Street, Chicago, in spite of the fact that the advertisement of his Correspondence Course gives no hint of attempts at interpretation in terms of Western religion. Like Yogananda also, he claims that his lectures are practical, non-sectarian, and do not interfere with any religion. The courses of ten lessons, "gifts of the Great Sages of India for the good of all Humanity," is published in the form of a booklet which can be purchased for twenty-five cents. It aims to inculcate physical, mental and "spiritual" development, and deals with the "Subtle Spiritual Centers" of the body, presumably the lotuses of the *Kundalini*. Here I shall let the announcement-folder speak for itself.

YOGA NAVAJIVAN
(Path to New Life)
Correspondence Course
Taught by SRI DEVA RAM SUKUL
Brahmin Philosopher and Metaphysician
President and Director APPLIED YOGA INSTITUTE
and HINDU YOGA SOCIETY
Editor "PRACTICAL YOGA"

Spiritual-Will Control of Cosmic Divine Energy for Highest Physical and Mental Perfection.

Yogi Technique of Concentration and Meditation for Spiritual Realization.

How to maintain the Highest Rhythm of METABOLISM and CIRCULATION in all parts of the body.

Higher Law of Transmutation and Conservation of Vital Life Fluid for Rejuvenation and Regeneration of Body.

Conscious Control and direction of Life Energy for the Harmonious natural functioning of the Ductless Glands, thus Eliminating the infirmities and Debilities of advancing age and insure Everlasting Youth.

* * *

A folder entitled "YOGESSAR" announces lectures by Swami Bhagwan Bissessar of Ajodhya, India, in the Junior Pioneer Association Building in St. Paul, Minnesota, beginning May 15, 1929. This swami's American address is P. O. B. 3, Oakland, California, and his folder presents him to the American public as follows:

SWAMI BHAGWAN BISSESSAR was born of High Caste Hindu Parents of Aryan descent. When a boy he was sent to England to be educated and attended Eton College and Oxford University. Several years later the Swami made a trip around the world for the sole purpose of studying the religions, the philosophies and the mode of living of the various nations. This gave him a broad and tolerant view of life and a keen understanding of the world's peoples. He then went up into the Himalayan Mountains, where he spent years at the feet of the Masters, studying and absorbing the Ancient Wisdom of India.

At the completion of his studies he was given the title "Swami

Bhagwan Bissessar," which means a Spiritual Teacher of God, and was sent out to teach humanity the way to NIRVANA. After remaining in India for some time he received the call to come to the Western World and impart his own interpretation of the Eastern and Western philosophies, having combined them in what he calls "YOGESSAR."

This "noted Hindu metaphysician," this "Distinguished Yogi Philosopher and Hindu Psychologist, called the Foremost Philosopher of Asia by the American Press," teaches, as might be expected, the way of "spiritual" realization, which is intended to give "health, youth, success and happiness." His lectures and private classes in the *jnana* and *raja yogas* deal with such subjects as *Prana* and *karma,* eating and breathing, relaxation and sleep, and the easy acquirement of wealth. His tuition fee is twenty-five dollars.

One cannot refrain from wondering how the swami reconciles the way to Nirvana with the way to easy wealth. And it seems strange that a swami, or one who has supposedly renounced all property, should teach others how to get it. But the old Hindu custom is for each man to stick to his function regardless of another. Thus the swami may stick to his wealth-renouncing, and the man of the world may stick to his wealth-getting, and each may encourage the other to be true to his own duty, or *svadharma.* But can a swami living in America actually be a wealth-renouncer?

* * *

In 1917 a young Madrasi Hindu known as His Holiness Srimath Swami Omkar established his Santi Asrama in the Totapalli Hills of southeastern India after clearing a fifty-acre spot of jungle with much strenuous toil. This Peace Retreat, which can be reached by mail at Santi Asrama Post, Godavari District, Madras Presidency, South India, was founded in memory of Swami Rama Tiratha, a Hindu mystic of considerable Christian understanding, who graduated from Forman Christian College, Lahore, taught mathematics there, and later made a preaching tour of America. To Omkar's Retreat came men and women of various faiths to find rest for body and mind among the beautiful shade trees and fruit trees of the garden, and the Santi Mission which preserves the Retreat also runs a children's secular school and publishes works on the spiritual life, including *Peace*, "an English Monthly Journal of Life, Light and Love," and *Santi*, a monthly magazine in the Telegu language.

In 1923 the first American branch of the Indian Asrama was established in Philadelphia under the name of Sri Mariya Asrama. Its president is Sister Mariya Iona, its secretary Brahmacari (or student) Suryananda, and its latest address 1928 North 61st Street, Philadelphia. Perhaps Swami Omkar can now be reached at this place. Another branch is the Peace Center at 1111 South Alvarado Street, Los Angeles. Among the swami's pamphlets for sale at this center are *My Creed, Meditation, Christ the Savior, Do You Want God, Daily Prayers, Tears Divine, The Coming of the Master, Are You Preparing for the Crucifixion, Christmas Tidings, Outcaste, The Divinity of Man,* and *Mother America.*

As a swami, Omkar is a follower of the first swami, Sri Sankaracarya, the great Hindu theologian whose name is often abbreviated to Sankara. As an admirer of Swami Rama Tiratha, Omkar is somewhat familiar with Christianity. Accordingly, he selects those aspects of Christian teaching which coincide with the teaching of Sankara, especially Christ's feeling of oneness with God, humanity and the world, and his universal love and pity. In his leaflet *Message of Niagara Falls,* Omkar hears the mighty cataract speak to him as follows:

Dear child of God, my message to you . . . is . . . to pour out all that you have . . . in a continuous and never-ending flow of service. . . . As an image of God, you can afford to give . . . infinite love and eternal peace. Peace and Love are your own Birthright. Do not withhold these precious gifts like a miser. Share all your perishable and imperishable riches with the whole of humanity. Drown the world in peace and joy. Bathe humanity in health and glory. . . . I give because I cannot keep. Behold how the whole world gazes at me . . . in awe and admiration. How beautiful is the giver. So, my sweet brother, be a giver of peace, love, harmony, bliss and glory. . . .

Likewise in his *Daily Prayers,* the swami suggests the following passage for meditation:

I will shower flowers of hope and love wherever I go. Help me to cheer, to encourage, to strengthen, to uplift . . . the downtrodden with Thy blessings. Above all, allow me to recognize nothing but Thee in every face I meet. Let me realize that in serving others I am serving Thee and Thee alone, for Thou art the all-pervading and all-interpenetrating Life, Light, and Love.

Thus Omkar appreciates the similarity between Jesus and Sankara owing to Sankara's so-called lower belief in God as the ground of the world. But at the same time he follows Sankara in the so-called higher belief in God as a transcendent realm of bliss wholly unattached to the world, which is thereby considered illusion. In his pamphlet *Do You Want God* he cries, "Let us feel that God alone is the only Reality, and all else is mere delusion." In like manner he denounces all sects and creeds, and exalts private meditation as the simple, silent "realization" of God conceived as a state of "superconsciousness," which in common with many Hindu preachers in America he calls "Christ-consciousness." In like manner also he interprets the resurrection of Christ as a leap beyond the world of name and form, with all its distinctions of good and evil. In his pamphlet *Are You Preparing for the Crucifixion* he cries:

O dear beloved ones! How can I attempt or succeed in describing or expressing the Glory of this Christ-consciousness? In this exalted state there are neither the blamed nor the blamer. . . . Here there are neither forms nor names. . . . It is a state of Changeless Peace.

But the swami comes back to the world of good and evil when he blames Miss Mayo for blaming Mother India. In his booklet *Mother America* he writes:

Here is our sister Mayo . . . engaged in ruthlessly wounding the feelings of three hundred and twenty millions of calm, forbearing and undefending Indians, and in singing lullabies to herself for so doing. She is doing harm not only to the Indian nation but to all lovers of India and Truth both in the East and in the West . . . inestimable harm to the whole world. . . . She had no love in her heart; hence she could find none lovable. She came with a repulsive spirit, and the same condition greeted her eye wherever she went.

Now I am not blaming Swami Omkar for blaming Miss Mayo. Nor am I blaming Miss Mayo for blaming Mother India. I am simply pointing out the swami's loyalty to Sankara and the *Upanishads* whereby he holds two different conceptions of God, the "higher" conception in which "there are neither the blamed nor the blamer," and the "lower" conception in which blaming may be considered a just and creative act, as when Sankara blames the Buddhists for unsettling the minds of the people. According to the "higher" conception Swami Omkar does not blame Miss Mayo: according to the "lower" conception he does blame her. Whether the contradiction here be real or apparent, the swami makes no attempt to explain it. In short, what Swami R. S. Narayana of Lucknow says about Omkar's booklet *Meditation* (in the Foreword) may be said about Omkar's whole preaching: "Without caring in the least for language or logic . . . he has freely given vent to the free flow of his inner feelings. . . ." And these feelings are sweet feelings of love. It is love for

India that leads him to blame Miss Mayo: how can love remain indifferent?

* * *

Yogi Ramacharaka teaches a system that is none the less Hindu because he happens to be an American named William Walker Atkinson.[3] His books, which deal with most of the *yogas* and with much oriental occultism, are obtainable at the "Yogi Publishing Society," 80 North Clark Street, Chicago.[4] Many of these teachers of wisdom from abroad are more than lecturers, and yet can hardly be called founders of new cults. Even the cults they represent cannot be called cults in the full sense. A fairly new religious form seems to be developing in America: something in between a sacred community and a secular audience, which might be called a supplementary cult, or a religious class that appeals chiefly to chronic "seekers."

* * *

The *Dharma Mandal,* or "Aryan Religious Association," organized by Kedar Nath Das Gupta, a Bengali of long residence in London and New York, features less lecturing and class work, and more worship and entertainment. I can describe the aims and methods of the association no better than by herewith presenting *its* constitution:

THE DHARMA MANDALA

1. This Society shall be called DHARMA MANDALA—Association for the cultivation of *Dharma.*

(a) "*Dharma* is that which promotes spiritual growth and evolution and leads to the realization of the unsurpassable Good, the Supreme Worth."

(b) *Dharma* is Religion as spiritual endeavor without the necessary acceptance of a religious "creed."

(c) *Dharma* is practical Philosophy which satisfies reason and enables Man to attain full Self-realization, divine Perfection and unconditional spiritual Freedom while still living here on earth.

(d) *Dharma* is in complete harmony with Science in so far as Science is ascertained truth, not mere speculation.

2.   The objects of the *Dharma Mandala* shall be:

(a) To promote life's onward march and uttermost fulfilment by the realization of the Supreme End of all human endeavor.

(b) To meet the spiritual requirements of those that are dissatisfied with dogmatic forms of religion and religious "creeds."

(c) To meet the spiritual needs of Hindus outside of India, including followers all of Aryan Paths such as the Vedic, the Puranic and the Tantric, as well as the Jaina, the Buddhist, the Sikh, the Brahmo and any others originating from Aryan life and thought.

(d) To bring about a better mutual understanding, sympathy and co-operation between the Aryan forms of *Dharma* and all other endeavors for the spiritual advancement of Man.

3.   The means to be pursued for the carrying out of the aforesaid objects shall be religious services, rites, ceremonies, social and religious plays, fairs and festivals, spiritual instruction and guidance of a special and personal kind and other practices of *Dharma;* as well as all forms of educational activity conducive to *Dharma* and to the growth of mutual understanding, sympathy and co-operation among aspirants to spiritual development in all races of mankind.

4.   The membership of the *Dharma Mandala* shall be open to anyone in sympathy with its objects.

5.   No one is required to renounce his particular form of religion to be a member.

The significance of this movement for America lies in the fact that it tends to bring Hindus and American Theosophists even closer together than they are at present. The brief history of the association is given by Mr. Das Gupta as follows:

The inaugural meeting of the *Dharma Mandal* was held in America at Carnegie Hall in New York on June 23rd, 1928, and in England at the Grotrian Hall in London on November 11th, 1928.   Since then several meetings were organized very successfully in London and New York and were highly appreciated by the large congregation.

Endorsers in India include—

His Holiness Shri Shankaracharya Dr. Kurtkoti of Bombay;
Swami Gnanananda of Benares;
The Maharajah Sir Pradyot Coomar Tagore of Bengal;
Shrijut Jugal Kishor Birla of Calcutta.

Extracts from "The Times of India," February 4, 1929:

"A public meeting was held at Girgaum, Bombay, on Thursday night, January 31st, under the presidentship of His Holiness Shri Shankaracharya Dr. Kurtkoti to inaugurate a home and a foreign mission to propagate the Vedic *Dharma.*

"Dr. Kurtkoti in his introductory speech said that it was essential to coordinate the secular and spiritual life of society at home and abroad through the medium of the Vedic *Dharma.* The first step in this direction was to organize a mission in India with branches in London, Paris and New York. Several persons, including princes and prominent among them, Sir Tukoji Rao Holkar of Indore, had offered their services for this work."

The first number of the magazine *Dharma,* managed and edited by Mr. Das Gupta, Suite 829, 152 West 42nd Street, New York, aims to "present India from India's own point of view," the view in which the divine appears everywhere, the view that Rabindra Nath Tagore describes as follows:

There sounded a voice in the ancient forest-shade of India proclaiming the presence of a soul in the burning flame, in the flowing water, in the breathing life of all creatures, in the undying spirit of Man. Those men who awoke in the world's early surprise of light were free and strong and fearless, crossing the barriers of things in joy and meeting the One in the heart of the All.

2. HINDU CULTURAL MOVEMENTS

Perhaps the most impressive form of cultural Hinduism in America at present is the Threefold Movement. One day I decided to pay a visit to its sponsor, Mr. Kedar Nath Das Gupta, who had arranged for Yogananda's lectures at the Union Methodist Episcopal Church at the beginning of 1929. I had already met this Hindu promoter at the first lecture, and having received a cordial invitation to visit him, went to his office at 152 West 42nd Street, New York. This address I found to belong to the Knicker-bocker Building, in view of Times Square. The Threefold Movement uses two rooms on the eighth floor. Mr. Das Gupta, I discovered, is the same man who organized the *Dharma Mandal:* he is promoting both a cult and a cul-tural movement. He is just past middle age, with gray hair and a rotund figure, a man of benevolence and simple charm.

"When did you start the Threefold Movement?" I en-quired, getting down to business.

"Over twenty years ago, I dreamed a wonderful dream."

"In Calcutta?"

"Yes. Struck with the fact that in spite of her variety of communities, castes and cults, India has a common background of culture, I dreamed that all the world, with its various nations and races, might some day live and move in cultural unity. So first of all I joined my country-men in the fight for *svaraj,* or self-rule. For I realized that world unity depended on mutual freedom and respect. We saw we couldn't get rid of British rule until we had first got rid of our economic slavery. So in 1902 we strove for *svadesi,* or home industry. We vowed hand on heart not to sell our souls to the luxury of the West, but to keep happy with the *khaddar,* or coarse cotton cloth spun and woven in our native land. Encouraged by Rabindra Nath Tagore, I opened a *svadesi* store, and became Secretary of Industrial Exhibits in Calcutta. I even sailed to London, to establish there a market for our goods. But at that time I was young and inexperienced. The big British capitalists soon killed my little business."

"What then?"

"I began to give lectures on India, and present our classic dramas, such as Kalidasa's masterpiece *Sakuntala* and Sudraka's *The Little Clay Cart*. Also Tagore's lyrical plays, and *Savitri,* an adaptation of my own. Here was a chance for me to help India and advance world unity at the same time. In the field of culture, at least, the British were approachable. So in 1910 I founded my 'Indian Art and Drama Society,' which in 1912 became 'The Union of East and West.' I laid down the rule that all controversy whether political or religious must be avoided. My society was like a green bamboo. It could be made into a flute of praise, but not a stick of censure."

"But what brought you to America?"

"In 1920 I met Tagore in London. He told me America was wonderful, and urged me to go there with him. I scraped up all my money and went. I was now convinced that the stage was the most effective way of presenting truth. I engaged the Garrick Theatre and put on one of Tagore's plays. Alas, I lost eight thousand dollars. But the cultural success was worth it! Then I got permission through Margaret Anglin to use the Frazee Theatre free. Later I said to myself, Look at all the church auditoriums going to waste on weekdays! I went to John Haynes Holmes. He allowed me to give in his newly reconstructed church building two performances of *Buddha,* adapted from Edwin Arnold's *Light of Asia.* Likewise, William Norman Guthrie let me use the auditorium of St. Mark's in the Bouwerie, and Rabbi Wise put the hall of the Free Synagogue at my disposal."

"How did you manage the stage settings?"

"Well, I came to realize that such accessories only obscure the profound message of the play. So bit by bit I gave them up, till I surpassed Ben Greet in this direction. Sometimes I even gave up costumes. But costumes in a garden make the best effect. I once produced a play in George Gray Barnard's Cloister."

"But when did you start the Threefold Movement?"

"It came about in this way. In 1924 I met Charles Frederick Weller, who was running the 'League of Neighbors' in Elizabeth, New Jersey. He is a great social worker. His aim is to help the stranger within the gates, whom you Americans call 'the dirty foreigners.' Weller and I decided to join our two movements and also create a third—the 'Fellowship of Faiths'—based on a principle too seldom put into practice, the principle of *appreciation*. Brotherhood is more than mere peace or tolerance, and in my opinion, it can be encouraged best by art—by sacred songs, dances, and the drama. I appealed to the ministers. The response was surprising. We opened centers in New York, Philadelphia and Boston. Also in London and Dublin."

"Where do you get your money?"

"Mostly from wealthy individuals. We also make a general appeal."

I thanked my kind informant, and departed to study the literature he gave me.

The *message* of the Threefold Movement is quite simple: mutual appreciation of East and West. It stands for "the Realization of Peace and Brotherhood—through Understanding and Neighborliness—uniting people of all Races, Religions, Countries, Classes and Conditions—not merely by Preaching but by Practice—by building Bridges of Mutual Appreciation across the Chasm of Prejudice." It has "no creed to 'put over,' no institution. It does not seek to change or weaken anyone's traditions or convictions. It enables individuals and groups to enlarge their own souls by appreciating unfamiliar neighbors throughout the world. By understanding and serving his country as a whole, a citizen becomes more useful to his native town. Similarly, an American Christian will the better serve his own nation and his church by also appreciating the people of other creeds and countries." Both National

Prosperity and International Peace are essentially spiritual. The Threefold Movement seeks to develop a *consciousness* of unity adequate to the *fact* of unity created by modern means of communication.

The methods of the Threefold Movement are likewise patent to the Western mind. The organization is federal and democratic, including "Committees of One Hundred" in fourteen cities of nine countries, namely, New York, Boston, Philadelphia, Washington, Baltimore, Chicago, London, Dublin, Paris, Geneva, The Hague, Berlin, Peking and Calcutta. At present the main center is in New York where the general executives, Mr. and Mrs. Weller and Mr. Das Gupta, carry on their work. The Rev. Robert Norwood, D.D., is the president of the New York Committee, while the chairmen of other committees are, for example, the Rev. Joseph Fort Newton, D.D., in Philadelphia, and Sir Francis Younghusband in London.

This organization seeks to work with others without overlapping or competition. It is not a Hindu sect, and it has no cult. It presents its message through settlements, churches, colleges, the Young Men's Christian Association and similar institutions. "It is not a machine but a movement." Its publications include bulletins, reports, *Messages,* newspaper contributions, and a bound book by Dr. Alfred W. Martin, entitled *The Fellowship of Faiths.* For one of the *Messages* Das Gupta has compiled a "Fellowship of Worship" which includes prayers, hymns and poems selected and adapted from Western poets and the scriptures of the world. For example, one hymn is "Akbar's Dream," a paraphrase of Tennyson's poem by Will Hayes. It begins:

> Of each fair plant the choicest blooms I scan,
>> For of the garden of the King I'm free
> To wreathe a crown for every Mussalman,
>> Brahman and Buddhist, Christian and Parsee.

Another method of work is the production of classical plays of the Orient, such as the Hindu *Sacrifice* by Tagore, with Hindu music and dancing, and *The Crimson Camellia,* a Japanese drama acted in English by Japanese players, with Japanese music. Exhibitions of Eastern arts and crafts have been organized in England and America, and neighborhood service has been rendered to needy individuals, especially bewildered foreigners.

In four years, meetings have been held on an average of about one a day, with a total attendance of about 100,000. These meetings include select dinners, mass meetings, festivals and popular lectures such as "Pictures of Hindu Life" by Dhan Gopal Mukerji, and "Glimpses of Chinese Manners and Customs" by Dr. Inming C. Suez, the Chinese Consul General. In Chester, Pennsylvania, under the auspices of the League of Neighbors, a large hall, decorated with flags of many nations, was filled with people of various communities in picturesque national costumes. An outstanding annual event is "Peace Week," observed in May with large cosmopolitan gatherings.

In London, England, one of the meetings of the Fellowship of Faiths gathered together in common "Tributes to Christianity" notable representatives of eight different faiths, including:
1. Dr. A. D. Jilla, a Zoroastrian
2. Abdul Majid, a Muslim
3. the Maharajadhiraja Bahadur of Burdwan, a Hindu
4. the Hon. Dr. W. A. de Silva, a Buddhist
5. Sir A. Conan Doyle, a Spiritualist
6. Rabbi Moses Gaster, a Jew
7. Dr. Annie Besant, a Theosophist, and
8. Dr. F. W. Norwood, a Christian

The intellectual character of the Threefold Movement may well be described by selecting a few of the statements purporting to express what the Movement "has learned":

The real conflict is not between France and Germany, or East and West, or between any other nations, but between the forward-moving idealists in each country and their own backward-looking fellow-countrymen.

Culture is a potent means of unifying people of divergent races, languages and religions—as illustrated in the cultural unity . . . of the peoples of India . . . who differ extremely in religion, race and language.

Unity cannot be achieved through enforced or attempted uniformity. Increasing differentiation is God's and nature's way of life. Each must cherish that consciousness of unity which is enriched by free variety and differences.

Consciousness is the determinant of external facts and forces. The internal, the unseen, the mental-emotional-spiritual faculties in every man enable him to *create anything he can conceive and hold faithfully in consciousness*—not only personal health and prosperity but social relationships and conditions, local, national and international.

*　　*　　*

The International School of Vedic and Allied Research, if not so demonstrative at present as the Threefold Movement, is perhaps even more venturesome in its ideal, which is nothing less than complete Western appreciation of Aryan culture. Its motives are the desires of Easterners to promote their ancient culture in the West, and the desires of Westerners to enlarge their vision and profit by the culture of the East. Its methods are purely academic. The Director is Pandit Jagadish Chandra Chatterji, and the Secretary Dr. George C. O. Haas, an American Sanskrit scholar with a deep appreciation of Hinduism.

The pandit and his co-worker feel that the truths of Hinduism and other eastern systems of thought have not had a fair chance in the West. Until now Hinduism, for example, has crept in unbidden, and masked by such movements as Theosophy and New Thought. Or it has been stored away in American Hindu cults such as Vedanta and Yogoda that have only a weak connection with the dominant concerns of the West as a whole. Accordingly, these scholars are adopting methods calculated to weave Hindu ideals into the very fabric of Western culture and education.

In the mind of the West until now, they say, Hindu notions have been rare and curious specimens from a strange land, carefully labelled and stowed away in libraries by Western scholars, many of whom have never been to the East nor understood the meaning of the concepts they handle. Accordingly, the aim of the friends of Eastern culture must be to furnish Western universities with genuine professors of Aryan learning, that is, scholars who shall be able to present Eastern learning from the standpoint of the East.

So Pandit Chatterji and his colleagues have created the International School of Vedic and Allied Research, with centers in America, Europe and India. The Executive Council of the American Section is composed of well-known university men such as John Dewey, John H. Finley, Stephen P. Duggan, Paul Munroe, and William E. Hocking. Its president is Charles Rockwell Lanman, Professor Emeritus of Sanskrit, Harvard University. The president of the British Section is the Marquess of Zetland, while the temporary president of the All-India Committee is Mr. M. R. Jayakar.

The Director of the whole School, of course, is Pandit Chatterji. The title of pandit proclaims him a Hindu Sanskrit scholar of the ancient orthodox way. He studied in the Government Sanskrit College, Calcutta, and obtained from the *Bharata Dharma Maha-Mandala,* or All-India Religious Association, Benares, the title of Vidya-Varidhi, which means Ocean of Learning. He received a degree also at Cambridge University, England. He was formerly Director of Oriental Research and Archæology of Kashmir, and Chief of the Department of Religious Administration and Education of Baroda. Finally, he is the author of several books, including *Hindu Realism,* which presents the metaphysic of the *Nyaya-Vaisesika* School in a form intelligible to the modern reader.

In support of its position that the mutually complementary nature of the cultures of East and West is of vital and practical interest, the School has announced four definite aims:

1. The establishment of educational relations and exchange scholarships as between the universities of America, Europe and the East, especially India.

2. The development of a wider interest in the languages and literatures of Vedic origin and affinity as an aid to general culture and in particular to humanistic studies.

3. Systematic studies in Vedic, Indo-European (Aryan), Sumerian, Semitic, Hittite and other "West-Asiatic" and allied subjects, in the light of the latest archæological discoveries.

4. Continued archæological research in Armenia and other places where such discoveries have already been made or may be made in the future.

A special department corresponds to each of these aims.

1. *The Department of Educational Exchange and Relations* aims to equip both Easterners and Westerners with Eastern lore. Western universities that at present do not offer courses in Oriental studies will be urged to do so, those that do offer them will be requested to include them in general courses for the Bachelor of Arts degree, while those that go this far will be encouraged to prepare their teachers to impart Eastern culture with a sympathetic understanding.

Hindu students will come to the West to study Western science, sociology and methods of research with a view to making an accurate study of Hindu thought from an appreciative standpoint. To this end an Indian University is being planned for America, and another for Europe. Western students will be sent to India to study Hinduism in "living contact with Hindu scholars." To this end an American University is being planned for India "like the American universities at Peking, Cairo and other centers in the Orient." This means that the funds and teachers will come chiefly from America. The International School's American university in India "is to be housed in the well-known palatial building known as Radha Vilas, situated directly on the banks of the Ganges, opposite the palace of the Maharaja of Benares and close to the Benares Hindu University."

2. *The Department of Vedic, Indic and Indo-European Studies and Research* aims to bring before the public eye in the West the whole mass of Hindu lore in all its original garb and meaning. To this end many massive encyclopedic works will be produced, and a special effort made to exhibit Hindu philosophy as the practical search for "a state of unlimited bliss and enlightenment," as a body of doctrine in harmony with Christianity, and as "the fulfilment of Western thought." Moreover, the School has announced three courses, which will be given as soon as a sufficient number of students have registered for them: "Introduction to Hindu Philosophy" by Director Chatterji, and "Sanskrit" and "Readings in the Upanishads" by Professor Haas.

3. *The Department of Allied Studies and Research* aims to make a detailed investigation of the possible points of connection between the Hindu Aryans and the more Western races like the Semites. Why, for example, do the childhood stories of Krishna and Christ have so much in common—miraculous birth, slaughter of the innocents, and so on?

4. *The Department of Archaeological Research* aims merely to carry on the field work required by the third department.

The School will include a bureau for supplying information about the East, and also a reference library. Two numbers of its quarterly *Journal* have already appeared, published by the India Institute Press, Times Building, New York, where the School has its main office. "All persons who are interested in the work of the School and desire to participate in its benefits, while at the same time assisting it in carrying out its plans, are invited to become members of the India Institute."

Many of the proposals that are to be realized in the School were advanced by Professor Lanman in his presidential address before the American Oriental Society in 1920. The following quotation will give in a nutshell the attitude of the Eastern and Western promoters of this and similar institutions supporting the advance of Hinduism in America:

The business of us Orientalists is something that is in vital relation with urgent practical and political needs. The work calls for co-operation, and above all things else, for co-operation in a spirit of mutual sympathy and teachableness. . . . India with her great learning is eager to adopt modern methods to make that learning available to her own sons and to us, and is ready to join hands with us of the West in order to make her spiritual heritage enrich our too hurried life.[5]

* * *

Another cultural movement is the Hindustan Association of America, Inc., 500 Riverside Drive, New York, which aims to ease the way for young Indians to come and study in America, and to promote Indian culture. Its declared purpose is to interpret India to America and America to India. To this end, literary and social gatherings are arranged, bulletins[6] published, and an official monthly circulated, entitled *The Hindustanee Student,* of which the editor is a young Bengali by the name of Hemendra Kisore Rakhit. Of course, Hindustan means India, and India is not wholly Hindu; yet in numbers and age of culture the Hindus are dominant, as well as by far the most plentiful in America, so that any all-India movement, especially in America, is apt to be mainly Hindu, and so can be included in our study.

*   *   *

A cultural movement similar to the Hindustan Association, but working among the public at large instead of chiefly among students, is the India Society of America, Inc. The director, Hari G. Govil, whose office at present (1930) is in the Times Building, New York, is a Hindu of the *Vaisya* caste, and hails from the city of Bikanir in the country of Rajputana, West India. At the National Hindu University, Benares, Govil read for the Bachelor of Science degree, and in 1920 came to America to enter the Boston Institute of Technology. Meeting difficulty here, he began to study electrical engineering in the College of the City of New York. But the need of making a living was so pressing that he was forced to abandon his technical career, and work at odd jobs including lecturing and manual labor. Of these two kinds of work, the lecturing proved to be the more fruitful, for many Americans were interested in what he had to say about India.

Thus Govil turned from the study of engineering to the teaching of Hindu culture. Encouraged by the growing group of India enthusiasts, he published the first issue of his bimonthly *Oriental Magazine* in 1922. Out of the interest created by this magazine grew the India Society, founded in 1924 and incorporated in 1925. The purpose of this society is "to promote cultural relations between India and America," and its methods also are cultural, for while it desires to promote Indian independence, it seeks to exclude all political and sectarian controversy. Like Jagadish Chandra Chatterji of the International School and Hamendra Kisore Rakhit of the Hindustan Association, Govil deprecates all religious propaganda whether Christian or Hindu on the ground that it excites animosity and interferes with the deeper exchange of culture which is the best way of promoting freedom, peace and brotherhood among the nations of the world. The honorary president of the Society is Ananda K. Coomaraswamy; the president, J. T. Sunderland, D.D. The Advisory Council includes Upton Close (Joseph Washington Hall), Sidney L. Gulick, Jane Addams, Ruth St. Denis and Heywood Broun. The record of the Society up to date may now be presented in its own words:

PLAN AND PURPOSE

Through its mastery of physical science, America holds the key to power in the world without—through the knowledge of the inner forces, India holds the key to the world within. Just as America represents the highest achievement of the scientific West, India represents the lofty spiritual achievement of the East.

For the unity of mankind and its fullest harmony, the intellectual and spiritual aristocracy of America and India should unite in an effort to attain to a more sympathetic understanding of each other.

Towards this end, the India Society of America has undertaken to establish the first India Center in America to promote cultural relations between India and America. . . .

Origin

The India Society of America was founded by Hari G. Govil in 1924 and sponsored by such distinguished men and women as Prof. Edwin R. A. Seligman, Columbia University; Oswald Garrison Villard, editor of *The Nation;* Prof. John Dewey, Columbia University; Prof. William R. Shepherd, Columbia University; Dr. Alfred W. Martin of the Society for Ethical Culture; Rev. Dr. John Haynes Holmes, minister of the Community Church; and Rev. Dr. J. T. Sunderland of the Unitarian Church. . . .

Our Object

In 1925 the India Society was chartered under the laws of the State of New York as a membership corporation with the following purpose:

To promote a broader and more intelligent understanding be-

tween the peoples of India and America through the study and appreciation of India's art, literature, philosophy and culture;

To disseminate a more accurate knowledge of the Hindu people, their life, ideals and aspirations.

ACTIVITIES

During the five years of its existence the Society has successfully carried on its work of interpreting India to America through various activities which may be briefly summed up as follows:

Lectures

The Society has arranged lectures on Hindu art, literature, philosophy, religion, science and contemporary life of India by prominent authorities and leaders, among whom may be mentioned: Dr. Ananda Coomaraswamy, Dr. and Mrs. James H. Cousins, Rev. C. F. Andrews, Mme. Sarojini Naidu, Prof. S. Radhakrishnan, Prof. Surendra Nath Das Gupta, Pandit Jagadish Chandra Chatterji, Dhan Gopal Mukerji, Prof. Herbert Adams Gibbons, Prof. Robert Morss Lovett, Prof. Harry F. Ward, and Dr. Jagadisan M. Kumarappa.

Social Gatherings and Receptions

Special functions have been arranged in honor of distinguished visitors from India to give an opportunity to members and friends of the Society to make personal contact with some of the outstanding personalities of India.

Art Exhibitions

The Society, in cooperation with the Corona Mundi International Art Center and the American Federation of Arts, sponsored the first Exhibition of Modern Hindu Paintings in New York City, with a lecture on *Renaissance in Hindu Art,* by Hari G. Govil, Director of the Society. Under the joint-auspices of the India Society and the Art Alliance of America, another Exhibition of Modern Hindu Art, consisting of water-color paintings by contemporary artists of India and brought by Dr. James H. Cousins, was arranged at the Art Center, accompanied by lectures on *The Art and Culture of India,* by Dr. James H. Cousins. The Society also introduced to American art lovers, the Exhibition of Heerameneck Collection of Rare Asiatic Art at the American Art Galleries with an illustrated lecture on *The Art of India,* by Dr. Ananda Coomaraswamy, Hon. President of the India Society.

The Society represented India at the First Oriental Exposition held in New York City in 1927-1928 and arranged an India program.

Hindu Films

With the cooperation of the India Society, the premiere showing of *The Light of Asia,* produced in India by an all-Hindu cast and portraying the life of Buddha, was given at Carnegie Hall by the Film Arts Guild.

Shiraz, another film made in India with an all-Hindu cast recounting the romantic tale of the creation of the world-famous Taj Mahal, was also presented with the cooperation of the India Society.

Radio

The Society arranged India programs of lectures and musical recitals over the broadcasting stations WEAF and WJZ . . . station WGL . . . and other stations. . . . More than thirty programs have been broadcast. . . .

Publications

The Society has published informative literature on India for free distribution among members, public libraries and educational institutions. The following monographs . . . may be secured by writing to the Secretary: *India and America* by Dr. Ananda Coomaraswamy, *The Marriage of East and West* by Claude Bragdon, *The Western Discovery of the Orient* by Dr. Louise M. Keuffner Avery, *India's Place in the World's Civilization* by J. T. Sunderland, *East and West* by Rabindranath Tagore.

Library

The Society has a selected collection of books on India and Asia available to members. New books are constantly being added. The Society has presented significant books imported from India to the important libraries in America.

First India Conference of America

As an outstanding achievement, the Society organized the First India Conference of America, held in New York City during the three weeks from October 4th to November 5th, 1928, to present a comprehensive survey of India's life and thought, art and culture. The Conference opened with the First Exhibition of Modern Hindu Paintings. A recital of Hindu instrumental and vocal music was included in the program. More than 50 lectures were delivered from the platform and more than 25 over the radio. The Conference aroused great interest and received much favorable comment in the press. Many prominent speakers from

India and America participated. Mme. Sarojini Naidu, co-worker of Mahatma Gandhi and formerly president of the Indian National Congress, made her first New York public appearance at the Conference.

INDIA CENTER

As the outcome of the round-table discussions of the First India Conference of America, it was decided at the annual meeting held in January, 1929, that in view of the growing interest in India's art and culture and in the work of the India Society, definite steps be taken to establish . . . the India Center, where all the activities of the India Society will be concentrated.

Endowment Fund

In line with this general resolution of opening a Hindu Center for the cultivation of cultural relations between India and the United States it was decided to raise an Endowment Fund of $300,000 in India and America to finance the purchase of the building and to create a Permanent Endowment Fund to sustain the work and enlarge the program of the Society.

Location

The six-story building at 334 Riverside Drive, near 106th Street, New York City, has been purchased for the India Center. The location of the building is ideal in every respect.

Facilities

After thorough alterations, for which Frederick Kiesler, the noted Viennese architect, has been engaged, the premises of the India Center will provide the following facilities:

Auditorium

(a) for holding lectures and other functions.

(b) to present Hindu films to depict a true picture of the life and customs of India. Arrangements are being made to import Hindu films directly from India for this purpose.

(c) Hindu dramas and musical recitals will be presented occasionally. Negotiations are being made to invite a group of Hindu musicians from India to demonstrate this art of India that is so little known in this country.

Art Gallery

There will be a permanent exhibition of the contemporary and classical art of India—paintings, sculpture, wood-carving, metal-works and bronzes, textiles and prints, and other handicrafts of India. Parts of this exhibition will be circulated all over the country through important art centers.

Conference Rooms and Lounge

These will provide all the facilities of a social and intellectual center for the members and friends of the Society.

Library and Reading Room

The Center will contain a comprehensive reference library of books on India and Asia. . . . Magazines and newspapers from India, Asia and Europe will also be made available.

Studio Apartments

The Center will also provide living-quarters through its six one-room apartments, equipped with all modern facilities. . . . Visiting professors, scholars and business men, as well as tourists from India, will find an ideal home at the India Center.

Restaurant

A well-appointed eating-place will be opened in the building, where both American and Hindu dishes will be served.

International Institute of Hindu and Buddhist Culture

The purpose of the Institute will be: (a) To coordinate the activities of the various learned societies and institutions all over the world in the study and appreciation of India's culture; (b) To provide for scholarships and fellowships for exchange of professors and scholars between India and America; (c) To arrange, in cooperation with other institutions, courses of study in Hindu and Buddhist art, literature, philosophy, science and history; (d) To encourage the study of Hindu and Buddhist culture in the universities of America.

American Cultural Expedition to India

Members of the Society have often approached the Director with the suggestion of conducting a party of American friends to the heart of India and to interpret her life and thought. A group of more than a dozen is already formed as the nucleus of the party. In order to make the party comprehensive in its interests, it has been decided to include a few more members such as artists, writers, journalists, photographers and students and professors who are capable and willing to approach India with an unbiased mind. The party is expected to start in November, 1930, for a period of from six to eight months.

This "Passage to India" would mean a tour round the world —going via Europe and returning via the Pacific. The party will visit the various cultural centers in India such as Tagore's International University at Shantiniketan, Gandhi's Satyagrah Ashrama at Sabarmati, Bose's Science Institute, Calcutta, Brahma-Vidya

Asharam at Adyar, Benares and other important cities and historic sites of India.

The tour will be conducted by Hari G. Govil with the co-operation and supervision of the American Express Company.

This tour will be similar to the fourth Far East Cultural Expedition conducted by Upton Close, leaving Seattle July 2, 1930, and returning to America by way of Siberia and Russia after having visited South America and the islands of the Pacific. In 1927 began Govil's new series of the *Oriental Magazine,* which includes Bertrand Russell, Count Keyserling, Anatole France, Rabindra Nath Tagore and the well-known Gandhi among its contributors. In October 1930, will be held the Second India Conference of America, most probably in the new India Center. For the International Institute of Hindu and Buddhist Culture there has been arranged a series of lectures by Kalidas Nag, Ph.D., Secretary of the Greater India Society, Calcutta, an institution very much like the India Society of America; A. E. (Charles Russell), the Irish poet; T. L. Vaswani, M.A., Principal of the National University in Karachi; V. R. Kokatnur, Ph.D., a Hindu chemist in New York; Felix Valyi, a Swiss writer; A. K. Coomaraswamy, and H. G. Govil.

* * *

Representing Indian nationalism in its political aspect is the American branch of the Indian National Congress, called the *India Freedom Foundation,* of which the Director is S. N. Ghose, whose office is at 31 Union Square, New York. Just how much political propaganda may lie hidden in other Hindu movements in America is from the nature of the case hard to tell. I have discovered none, and have made no attempt to do so. But whatever may be the influence of Indian political leaders on these movements, there is naturally at this time of political crisis in

India a very sensitive national consciousness among Indians in America.

3.   LEARNED HINDU LECTURERS

As early as 1886, a certain Mr. Joshee[7] lectured before Theosophical societies in America. How learned or scholarly he was I do not know, but he is the first Hindu teacher in America of whom I have record. In 1905, about twenty years later, Paul Ramanathan, who was not a Christian although his first name was Paul, delivered a lecture on "The Spirit of the East contrasted with the Spirit of the West" at the Brooklyn Institute of Arts and Sciences.

Two years previous to this came Swami Rama Tiratha, a Brahman from the Panjab, about whom we have copious information. He arrived at San Francisco at the close of the year 1903. As the steamer reached the harbor, he was standing on deck calm and luminous in his flame-colored robe, amid the surrounding hustle and bustle of landing. No one would have taken him for the university professor he was—a teacher of mathematics, if the truth be told.

"Where is your luggage?" inquired an American fellow-passenger.

"Rama keeps as much as he can carry himself," was the serene reply.

"Have you any money?"

"No."

"Are you landing here?"

"Yes."

"Then you must have some friends to help you."

"Yes, there is one."

"Who is he?"

"You!" breathed Rama, touching his companion's shoulder.

An electric touch that produced results. This man took care of the swami during his whole stay in America, and later wrote of him: "He is a torch of knowledge hailing from the Himalayas. Fire cannot burn him, steel cannot cut him. Tears of ecstasy flow from his eyes, and his very presence gives new life." [8]

Such was Swami Rama. His message was simple, but deep, for his soul was fed by Christian love and service as well as by the Hindu feeling and conviction, "I am God." In Forman Christian College, Lahore, he consumed his body at the altar of Western learning, and then grew strong and robust on the diet of *Vedanta* assurance and *yoga* body building. To India his message was patriotism and reason, the abolition of caste and the adoption of modern education.

Accept not a religion because it is the oldest. . . . The latest innovation, if it can stand the test of Reason, is as good as the fresh rose, bedecked with sparkling dew. . . .

Accept . . . a religion on *its own* merits. Examine it yourself. Sift it.

Renunciation does not require you to go into the . . . forests . . . to strip yourself of all clothing. . . . To realize God, have the Sannyasa *spirit,* i. e., entire renunciation of self-interest, making the little self absolutely one with the great self of *Mother India.*[9]

To America his message was peace, and confidence in the self as God. It is useless to send Christian missionaries to India, he insisted. Just let the Hindu come to America for modern education, and then return.

Cultivate peace of mind, fill your mind with pure thoughts, and nobody can set himself against you. That is the Law. . . .

Have you a doubt as to your own Divine Self? You had better a bullet in your heart than a doubt there. . . . The whole Universe serves one as his body, when he feels the Universal Soul as his very Self.[10]

In all and above all, Rama Tiratha was a universal mystic.

Rama brings you a religion which is found in the streets . . .
written upon the leaves . . . murmured by the brooks . . .
whispered in the winds . . . throbbing in your own veins and
arteries; a religion which concerns your business and bosom;
a religion which you have not to practice by going into a particular church only; a religion which you have to practice and
live in your everyday life, about your hearth and in your dining
room, everywhere you have to live that religion.[11]

*   *   *

After Swami Rama, came Rabindra Nath Tagore,[12] another uniter of East and West, who made flying trips to
the United States in 1910, 1917 and 1921. He expects to
come again soon. Poet of joy and love and play, a man
of ceaseless activity and variety of effort, shifting back and
forth like Tolstoy from public to private life, plunging
through political and social reform into education and
religious peace, observant and critical, sweeping in praise
or blame, blurred by popularity, rejected in his native
province of Bengal, but accepted by the world, a champion
of freedom for women and for subject races, Tagore himself is his message.

The poet is no exact philosopher—his mind is too sentimental and glancing. Nor is he bound by Hindu or
Christian tradition. He once repelled the suggestion that
he had been directly influenced by Christian thought when
he wrote *Gitanjali* by saying that he had never read the
Bible. In similar vein, he once dubbed the ordinary Hindu
doctrine of transmigration a "fairy-tale." And this from
a Brahman! He frowns alike on the methods of Christian
missions, and the custom of Hindu caste. Tagore is just
Tagore, and his message is no more strictly Hindu than
his life.

*   *   *

In 1909, the year before Tagore's first visit, another
Brahman received the degree of Doctor of Philosophy in
sociology at Cornell University, Ithaca, New York. His

name was Shridhar Venkatesh Ketkar, and he hailed from a western part of India called Maharastra. Encouraged by the favorable reception of his dissertation on Hindu caste, he wrote another book called *Hinduism: its Formation and Future*. He did it by himself, without the critical help of his teachers.

This Brahman does not preach to America—he just describes the future of Hinduism. Hitherto it has regarded cultured Westerners as Barbarians like the outcastes and the jungle tribes. From now on, however, it will take them into its fold. Under the pressure of Islam and Christianity it will develop a national brotherhood of "Indianism" without forming a new religion. On this basis, it will proceed to conquer the world with its culture. "The work for the future for Hinduism to perform is the creation of a *manava-dharma*, a common tradition for the whole world." [13] Of this common tradition, the Brahmans will be the priests. Already they are virtually world-teachers—their universal *Dharma*, or eternal religion, is the basis for all particular cults or temporal religions such as Hindu sectarian devotion and Christianity. But their teaching will not be universally accepted until the West prepares itself intellectually to appreciate the higher philosophy of the Hindus.

* * *

After Shridhar Venkatesh Ketkar the sociologist, came Sarvapalli Radhakrishnan the philosopher, and in 1926 delivered the Haskell Lectures[14] in the University of Chicago. He spoke somewhat as a preacher proclaiming a gospel, somewhat as a lawyer defending a case. The Hinduism he advocated was not the orthodox Hinduism of the pandits, nor yet the reformed Hinduism of the Brahma Samaj, but something between the two. He seemed to be interpreting the substance of classic Hinduism according to certain familiar conceptions of Christianity and Western idealism.

In his lectures the doctrine of rebirth is scarcely mentioned, while *karma* is presented as the "embodiment of the mind and will of God," an instrument for effecting divine mercy and forgiveness. The *sannyasi* of India, that wandering, saintly mendicant, is pictured as a solicitous charity worker, whose aim is "not to free himself from the cares of outward life," but to "suffer and sacrifice and die" for mankind. His renunciation is not detachment from the world as is commonly supposed, but "attachment to the finite as the embodiment of the infinite.[15] Yet Radhakrishnan also calls the *sannyasis* "solitary souls who have not any personal attachment." [16]

Even caste, which Tagore and the West denounce as the bane of Indian life, is to Radhakrishnan really a model for imitation, if properly understood. For there are only four ways of dealing with a conquered race. Three of these are bad: slaughter, enslavement, and absorption by intermarriage. Only the way of caste-organization is good, for this preserves individuality with peace, and prevents a degrading fusion of blood. But he omits the fact that caste did not prevent this fusion in India. Even the code of Manu allowed the fair Brahman to have four wives, one of whom could be a Sudra, or dark-skinned person.

Amid the "flow of strife and opinions" Radhakrishnan finds one firm foundation for his teaching, "since every form of Hinduism and every stage of its growth is related to the common background of Vedanta." [17] In the spirit of universalism, the professor declares, "The Vedanta is not *a* religion, but religion *itself*." [18] This religion is true in itself—ineffable, incomparable, sublime. It is not dogma but experience, beyond the reach of reason to condemn. In brief, *it is the reality of the mystics, and mystics are all alike*. "Judged by the characteristic religious experience, St. John and St. Paul have not any material advantage over Plotinus and Sankara." [19] This ineffable reality is perfection, and perfection is inactive, unhistorical, unknowable. Such wise agnosticism prevents intolerance and heresy-hunting.

To attain *moksa,* or salvation, in this perfection, you may believe anything you please, so long as you strictly follow certain prescribed rules of conduct, bound together in *Dharma,* or right action. Freedom comes only through law. For the individual this law means the four stages of life, in which he becomes first a student, then a householder, then a hermit, and finally a wandering beggar. For society this law means caste. In Hinduism, then, you may believe what you please, if only you *do* what Vedanta believes.

*   *   *

In 1926 again, the same year that Radhakrishnan lectured in the University of Chicago, Surendra Nath Das Gupta, his colleague in the University of Calcutta, and a Brahman of Bengal, delivered the Harris Lectures[20] of Northwestern University in Evanston, Illinois. Like Radhakrishnan, he presents Hinduism as fundamentally a non-rational mysticism, "a view which considers reason to be incapable of discovering or of realizing the nature of ultimate truth . . . but at the same time believes in the certitude of some other means of arriving at it." [21] The "lower" mysticism is worldly and magical, but the "higher" is "directed to the liberation of the spirit and the attainment of the highest bliss." [22]

*   *   *

Another Bengali Brahman, who in spite of conservative protests married into another caste in Hyderabad, South India, is Mrs. Sarojini Naidu, India's foremost woman.

A peerless orator, once president of the Indian National Congress, a distinguished poetess, and a tireless worker in the cause of social and political freedom, she came in 1929 at the request of the Feakins Lecture Bureau to lecture in America with the avowed purpose of interpreting India's womanhood and national aspiration, in order to weld a bond of fellowship between East and West.

* * *

In the Fall of the same year, Harindra Nath Chattopadhyaya came to America as a "cultural ambassador from Young India." He is the youngest brother of Mrs. Naidu, and like his sister, he writes poetry that has received the admiration of many, including Rabindra Nath Tagore and Manmohandas Karamchand Gandhi. Like his sister, also, he toured the country under the Feakins Lecture Bureau, Times Building, New York. He is a musician and a playwright as well as a poet, and is a vital force in the Hindu art renaissance. His Farewell Address at the Town Hall Club, April 15, 1930, was on "The New Theatre Movement in India."

* * *

These lecturers have gone back to their work in India, but many of their compatriots are still in America today. On Hollywood Boulevard[23] in Los Angeles, Jogdesh Misrow, a fourth Bengali Brahman, is holding forth on *karma* and rebirth and other topics dear to the Hindu mind. Dhan Gopal Mukerji, likewise a Bengali Brahman, lecturing here and there on Hindu drama, jungle life and other interesting topics for the Feakins Lecture Bureau, is telling delightful stories culled from Oriental lore, praising the position of Hindu women, and denouncing the West for its greed. Harendra Nath Maitra, a sixth Bengali Brahman, in his book *Hinduism: the World Ideal* offers his native culture complete as a balm for the wounds of the world. Says he:

In studying Western civilization I have felt that there is something wanting. This something India has. I can express the distinction in one sentence. India looks within; the West without. It was the uttering of the Great Teacher who is known in the West that the Kingdom of God is not without but within. The real crux is there. To find out that *within* is the basis of India's civilization; and that, I boldly state, must be basis of the World-ideal. The West is mad for the outer. She has sought the help of science not to gain life, but death. . . . She must learn meditation.[24]

* * *

Ananda K. Coomaraswamy, of Ceylon, Curator of the Oriental Department of the Museum of Fine Art in Boston, also looks askance at Western civilization. Opposite the titlepage of one of his books, called *The Dance of Siva,* is the plate of a bronze figure with two legs and four arms, executing a whirling, elaborate dance. The figure is symbolic, and replete with meaning. It is the image of Siva, the God of primitive, rhythmic energy, who with Visnu divides the honors of popular Hindu devotion. Says Coomaraswamy:

Amongst the greatest of the names of Siva is Nataraja, Lord of Dancers, or King of Actors. The Cosmos is His theatre, there are many different steps in His repertory, He Himself is actor and audience—

"When the Actor beateth the drum
Everybody cometh to see the show;
When the Actor collecteth the stage properties
He abideth alone in His happiness."

Whatever the origins of Siva's dance, it became in time the clearest image of the *activity* of God which any art or religion can boast of.[25]

But the activity of God, according to the dominant Hindu position, is only on the surface. There is another and deeper phase of the divine rhythm, and this is God's *passivity*. After the dance is over, the Actor abides still and alone. In reality, God is the bliss of solitary repose. It is this passive oneness that lies in the background of Hindu art as India's only contribution to the world—"her philosophy." This philosophy "is equally the gospel of Jesus and of Blake, Lao Tze, and Rumi—but nowhere else has it been made the essential basis of sociology and education." [26] The result is Hindu society, which appears to many "infinitely superior to the social order which we know as 'modern civilization'." [27]

According to this Hindu view, the history of Western progress, with its achievements in science and industry, is nothing more than the dance of Siva, a bit of activity that must come to an end, an illusion that will ultimately vanish. [28]

However much the Brahmans in their mature wisdom believed in renunciation, says Coomaraswamy, they had no desire "to impose the natural asceticism of age upon the young," and so tolerated all kinds of self assertion in men of lower rank. From this tolerance arose the Hindu social order with its reincarnation and caste. The doctrine of reincarnation is just "an artistic or mythological representation" of the fact that the souls of men vary in age, irrespective of the age of the body. Young souls revel in action, but wise old souls prefer repose. By natural law according to this preference, each soul is nearly always born into its own befitting environment, and thus becomes a member of a certain caste, low for the young soul, high for the old soul. "To those who admit the variety of age in human souls, this must appear to be the only true communism." [29]

This coöperative scheme of Hindu life, the only hope of the world, is now unfortunately the victim of materialistic competition and exploitation.

The rapid degradation of Asia is thus an evil portent for the future of humanity, and for the future of that Western social idealism of which the beginnings are already recognizable. . . . There will come a time when Europe will not be able to fight Industrialism, because this enemy will be entrenched in Asia. . . . What has to be secured is the conscious coöperation of East and West for common ends . . . for if Asia be not with Europe, she will be against her, and there may arise a terrible conflict, economic, or even armed, between an idealistic Europe and a materialized Asia.[30]

* * *

Rama Krishna Lall is a young "Hindu metaphysician" who began his lecturing career in America by utilizing vacation periods while studying in Cornell University, Ithaca, New York, from 1927 to 1929. At present (1930) he is delivering lectures under the Emilie Sarter Lecture Management, New York, some of his titles being: "India, Her Virtues and Her Handicaps," "India's Contribution to World Civilization," "India in Transition," "The Youth Movement in India," and "The Hindu Way of Life." In expounding the Hindu way of life, he passes over from the mere description of culture to the definite teaching of religion and philosophy, and is thinking of expanding this side of his work by starting a *"Dharma Center"* in New York. While he is an adept in producing illusions of mind reading and other works of wonder for the sake of entertainment, he does not pose as a supernatural seer, but presents his Hindu message on its own merits.

Like many other Hindu lecturers in America, Lall is a product of East and West, for in his native city of Allahabad in the "United Provinces," North India, he sat at the feet of his revered *guru*, or Hindu religious tutor, during all the years he attended the elementary school and the high school conducted by the American Presbyterian Mission. But he does not vacillate between two religious positions: he is a thoroughgoing Hindu with a knowledge of Christianity. Later extensive travels, including sojourns in British Guiana and New York City, where he landed in America in 1924, did not shake his faith in his original religion and culture; and while he worships Christ as an outstanding moral teacher and artist in parable along with other "masters" of his country, he regards the intricate theories and exclusive claims of the intolerant sort of missionaries as a bit of hypocrisy. The main source of religious illumination, he feels, is his own India, which has contributed much in the past, including the lure which led to the discovery of America, and will contribute more in the future along the spiritual line.

*　*　*

Hari Das Mazumdar, another young Hindu, who in 1928 received a fellowship in Sociology in the University of Wisconsin, at Madison, Wisconsin, is also lecturing in America, and has written a book entitled *Gandhi the Apostle.*

*　*　*

Shri Vishwanath Keskar, like Shridhar Venkatesh Ketkar, is a Brahman from Maharastra. He came to America in October, 1929, and at present (1930) is staying at the Roerich Museum (a huge building including apartments), Riverside Drive and 103rd Street, New York. Here he received me in the quiet manner of the classic East, and kindly gave me his story, which I now set down. While he is a university man, he represents no university or academic institution. He speaks only for himself, lives on private funds, and demands no fees for his lectures.

Graduating from the Poona College of the Bombay University, he spent five years at the National Hindu University at Benares teaching philosophy of East and West.

But studying rather than teaching was his main interest at that time. So he left Benares and wandered about the country, visiting all the universities in India and Burma. Then feeling the urge to develop a more profound inner life, he retreated to the lofty Himalayas, where he engaged in private meditation for a period of about five years. This part of his life must remain a closed book to the public. His next step was to visit a multitude of holy places including monasteries and secret abodes. All this he did to prepare himself to be an accomplished teacher of religion and philosophy. After filling the office of principal of a large high school in Poona for nine years, he steamed away from Bombay in April 1929, traveled in Europe and Britain for several months, and then came to America.

Piles of manuscripts embodying the results of his researches and reflections are waiting to be printed. And the call is about to come, for the inner voice has sounded. Everything goes according to the plan of this inner voice. No haste, no waste. No hurry, no worry. All is calm and serene. One of the forthcoming books will deal with personal experiments on "different planes of life and matter." Another will describe "great teachers and masters who are not to be found in the schools." Another will go into psychoanalysis. Others will treat culture and civilization, the purpose of man, the fundamentals of education, and the problem of sex.

In his youth Professor Keskar was a skeptic. Like Descartes he resolved to accept nothing on authority. But on the basis of experience and intuition he has reached a position of "scientific insight and religious fervor" which supports the following message for the world. Science is good and true, but limited. Art is beautifying, glorifying, but likewise limited. A harmonious adjustment is needed, and this is supplied by religion and philosophy, which are really one and the same. The greatest need at the present time is for religion as a sweet harmonizing influence, religion without exclusive creeds or dogmas. Every religious cult, such as Visnuism, Sivaism, Judaism or Christianity, has a place to fill in the cosmic *Dharma,* or universal religion, which the West labels Hinduism. Visnuism contributes devotion; Sivaism, discipline; Judaism, law; Christianity, sacrifice; and so on. But Hinduism gives them all a common goal in the final bliss of supermaterial activity of soul.

Four prepared lectures on "Spiritual Synthesis" present this message. Another four lectures deal with the *Bhagavad Gita,* and yet another four with the philosophy of art. The names and places of his lectures may be illustrated by the following samples. "The Message of the *Gita*" at the Vedanta Society, "Christ the Master" at Union Theological Seminary, and "The Fundamentals of Spiritual Life" at the Rosicrucian Society, all in New York. Then "The Spirit of India" at the Howard High School in Wilmington, Delaware, and "Education" at Swarthmore College, Pennsylvania. Professor Kesker expects to lecture also before Rotary Clubs and Ethical Culture and Psychical Research societies.

4. POPULAR LECTURERS ON HINDUISM

"Super Akasha Yogi Wassan" is the self-styled name of an uneducated Panjabi who seeks to convince gaping crowds of the superior merits of a cultivated solar-plexus.[31] Mr. Wassan's title alone is a sufficient index to the character of his teaching. To the great Sankara, *Akasa* signified the ultimate reality or bliss. Our yogi is just above this ultimate! There are a few other popular Hindu teachers lecturing here and there in America. K. D. Shastri is the author of a book entitled *Hindu Sexology in Spiritual Development,* published by a certain Indo-Aryan Publishing Company in Minneapolis in 1917, and

R. S. Gherwal is responsible for the book *The Great Masters of the Himalayas,* published in 1927 at Great Falls, Montana, by a firm called The Public Drug Company. Then there are certain very popular Hindu lecturers indeed, the famous Hindu "fakirs" who sometimes make a living on the American vaudeville stage by "mind-reading" or other "wonder-working" stunts.[32]

* * *

However, popular lectures on Hinduism, especially in its practical aspects, are not confined to Hindus. A number of Americans have also learned the art. "Oom the Omnipotent" is the self-styled Hindu name of Peter A. Bernard, of New York City and Nyack, New York. According to Charles Wright Ferguson,[33] he was formerly a professional baseball player. Swami Yogananda says "Oom" was once a barber, has been to India, does not pose as a native Hindu, and teaches *hatha-yoga* and a bit of the *tantra* practice. "Prince Ram Maharaj"[34] is another American "Hindu," who claims to have come from Tibet after enduring twenty years of hardship attending his initiation into Hinduism. He has announced his intention of establishing a Hindu center in Los Angeles. Baba Bharati also came from Tibet to Los Angeles. The "Great Masters" of the Theosophical Society likewise live in Tibet. Perhaps some day they too will come to Los Angeles.

These Americans often go so far as to establish novel Hindu cults as in the case of Yogi Ramacharaka.[35] America seems to be an exceedingly fertile field for the sowing of Hinduism. And we must remember that certain Americans, by virtue of their complexion, are naturally equipped to play the rôle of a popular Hindu teacher. We have heard of Hindu "fakirs"—let us now turn our attention to Hindu "fakes."

5. American Imposters

Swami Yogananda tells me that "Prem Lal Adoris," whatever else he may be, is not a Hindu. Let us take another case. The astute Joe Downing[36] of coal-black visage and some small town in Illinois appeared in 1918 on Keith's vaudeville circuit under the name of "Joveddah de Raja," an opulent nomenclature smacking of Roman divinity, French nobility and Hindu royalty all in one. With his wife, "Princess Olga," he did a "mind-reading" act. Circulating in the audience, for example, he would take a gentleman's ten-dollar bill, look at it intently, and then miraculously pass on its serial number to Princess Olga on the stage, who would at once proclaim it to the mystified onlookers. The couple worked hard at this trick, practicing their code on motor-car license plates while traveling.

In 1926 the princely Joveddah, now a profound "philosopher and psychologist," began broadcasting words of Oriental comfort and wisdom from radio stations in New York and environs, such as WHN, WPCH and WMCA. In one year he received over eighty thousand letters from wistful and eager admirers. No doubt he had genius. He charged fifty dollars for six lessons by correspondence or four lectures delivered in person. He engaged a private secretary—a mere youth in college—to conduct the correspondence course and answer the yearning letters. Taking his apprentice to Brentano's bookstore, Joveddah bought him eighty dollars worth of cheap books on love, marriage and fortune telling, and bade him go to work. The boy worked with a will, knowing full well that he held in his hands the fate of many a tender maiden. Soon the master was prosperous, and the apprentice content with his share of the loot. Alas! The police and the prince did not see eye to eye in what constituted public welfare, and the prince had to move.

Is Joveddah de Raja a part of American Hinduism? In a sense. To many Americans, his dusky visage and oriental gear hold just as much of the "unfathomable mystery of the East" as if he were the genuine article. Like certain real Hindus, he puts a price on his lessons, and makes supernatural claims. Indeed, the supernatural runs like a thread through the Hindu fabric from beginning to end. Professor Surendra Nath Das Gupta of the University of Calcutta calls this the "lower" mysticism, defined as "an obscure and supernatural method by which in some unaccountable manner, miraculous feats may be performed or physical advantages reaped. . . ."[37] No doubt there are thousands of more or less wealthy Americans who are willing to part with a considerable portion of their money in order to reap the advantages of this kind of mysticism. Since Hindu charlatans in America are not sufficiently numerous to supply such an enormous demand, certain Americans themselves have begun to enter the lucrative trade. But this aspect of Hinduism in America belongs to America rather than to Hinduism.

6. HINDU PROFESSORS AND STUDENTS

Aside from the leaders of religious and cultural movements, other Hindus have immigrated to America, of whom the professors and students are perhaps the most important from the point of view of the diffusion of Hinduism. It seems that the first Hindu students arrived in California in 1901. Certain educational societies in India sent six more in 1904, and by 1908 the number had risen to seventeen. By now they are quite plentiful, especially in the great universities and on the coasts. Their influence is exerted chiefly through conversations with American students and more or less informal lectures in Church organizations and similar institutions.[38]

7. ORIENTAL CULTS OF PARTLY HINDU ORIGIN

Preaching in America these days are heralds of several oriental cults of partly Hindu origin. Sikhism was founded in the fifteenth century by the saintly *Guru* Nanak, a poetic Panjabi who attempted to harmonize the Hindu and Muslim communities in the worship of the universal God. The Sikh community, composed mostly of Hindus, was militarized by the tenth *guru*, Govind Singh, in the face of Muslim oppression. Since then Sikhism has been even more decidedly Hindu than Muslim, and until recently many Sikhs counted themselves as Hindus in the census. In 1927, Dr. Bhagat Singh Thind (Devotee Lion Thind), a Sikh from Amritsar, the chief city of the Sikhs, gave in New York two courses of sixty lectures each, the first in September in the Hotel Majestic, and the second in November in the Pythian Temple. His announcements contain his photograph, which is quite striking, and the following caption:

To Know, to Dare, and to Keep Silent
Master Course in the Teachings of the

SIKH SAVIOURS

Sixty Free Lectures on Divine
Realization
By
DR. BHAGAT SINGH THIND
Author of *Divine Wisdom, Vol. I*

Psychologist, Metaphysician and Divine of Amritsar, India
Sixty Life-Instilling Lectures on the
Practical Realization of the
Eternal Truth for Every-Day Life and Life Eternal, and Ever
Increasing Prosperity and Happiness

For Harmony without Discord, Freedom without Bond, Reality
without Illusion, Satisfaction without Striving, Love without
Longing, and Life without Death

As might be expected, he preaches the Hindu *Dharma* of *karma* and rebirth, saying, "You Choose Your Own Parents." Like the Hindu yogi, he teaches "Scientific Breathing," and gives a lecture on "Jazz Mania: Its Cause and Cure and the Psychology of Relaxation." He seems to accept the *tantra* doctrine of the seven planes of the *Kundalini* in announcing this title: "Seven Centres—Is It Dangerous to Open Them?" He also presents the famous *Om,* or *Aum,* "The Sacred Hum of the Universe." Like the Hindu he speaks of cycles of existence, and puts special emphasis on food and fasting. In his lecture, "Can We Talk with the 'Dead' and How?" he comes into contact with spiritualism, while in treating autosuggestion, the ductless glands and the science of colors, he comes into line with modern psychology.

Like Swami Yogananda and other Hindu preachers, he conducts healing meetings, gives Christ an occult interpretation, believes in the "Transmutation and Conquest of Sex Energy," and proclaims "The Highest Technique of Concentration, Meditation and Spiritualization of Body, Mind and Soul." He seems to be making a deliberate attempt to Americanize his teaching, at least in style. The main center of the Sikh movement in America is somewhere in California, as might be expected, since Sikh immigrants are located there, and California is very receptive to new cults. There is also a Sikh center in Vancouver, British Columbia, called the "Khalsa Diwan Society."

*   *   *

Buddhist propaganda is gently carried on from the "Ceylon and India Inn" at 148 West 49th Street, New York, which sells the magazine, the *Maha-Bodhi and the United Buddhist World, a Monthly Journal of International Buddhist Brotherhood,* founded thirty-seven years ago by Anagarika H. Dharmapala, and still edited by him. On the outside of the issue for December, 1928 was pasted a subscription notice in red ink, with the appeal, "We want your support to Spread the Dharma." The present Buddhist preacher of the Maha Bodhi Society in New York is the Venerable Thera P. Vajiranana, who lectures on such topics as "Right Mindfulness," and "The Buddha on Theocracy."

Early in 1929 the Venerable Lord Abbott Tai Hsu, a fairly young and progressive Buddhist of the *Mahayana,* or more comprehensive sect, visited New York, making his center of operations the Chinese Institute, at 119 West 57th Street. He said he was traveling in the interest of universal peace and happiness to find the elements of unity that would integrate the various cultures of the world. Buddhism, he declared, is unfortunately misunderstood in the West, else it would be accepted as the universal, perfectly scientific and philosophic religion. It teaches *karma,* or the unchangeable law of cause and effect in the moral as well as the corporeal realm, and the ideal of happiness in the best possible environment, to be won by the humane method of non-injury. In short, says the abbott, Buddhism gives complete intuitive wisdom for life. In achieving world happiness, the first step is to unite all Buddhist sects, and then unite Buddhism with other religions. Even now plans are afoot for an "International Institute for the Study of Buddhism."

* * *

In 1901 there appeared in America a certain preacher who called himself Ottoman Zar-Adusht Hannish, and claimed to have come *direct* from Tibet and the mysteries of the Dalai Llama. Since this Llama is the head of the Buddhist order in Tibet, Mr. Hannish seems to have some

connection with Buddhism, and hence with Hinduism.
Someone suspected he was once a typesetter on the *Mount
Deseret News* in Salt Lake City.[39]   But in spite of that
handicap, he launched his oriental movement, and with
the help of Marie Elizabeth Ruth Hilton, the wife of Dr.
G. W. Hilton of Lowell, Massachusetts, began to teach a
special art of breathing and a very ethereal diet of rose
leaves and other delicate vegetables, presumably intended
to rid the soul of all material dross.

This new religious leader was eclectic: he included in
his practical instruction the daily adoration of the sun and
the worship of Ahura Mazda, the supreme Lord of the
Zend-Avesta, the Zoroastrian Bible.   The main temple of
this cult, called Mazdaznan, is on Lake Park Avenue,
Chicago, a lesser one is on the Hilton lawn in Lowell,
while ground has been consecrated for a third in Montreal,
Canada.   In 1912 the movement claimed fourteen thousand followers in thirty cities of the United States of
America, and in Canada, South America, England, Switzerland and Germany.

One Sunday afternoon in the season of 1929-1930, I
attended a Mazdaznan meeting in a small parlor of the
Hotel McAlpin, Broadway at Thirty-fourth Street, New
York.   In addition to listening to a lecture, the little congregation of men and women practices relaxation of body
and mind by means of a series of loosening exercises to
the accompaniment of piano music and group singing.
The jolly, lilting tunes are found in the special hymn book.
Most of the members seem to be from Continental Europe.
According to the "Standard Health Rules" of Mazdaznan,
meat should be avoided, and fruits and vegetables should
be eaten at different meals.   The kind of food required
by any individual depends on whether his "temperament
and basic principle" is "intellectual," "spiritual" or "physical." This classification seems to correspond to the *sattva,*

rajas and *tamas* principles mentioned in the *Bhagavad Gita.*

I noticed from the hymn book that Mazdaznan draws on Hinduism directly, as well as indirectly through Buddhism and Zoroastrianism. And the Hindu type of Islam is also a source. Since all of these religions are dualistic, it is only natural that Mazdaznan should be dualistic, making a sharp distinction between Matter and Intelligence. One article of the "Mazdaznan Confession" reads:

I confess all the painful in matter to be the result of obstinacy on the part of substance through its processes of creations and evolutions, declining to yield to the peaceful operations of intelligence, thus introducing repulsion and impelling resistance.

Yet the Hindu-like monistic conviction of the identity of the soul with God is also prominent, as can be seen from the first part of the "Mazdaznan Affirmation":

I am all in One individually and one in All collectively;
I am present individually and omni-present collectively;
I am knowing individually and omni-scient collectively;
I am potent individually and omni-potent collectively;

ALL IS OF GOD AND GOD IS ALL!

Individually I am in Part, collectively I am the Whole;
Individually I am Di-verse, collectively I am Universe;
Individually I am Limited, collectively I am Unlimited;
Individually I am Begotten, collectively I Beget.

The following selections from the "Mazdaznan Declaration of Freedom" will show its dependence on Hinduism:

Mazdaznan declares that the lower walks of life are repetitions of past incarnations called into existence through processes of reincarnation and transmigration prompted by pre-natal influence and inherited tendencies which in man constitute the cause for contention and struggle, thereby retarding progression.

Mazdaznan declares that the Infallible Plan of Salvation lies in the Application of Means of Purification leading unto Regeneration, with the first step essential unto Salvation from Ancestral

Ties through the efficacy of rhythmic Prayers and Songs breathed *on the breath* . . . filling the heretofore unclaimed tissues and energies with Galama, the centralizing life principle. . . .

Mazdaznan declares to be the oldest and most comprehensive Educational System of Individual-Collective Thought, embracing as it does every Essential Truth embodied in the Aryan or Zend race, substantiated through Ainyahita, revealed through Zarathustra, approbated and declared by Jesus, founded upon Genesis, and borne out by the Science of Evolution. . . .

Whoever is interested in the Mazdaznan cult may send ten cents for literature to the Mazdaznan Press, P. O. Box 1854, Los Angeles, California.

* * *

Sufiism and Baha'iism are two other oriental cults in America that exhibit certain Hindu traits, and may have some historical connection with Hinduism through Persian Islam. Although both these movements are usually regarded as Muslim sects, they are considerably different from orthodox Islam, and perhaps more Hindu than Muslim in temper.

Sufiism was brought to America in the Fall of 1910 by Pir-o-Murshid Inayat Khan of Baroda, India, who traveled in America from coast to coast until the Spring of 1912, when he returned to India. He passed away in 1927. The movement is now established in about eight centers in America, with the main-center at San Francisco, which is the place of residence of the head officer, Murshid Rabia A. Martin. The New York office is at 10 West 84th Street. The American branch of Sufiism is controlled by Americans, some of whom, at least, have assumed oriental names and titles. This esoteric cult claims to be unique in its openness to all truth, and its universal adaptability to all conditions of men in all times and places by virtue of its all-embracing tolerance. In view of the claims of Vedanta, Yogoda, Theosophy and other cults to be unique in their universality it seems that Sufiism shares its "uniqueness" with quite a number of like-minded movements!

*   *   *

Baha'iism also is one of these "uniquely" universal movements. It is especially akin to Sufiism, because its founder was a Persian Muslim of the Shiite sect which in Persia is dominated by the Sufi movement. The Baha'i cult first appeared in America in 1893, when it was represented at the Parliament of Religions at Chicago by a Christian missionary who had come in contact with it in Persia. But it began to flourish in America only after the advent of Abdul Baha in 1912. The present Guardian of the movement is Shogi Effendi, who lives at Haifa, Syria. He is quite young, being Abdul Baha's grandson. In the United States there are many Baha'i centers. The secretary of the National Board has his main office at 119 West 57th Street, New York, while a huge temple is being built on the shore of Lake Michigan. The New York center, under the leadership of *Mirza* Ahmad Sohrab, has formed "The New History Society," which meets at the house of Mrs. Lewis Stuyvesant Chanler, 132 East 65th Street.

*   *   *

Now Sufiism and Baha'iism are more or less connected with Hinduism through Gnosticism, Neo-Platonism and Buddhism, all of which give evidence of Hindu teaching.[40] In particular, it seems that the seven Neo-Platonists expelled from Athens by the Emperor Justinian when he closed the Platonic Academy in 529 were welcomed to the Persian court by the broad-minded Nowshirwan the Just, the last of the Sassanian kings.[41] Moreover, we are told that this great patron of letters commanded Hindu pandits to translate many philosophical works from Sanskrit into Pahlavi.[42] Since the triumph of the Safawids in 1500

brought to the Persian throne a line of Sufi saints, it is
quite posible that Sufiism, and later Baha'iism, have been
distinctly influenced by these Hindu works.

8. AMERICAN CULTS OF PARTLY HINDU ORIGIN

Theosophy, of course, is more Hindu than Christian,
in spite of its origin in a land of Christian tradition.   In
1877, two years after the Theosophical Society was
founded in New York,[43] Madame Helen Petrovna Blavatsky, its leading spirit, published her *Isis Unveiled*, in
which she presented some bits of Hindu lore.   But this
was only the beginning of Hinduism in Theosophy.
Madame Blavatsky soon left America with her "Theosophical Twin" Colonel Henry Steel Olcott, and reached
Bombay in June, 1879.   The teachings of the "Twins"
now became much more distinctly Indian, based on the
Society's fundamental dogma of the Great White Brotherhood, or occult lodge of supernormal, supertransmigratory
divine masters, or adepts, in the trans-Himalayan fastness
of Tibet.[44]   From age to age, as reckoned by Hindu chro-
nology, these masters supply mankind with esoteric wisdom through chosen agents — Madame Blavatsky, of
course, being the one selected for this age.

Yet Theosophy did not become thoroughly Hindu till
the advent of Mrs. Annie Besant, who succeeded Madame
Blavatsky as the spiritual guide of the movement.   Since
1893 Mrs. Besant has spent most of her time in India, and
is virtually a naturalized Hindu.   Since 1906 she has been
president of the Society, of which the main center is not
New York but Adyar, Madras.   The new leader has lectured repeatedly in every part of India, making the defense
and exposition of Hinduism her chief theme, and can point
with pride to the Central Hindu College which she helped
to found in Benares in 1898, an institution modelled on
the lines of a Christian missionary college, but giving

Hindu religious instruction.[45]   Thus Theosophy early in its career changed its diet from American Spiritualism to fairly pure Hinduism, and is now more Hindu perhaps than Yogoda.

*   *   *

Christian Science, unlike Theosophy, looks at first glance like a pure American product, founded in the little town of Lynn, Massachusetts in 1875 by Mrs. Mary Baker Eddy,[46] a woman who had never ventured out of America, and whose *Science and Health,* published the same year, was advanced as a key to the Christian Scripture. Yet when we read this Christian Science Bible we find that it out-Sankaras Sankara with its doctrine of cosmic illusion![47] Since spirit is the only reality, and matter is opposite to spirit, the belief in matter is only an "error of mortal mind."   Sankara had the common sense to explain the illusory world of matter as the magic of God, real and independent of mortal mind, but Mrs. Eddy, quite above common sense, sees the world of matter as dependent on mortal mind, and mortal mind itself an illusion without any clear origin.

Is this similarity between Hindu illusionism and Christian Science due to similar response to similar need, or to some historical transmission of teaching? If we read the Yogoda *East-West* magazine, we find light on the subject, for in the issue of May-June, 1926, in his article "Christian Science and Hindu Philosophy," Swami Yogananda has turned on the searchlight.   The current editions of *Science and Health* contain no Hindu references, but in the older editions, which the Christian Science Church has deliberately withdrawn from publication, references to Hindu teachings are quite clear and distinct. Says Yogananda:

It may be of much interest to many Christian Scientists to learn that the great founder of their faith, Mrs. Mary Baker Eddy,

was a student of the Hindu Scriptures. This fact is shown by
her quotations from them in her *Science and Health* up to the
33rd edition. We find in this edition[48] the following excerpts
from Sir Edwin Arnold's translation of *Bhagavad-Gita*:

"Never the Spirit was born; the Spirit shall cease to be never;
  Never the time it was not; End and Beginning are dreams!
Birthless and deathless and changeless remaineth the Spirit for-
    ever;
  Death hath not touched it at all, dead though the house of it
    seems!"
                  Edwin Arnold's Translation of *Bhagavad-Gita.*

Again, Mrs. Eddy makes reference in the same chapter to
another translation of *Bhagavad-Gita*.[49] On page 259 of the
33rd edition, she says:

"The ancient Hindu philosophers understood something of this
Principle, when they said in their Celestial Song, according to an
old prose translation:

" 'The wise neither grieve for the dead nor for the living. I
myself never was not, nor thou, nor all the princes of the earth;
nor shall we ever hereafter cease to be. As the soul, in this
mortal frame, findeth infancy, youth, and old age, so in some
future frame will it find the like. One who is confirmed in this
belief is not disturbed by anything that may come to pass. The
sensibility of the faculties giveth heat and cold, pleasure and pain,
which come and go and are transient and inconstant. Bear them
with patience; for the wise man, whom these disturb not, and to
whom pain and pleasure are the same, is formed for immortality.' "

Both these quotations from the *Bhagavad-Gita*, or Song Celestial, which contains the essence of the Vedas, or the Hindu Bible,
are to be found in Mrs. Eddy's 7th chapter on "Imposition and
Demonstration." This whole chapter has been omitted from
later editions of *Science and Health;* That is why many Christian
Scientists are not aware that their great leader Mrs. Eddy was
familiar with Hindu thought, and in her bigness did not hesitate
to acknowledge it in print. . . .

In this article my purpose is to show not only that the doctrine
of "mind over matter" had been worked out by the Hindus prior
to the birth of Christian Science, and that the similarity of the
message of Mrs. Mary Baker Eddy and the principles of Hindu
Vedanta is quite evident, but that the Hindus and Christian

Scientists will find mutual benefit and will add to their knowledge of the power of mind by a combined study of the *Bhagavad-Gita* and the Vedanta of the Hindus, and Mary Baker Eddy's *Science and Health*.[50]

Furthermore, Mrs. Eddy must have imbibed some of the teachings of the New England Transcendentalists[51] who made their influence widely felt through books, magazines and newspaper articles. Bronson Alcott, who was one of them, attended her services. Now most of the Transcendentalists, like Emerson, Alcott, and Thoreau, were profoundly influenced by Hinduism, with its spirit of breadth and tolerance and unity.

Says Pratap Chandra Mazumdar, "The character of Emerson shines on India serene as the evening star. He seems to some of us to have been born in India."[52] At the early age of nineteen, Emerson could find nothing better to express his conception of God than a passage taken from Sir William Jones' translation of *Narayana*.[53] At twenty-seven he wrote to a friend, "In the sleep of the great heats there is nothing for me but to read the Vedas, the Bible of the tropics. . . . Nature makes a Brahmin of me."[54]

When Emerson was fifty-two years old, his dear friend Thoreau received forty-four volumes of Hindu literature as a gift from a friend in England. To this store of Hinduism, Emerson doubtless had access, and two years later his famous *Song of the Soul*, or *Brahma*, appeared in the first number of the *Atlantic Monthly*. The first two verses are sufficient to reveal two messages of the *Bhagavad Gita*.

> If the red slayer thinks he slays,
> Or if the slain thinks he is slain,
> They know not well the subtle ways,
> I keep, and pass and turn again.
>
> Far or forgot to me is near;
> Shadow and sunlight are the same,

The vanished gods not less appear,
And one to me are shame and fame.

Emerson's "Over-Soul" is a translation of the Sanskrit *Paramatman.* He regarded matter as the negative, and mind as the positive pole of this universal Spirit. Perhaps this is where Mrs. Eddy got her notion of mind and matter as *plus* and *minus* electricity. Emerson repeats both the monism and the dualism of the Upanishads: he sees man both one with the Universal Spirit, and different from the material organization.[55]

The world seems very simple and easily dispatched. . . . There are but two things, or but one thing and its shadow. . . . Cause and Effect, and Effect itself is worthless if separated from Cause.[56]

This is precisely the way that monism combined with dualism in the *Upanishads* to produce acosmism, including illusionism.[57]   And when Emerson gives us his poem called *Maya,* history repeats itself.

Illusion works impenetrable
Weaving webs innumerable,
Her gay pictures never fail,
Crowds each other, veil on veil.
Charmer who will be believed
By man who thirsts to be deceived.[58]

Thus through Mary Baker Eddy and Ralph Waldo Emerson, Christian Science is closely linked to Hinduism.

Unless we dig still deeper, however, we do not get to the bottom of Hindu influence on Christian Science. In 1861 Mrs. Mary Baker Patterson, who later became Mrs. Eddy, was cured of nervous depletion and stormy hysteria by Phineas Parker Quimby, a wandering healer whose practice was based on a strange conviction.[59]   After receiving treatment for some time, the patient took this conviction and developed it along her own lines into the cult now flourishing as Christian Science.[60]

Quimby's conviction was that health and sickness depend largely on the patient's belief. This was his own conclusion, which he reached by keen observation while practicing the mesmerism he had learned as a youth from Charles Poyen, a Frenchman who had come to America in 1836.[61] Now mesmerism goes back through Mesmer and the Nancy school of Charcot, Janet and Coué to the Swiss doctor Paracelsus in the fifteenth century, who believed in an all-pervading vital magnetic fluid directed by the indwelling spirit, which could be used by the well to cure the sick.[62]

This sounds like the *Prana*, or Cosmic Energy, proclaimed by Yogananda and other swamis and yogis today. Has Paracelsus any connection with Hinduism? His characteristic doctrines may be traced to Neo-Platonism,[63] of which the chief representative was Plotinus, the Alexandrian philosopher of the third century after Christ. Students of Plotinus know that his system stands nearer the Vedanta than any other Western system, including that of Schopenhauer. The similarity between Plotinus and the *Bhagavad Gita* is quite striking. An historical connection between Plotinus and India is suggested in many ways, especially by the treatise of Bardesanes on the Indian "Gymnosophists," or *risis* and yogis, a treatise used by Porphyry, who was the intimate companion of Plotinus.[64]

Christian Science, of course, is first and foremost an American movement, based on the personal experience of its founder, who was typical of many nervous Americans, and also on the personal conviction of Quimby, which was the conviction that belief largely determines health. But it seems clear also that Christian Science has certain historical connections with Hinduism through Mrs. Eddy's use of the *Gita*, through New England Transcendentalism, and through the very indirect influence of a certain Hindu view on Quimby.

The first New Thought[65] Society with a regular leader and organization was established as the "Church of the Higher Life" at Boston in 1894, the same year that Swami Vivekananda founded the New York Vedanta Society.[66] New Thought soon showed its hospitality to Hinduism by inviting Swami Abhedananda to speak at its second convention, held at New York in 1900.[67] Such a gesture is only natural in view of the fact that this young cult, even more than Christian Science, owed its birth to Quimby, the American herald of spiritualistic mesmerism, and Emerson, the American herald of transcendental pantheism.[68] Mrs. Eddy and the Dressers were the outstanding members of Quimby's little group of disciples,[69] but Mrs. Eddy soon branched out for herself, and Quimby passed away, leaving the Dressers and their friends moving at a slow pace until Charles M. Barrows adopted Emerson as the father of the movement. The words of the Concord sage have now become the unofficial Bible of the New Thought Church. A booklet called *Emerson's Conception of Truth* has been compiled by Henry Richardson Thayer, who explains that "not a word of Emerson's has been changed or added to, but widely separated sentences have been brought together." [70]

Thus New Thought contains some very old elements which can be traced partly and indirectly to the *Upanishads* by way of Quimby and Emerson. And what applies to New Thought applies also to "Divine Science," or "Practical Christianity," which is just that form of New Thought developed mainly in the west of the United States.[71]

*   *   *

The Unity School of Christianity, founded at Kansas City in 1899,[72] seems to be connected with Hinduism on account of the broad and tolerant attitude of its founders,

Charles and Myrtle Fillmore. As Mrs. Fillmore lay musing
one night on what name would symbolize their "sympathy
for all movements helping in the uplift of humanity," she
thought of the word "Unity," which suggested not only
the oneness of man with God, but also the oneness of all
religions.[73] These, of course, are primarily Hindu conceptions. By 1899 these principles had been preached by
Emerson and Vivekananda, and it is very likely that since
its foundation Unity has absorbed Hinduism in yearly increasing measure from Theosophy, Christian Science, New
Thought, and the Hindu cults themselves.

Says Charles Wright Ferguson, "According to its own
claims, Unity sprang into being quite independently of all
cults and with equal independence reached maturity. But
its stuff is too closely akin to the stuff of *Nautilus*[74] and
Orison Swett Marden[75] to be mistaken in identity. It was
undoubtedly joined by an umbilical cord to New Thought,
and sired by Christian Science. Over in New England
Mother Eddy had already published several editions of
Science and Health. . . . By the time Unity arose Mrs. Eddy
had fairly well demonstrated that she could cure disease
by philosophy, and Warren Felt Evans[76] had begun to
give the world his commentaries on the work of Quimby.
It is obvious that the teaching of the Fillmores partakes
largely of both the unwieldy and amorphous body of
doctrine known as the New Thought and the solidly con-
trived dogmas of Christian Science."[77] Unity's doctrine of
reincarnation in itself is enough to make its members
eligible for Das Gupta's *Dharma Mandal*.

* * *

The Liberal Catholic Church is not a cult of American
origin. And of course it does not come originally from
Hinduism. But it may just be mentioned here as a cult
which is now established in America as well as in Eng-

land, Australia, New Zealand, South Africa, Holland and Java, and which is *now* connected with Hinduism through the Theosophy of its presiding bishop, Charles W. Leadbeater. As Theosophy turned from American Spiritualism to Hinduism, it seems that this strange church is now turning from Dutch and English Catholicism to Theosophy.[78]

* * *

In addition to these well-organized American cults, there must be scores of independent American lecturers in the large cities of the United States strongly influenced by Hinduism. Any one of these lecturers is a potential or actual cult leader, as for example George Edwin Burnell, the teacher of "The Absolute Truth," whose *Book of Axioms* may be purchased at the Good Year Book Shop, at Broadway and Forty-second Street, New York, in the George Cohan Theater, downstairs.

* * *

Thus we see that Theosophy, Christian Science, New Thought, Unity, and other systems, all originating in America, are more or less Hindu in character and connection. American Hinduism, then, may be said to embrace both Hindu and Hindu-like movements. Furthermore, if traces of Hinduism can be found in Plotinus and other Western thinkers, America must be indirectly learning some Hinduism in its colleges, seminaries and universities, in spite of the fact that Hinduism as such is studied very little in the West, and less in America than in Europe. In view of this fact, let us now endeavor to understand American Hinduism more fully, to see it as a part of the vast vague Hinduism that seeps into Western culture first through Plotinus and later through translations of the Vedanta works themselves.

9. HINDU INFLUENCE ON WESTERN THOUGHT

Plotinus is the main early source of Hindu-like teaching for the West. Dissatisfied with Stoicism, Epicureanism, Scepticism and Eclecticism, he harked back to the ancient glories of Greece and India, and crowning Plato's Idea of the Good with the Hindu Absolute above all good and evil, he developed a mystic plan of salvation. Plotinus was a fellow townsman of Origen, the first great Christian theologian. Both were immersed in the oriental atmosphere of Alexandria, and attended the lectures of Ammonius Saccas. According to Dean Inge, "Origen attempted to do for Christianity very much the same that Plotinus attempted to do for paganism." [79] According to Wilhelm Windelband, "Neoplatonism and Christianity had a community of purpose and a common origin. Both were scientific systems that methodically developed a religious conviction and sought to prove that this conviction was the only true source of salvation for the soul needing redemption." [80] Both systems were Platonic. Yet the heart of the one was Hebrew, while the heart of the other was Hindu.

For six centuries after his earthly life, Plotinus molded the mysticism of the West, and even today Idealism depends on him for its distinction between body and mind, for he stamped the vague term "spirit" as pure immateriality. In the Eastern Empire, says Thomas Whittaker,[81] "Greek ecclesiastical writers such as Nemesius (fl. 450), who had derived their culture from Neoplatonism, transmitted its refutations of materialism to the next age. In the West, St. Augustine, who . . . was profoundly influenced by Platonism . . . performed the same philosophical service." Throughout the Dark Ages, the task of replenishing the faintly burning lamp of culture was handed on by men of Plotinian cast — the moralists Boethius and Macrobius, the fervent, mystical author of

"Dionysius," and the bold Scotus Erigena. Thomas Aquinas himself, the greatest philosopher of the Middle Ages, and the official source of Roman Catholic theology today, absorbed Plotinus not only directly through *"Dionysius,"* but also indirectly through Augustine, Erigena and Anselm, the Plotinian psychology, and the system of Aristotle worked over by the latest school of Neo-Platonism.[82] We should not be surprised to find Hindu-like dualism in the creeds of Christendom, both Catholic and Protestant, owing to the dominant influence of the "angelic doctor." And if we find the strain in Dante, it may possibly be traced to Proclus, and through him, indirectly to the *Upanishads.*

The rise of Humanism, which threw off the shackles of Scholasticism and ushered in the Renaissance, was accompanied by a return to Plato, studied for his own sake, and read through the eyes of the Neo-Platonists. In philosophic expression Bruno always falls back on Neo-Platonic terms. Nor did the modern scientific upheaval dim the luster of Plotinus in the eyes of certain thinkers, for his own interest in science and keen distinction between spirit and matter left him peculiarly available to scientific men of the idealistic type. Thus, the Cambridge Platonists felt they could adopt the corpuscular physics as not incompatible with "the true intellectual system of the universe," and Descartes could view the world as a vast machine, while saving God and the soul in the realm of absolutely immaterial spirit. On the other hand, the monism of Spinoza,[83] which seems to have come indirectly from a certain element implicit in Hinduism, provides a basis for modern science, especially in its philosophic mood.

In spite of his modern regard for the test of experience, and his official Christian viewpoint, Bishop Berkeley, it seems, found in the ancient "pagan" Plotinus hints towards the solution of the ultimate problems he had first

proposed to settle by developing Locke's position. Without imitating the detail of Plotinus, the Platonic English
poets from Spenser to Shelley, as well as the Romanti-
cists and Neo-Christians of Germany lived and moved in
his atmosphere of pure spirituality. The simple German
mystic Jacob Boehme,[84] who seems to have received his
bold doctrines from a humble neighboring rabbi deeply
imbued with the Qabbala, was the last Western thinker to
depend on Hinduism only by way of Plotinus. With
Schelling and Hegel, Vedanta and Hindu thought in general began to be directly and assiduously studied in the
leading universities of Germany.

Friedrich Schleiermacher, with his definition of religion
as the feeling of utter dependence on the Infinite, and
Christian F. Krause, with his doctrine of the immanence
of all things in God, must have been influenced somewhat
by Vedanta by way of Schelling and Hegel.[85] Says Friedrich Schlegel, "The Indians possessed a knowledge of the
true God, conceived and expressed in noble, clear and
grand language. . . . Even the loftiest philosophy of the
Europeans, the idealization of reason, as set forth by the
Greeks, appears in comparison with the abundant light
and vigor of oriental idealism, like a feeble spark in the
full flood of the noonday sun." [86]

Arthur Schopenhauer felt the influence of Vedanta
through the work of Anguetil Duperron, a French traveler
who obtained in 1775 a manuscript of a Persian translation of the *Upanishads*. This he translated into French
and also into Latin, and in 1801 and the following years,
the Latin version was published under the title of *Oup-
nek'hat, i. e., Sacretum Tegendum,* meaning "Deep Mystery." This unusual piece of work was neglected till
Schopenhauer took it up and told the West that "the ancient Hindus may have had perhaps more to say about
philosophy and fundamental truths than many of our mod-

ern writers." [87]   In the preface to the first edition of his *World as Will and Idea* he tells the reader that the discovery of the *Upanishads* is the greatest privilege of the century.

The Indian air surrounds us, the original thoughts of kindred spirits. . . . And oh, how thoroughly is . . . the mind washed clean of all early engrafted Jewish superstitions, and of all philosophy that cringes before these superstitions. . . . In most of the pagan philosophical writings of the first Christian centuries, we see the Jewish theism—which as Christianity was soon to become the faith of the people—shining through, much as at present we perceive . . . in the writings of the learned, the native pantheism of India, which is destined sooner or later to become the faith of the people.[88]

Sir William Jones, one of the first Sanskrit scholars of the West, says of Hinduism, "It is impossible to read the Vedanta . . . without believing that Pythagoras and Plato derived their sublime theory from the same fountain with the sages of India." [88] Friedrich Max Müller, who used to be the Nestor of Western Sanskrit scholars, was drawn to the *Upanishads* while attending the Berlin lectures of Schelling, who used "rapturous language" about these Hindu works. Says Müller, "The earliest of these *Upanishads* will always maintain a place in the philosophic literature of the world among the most astounding products of the human mind." [89] Says Victor Cousin, the French educator and philosopher, "When we read the poetical and philosophic monuments of the East, especially of India, we discover there many a truth, and truths so profound, contrasting so favorably with the results of European genius, that we are constrained to bend the knee before the philosophy of the East and to see this the native land of the highest philosophy." [90]

Of considerable significance is the direct and potent influence of Plotinus on the modern revival of mysticism in the West in such persons as Dean Inge, Evelyn Underhill and Rufus M. Jones, and especially in Henri Bergson, whose stimulating conception of creative evolution is a unique combination of the pragmatism developed by William James and the vitalistic mysticism developed by Plotinus. Like Plotinus and Sankara, Bergson defines a sharp dualism between spirit and matter. Bergson's conception of life encased in matter is like the *Upanishad* illustration of the razor in its case to describe the relation of soul to body. In Hinduism the relation of the *Paramatman,* or universal soul, to the *jivatman,* or individual soul, is compared to the relation between a river and its rills. The same analogy is used by Bergson to relate the *élan vital* to the individual. And in Bergson the pragmatism of James is reversed in accord with the contemplative ethic of Hinduism and Neo-Platonism. We must strive to see in order to see, he says, and no longer to see in order to act.[91]

Thus Hinduism comes to America indirectly through the classic philosophy taught in American institutions of higher learning, and directly through American writers and poets such as Emerson, Thoreau and Walt Whitman. Even Muslim, Christian, Sikh and Parsi lecturers coming from India, including Christian missionaries, contribute to the spread of Hinduism in America. American professors of Sanskrit and oriental studies are not necessarily enthusiasts for Hinduism, but now and then they become lecturers and writers on Hindu subjects, and from this position may pass over into the work of organizing an American cult more or less influenced by Hindu religion or culture, as in the case of Dr. George C. O. Haas, who is a co-leader with Miss Beulah E. Thompson in the Universal Spiritual Church, Hotel Biltmore, New York, which holds meetings on Sundays at 8:15 P. M.

10. THE MODERN EXPANSION OF HINDUISM

In various ways, then, Hinduism has impressed itself on American life: on miracle-loving people through Hindu "fakes" and "fakirs," on individual religious truth-seekers through the Vedanta movement, the Yogoda Society, and other Hindu and Hindu-like cults, on cultural liberals through the Threefold Movement, and on students, teachers and scholars through the International School, learned lecturers, cultural organizations and certain Western philosophers and poets. Outside of America, moreover, Hindu missionaries are teaching and preaching their religion in both Eastern and Western countries. In India a certain "Hindu Missionary Society" [92] has been formed on these three principles:

    1.   He who calls himself a Hindu is a Hindu.
    2.   Any person wishing to come into Hinduism may be ad-mitted into its fold.
    3.   The religious status of all Hindus is the same. The Vedas and the Sanskars, including the Sacred Thread, hitherto confined to the three "twice-born" castes or orders are now free for all. Caste, food, dress and other outward forms are to be considered not religious but merely social matters.

A certain J. S. Rao writes in the *Hindustan Review*, Allahabad, "The Western frame of mind is so peculiarly promising for the reception of Indian ideas," that "it will be our own mistake if we do not make India the teacher of the West as it has already been of the East." [93] He is jubilant over the recent success of Hinduism, and sees Christianity in the throes of death. Its dogmas, he thinks, cannot withstand the scientific theory of evolution, while its claims to finality cannot be maintained in view of the modern study of religion. Hinduism, on the other hand, is fit to be the world religion, for it stands for culture rather than for dogma. Its principles of reincarnation and *karma* support the belief in a just and merciful God, while its repeated incarnations reveal more divine love than the single incarnation of Christianity.

Hindus never tire of insisting that they have principles, whereas other religions have only dogmas. It is true they eschew dogmas in the sense of detailed historical documents sanctioned by majority vote to bind the beliefs of future generations. But dogmas in the sense of hoary and authoritarian rules of belief and practice uncritically accepted and devoutly obeyed, they both cultivate and propagate. They do not shrink from embracing new ideas, but they are loath to give up the old. As Sir Charles Eliot says, "the guiding principle of the Brahmans has always been not so much that they have a particular creed to enforce, as that whatever is the creed of India, they must be its ministers." [94] And now that India is awaking to modern civilization, this principle is simply being extended to include all countries and races. Hitherto the Brahmans have been the preceptors of India. They now desire to teach the world.

This desire, moreover, is not confined to the Brahmans. Just as the range of Hinduism is being extended from India to the world, the privilege of teaching this supposedly universal religion is being extended from the Brahmans to the lower orders. Says Manmohandas Karamchand Gandhi, commonly called *Mahatma,* or Great Soul, a Hindu who is not a Brahman, "Why should you self-styled whites get it into your heads that Christianity is your special largesse to distribute and interpret? You have made a mess of it yourselves. As a matter of fact, Christ was originally Asiatic, as were all the founders of religions, and I think we understand him much better than you do. We would have thanked you for bringing his gospel before us had you not mingled it so much with your Western culture, dress and machinery. We will go on and present the true Christ to India." [95] And practicing what he preaches, Gandhi has ordered the New Testament read in all *Svaraj* schools. Like most of his countrymen in America, he will teach all religions with a Hindu interpretation.

This modern expansion of Hinduism is just a part of the great modern awakening of Asia. Although the other oriental religious leaders do not so often pose as world teachers, they nevertheless have a world outlook, and wish to propagate their own culture while absorbing the culture of the West. The Venerable Lord Abbott of Zojo, a progressive Buddhist of Japan, said in a public interview that it was a good thing for the leaders of various religions to meet often and discuss common problems, and the oftener, the better. He supports the *Shukyo Konwakei,* an organization for Buddhist-Shinto-Christian fellowship. The Y. M. C. A. and the Y. W. C. A. have their Buddhist parallels in Japan. Buddhist churches, conference organizations and Sunday schools have been formed, and the children sing Christian tunes to words such as "Buddha loves me, this I know. . . ." Imitating the Red Cross in the West is the "Red Swastika Society" of China and the "Red Crescent" in Turkey.[96]

A world-wide struggle for cultural influence is now taking place. The West has sent missionaries to the far away "heathen" lands, foreseeing and preparing for the day when India and China would become Christian, only to evoke a strong reaction of Eastern propaganda. Each community cries, "We have the universal religion!" Perhaps India is in the van of oriental religious imperialism because she has lived in the British Empire, and her intellectuals have learned a world language.

As oriental countries in the recent past furnished good soil for the sowing of Western culture because of their material helplessness and subjection, so America today offers good soil for the sowing of Eastern culture because of its growing liberalism. The enlarged conception of the universe presented by the telescope and the microscope, electrical research and mathematical progress, the advancing verification of the doctrine of evolution, the growth of Biblical criticism and comparative study of religions, the new psychology with its study of instinct, dreams, suggestion and the "occult," the increasing pragmatic and the eclectic habits of philosophy, the growing social unrest and the migration of populations—all these movements have tended to break down the original dogmatism and provincialism of American religious life.[97]

The American churches themselves are becoming more rational, social and spiritual.[98] The original Protestant idea of freedom in worship is working out to its logical conclusion. At first freedom meant only freedom for a particular church to be intolerant, sectarian and dogmatic. It is now coming to mean freedom for the individual to join or start whatever cult he pleases. The authority of Church and Bible are challenged, and for many, only the *individual* remains as the final ground and judge of religion. If the Hindu movements in America today are a part of the age-long Hindu influence on the West and a part of the modern awakening of Asia, they are also a part of American liberalism. To a large extent, Hinduism in America is American Hinduism.

CHAPTER VIII

AMERICAN HINDUISM, THE RESULT OF HINDU ADJUSTMENTS

In order to trace the adjustment of Vedanta and Yogoda to American life we must begin with the swamis in India. Before Vivekananda came to America, he was half Sankara Hindu and half dilute Christian.[1] His Christianity came to him from his college and the Brahma Samaj. His Hinduism came to him at birth (or before), and he followed Sankara after meeting Ramakrishna. In spite of his portion of Christianity, he did not cling to any reformed or liberal Hindu group, but merely held an advanced position among the conservatives. And as a monk he was a Hindu of the strictest and most medieval type, seeking to escape the world by condemning it as illusion. Vivekananda was indeed a strange mixture. As a modern preacher he was conservative, but as a medieval monk he was liberal. Thus when he came to conservative Madras, he created quite a stir by preaching such liberal ideas for a monk![2]

Before Yogananda came to America, he was one-third Sankara monk, one-third practical yogi, and one-third University of Calcutta graduate, all dominated by the *Bhagavad Gita*. Thus instead of wavering between Sankara renunciation and Christian creation like Vivekananda, he held to the *Gita*, which teaches in the main a kind of Stoic or Ramanuja resignation.[3]

Neither of the swamis came to America on their own initiative. Nor were they sent out by the spontaneous act of any Hindu organization. Each came as a delegate to a religious congress inspired and organized by liberal Christians.[4]   Thus the presence of Hinduism in America in the form of purely religious organizations is due primarily to the desire of certain American Christians for deeper and wider knowledge of the world's religious thought.   The Hindu preachers in the United States are not so much missionaries as "inductionaries."   The stimulus is American, the response Hindu.

But even the response is strongly influenced by Christianity and Western culture.   In sending Vivekananda to America, the Hindu enthusiasts at Madras did not send a monk of the old fashioned type to represent their religion before the world.   They sent a man with modern education, a command of English, and a spirit of freedom and expansion, all of which traits are primarily due to the British Government and Christian Missions.[5]   Yogananda likewise possessed these typically Western virtues.

And again, why is it that most of the Hindu preachers and teachers in America are Bengalis from the vicinity of Calcutta?   Because that locality was the first and foremost in India to feel the influence of Government and Missions.   Calcutta is so Western that, unlike most other cities of India, it has no "native" section, and Bengalis are famous for their prominence in government positions throughout the country.   They might be called the national westernizers of India.   Thus the response of Calcutta to the stimulus of Chicago in 1893 and Boston in 1920 was the West returning to the West bearing gifts of Eastern treasure.   The swamis come to America because of Christianity and Western culture rather than because of Hinduism of Eastern culture.   We see a rebound of the West on itself, and furthermore a second rebound of the West on the East in the work of the Ramakrishna *Mission*, which was organized by Vivekananda only after his experience in America.[6]

If now we ask why the swamis *stayed* in America after
they came, the answer is somewhat different. Western
Christianity is not as responsible for the founding of
Hindu cults in America as it was for the coming of their
founders. The driving power in both cults seems to come
mainly from those Americans who were already turned
toward Hinduism by American cults of partly Hindu
origin.[7] This is especially true of Vedanta, while Yogoda
relies on two other groups also—liberal Christians and
pure converted Yogodans.[8]

But whoever may be their supporters, these Hindu cults
persist in America only because they make some contribution to American religious life. In the Vedanta movement it seems to be mainly the peace that comes from
sympathy, tolerance and breadth of view, while in the
Yogoda Society it seems to be mainly the practice of body-
building and relaxation by means of calisthenics, concentration and meditation.[9] Aside from this main teaching,
the wealth of Hindu lore proves attractive to many.[10]
Whatever effect these cults have on American culture in
the ecclesiastical, political, industrial and social realms is
not direct but indirect, coming through individual influence.

Yogananda, however, has the desire if not the present
means to deal with such human problems as immigration,
the crime wave and sensational journalism, and hopes to
introduce his educational methods into churches and
schools.[11] Vivekananda, on the other hand, had little
social or even historical interest. Since his share of Christianity was not needed in America, he preached his share
of Sankara Hinduism, with the result that the members
of the Vedanta, or Ramakrishna, movement in America
today are on the whole more medieval and otherworldly
than all of the liberal and many of the conservative Hindu
groups in India itself.[12]

Now in making these contributions to American life, how have our Hindu cults adjusted themselves? As to message, we cannot expect them to revise their creeds deliberately, for the Hindu assumes he has no creeds, and possesses all doctrines to begin with. He does not care so much to preach any special doctrine as to be the special preacher of whatever doctrine he can understand.[13] And so far, the contacts of American Hindu cults with genuine Judaism and Christianity have not been serious enough to yield any profound understanding of these more Semitic religions. On the supposition that India is the "Mother of Religions," the Hindus seek to embrace the various elements common to all religions as children of Hinduism, while the distinctly Jewish or Christian elements they either overlook or interpret according to dogmatic Hindu principles.[14]

In the *presentation* of the message, however, we notice a decided shift of emphasis from Sankara to the *Bhagavad Gita,* from renunciation to resignation, from knowledge and meditation to devotion and work, in short, from *escape from the world* to *escape from anxiety.* Vivekananda used to tell us that we live in a hellish world, and that the quicker we deny it, the better. But his follower Paramananda proclaims today: "God is One . . . We are all children of that One, and we cannot serve and love that One unless one love makes us include all his children— east, west, north, south, everywhere. To uphold this unity is the chief aim of this work."[15] At first Yogananda used to tell us how to extract the Spirit from the baneful body. But now he tells us how to invigorate the body with cosmic electricity. He may formally believe in escape, but he actually teaches control. If the esthetic Plotinus had been given the work of running the Roman Empire and could have kept his health while doing it, would he not have become more like Marcus Aurelius? In the same way, the demands of organization and the environment of American industry have made Vivekananda and especially Yogananda more Stoical and even somewhat Christian.

Again, we see the Hindu preachers grappling with Western science and philosophy. At least, they talk more glibly about science than scientists and more deeply about philosophy than philosophers. And whatever their interpretation of religion may be, it is completely scientific and philosophic, so they say.[16] Perhaps this use of Western thought as a means of presenting an Eastern message will some day radically modify the message itself. Even now, however, the Yogoda Society, unlike the Vedanta movement, is making a deliberate attempt to reconcile the cultures of East and West, and has accumulated a wealth of inspiration and practice.[17] In this society, the Hindu *Kundalini* traverses the seven stars of Revelation in the Christian Bible, the Fourth of July is a fine day for a Hindu sermon, while the Heavenly Father in His warmth of love hobnobs with a divine principle as cool as a glass of distilled water!

It is in the realm of method, however, that the difference between the two movements is most striking.[18] In the Vedanta centers, the swamis sing their song, and those come to listen who will. But the Yogoda Society means business. It not only preaches "the Gospel of Getting On," but has also developed the *art* of getting on through high-pressure advertising and the community church. It literally proclaims its message from the housetops—by using the radio. And when the physical radio is inadequate, it resorts to the "spiritual" radio. The Vedanta centers are guided only by swamis and sisters, but the Yogoda Society with its national organization is built to endure even if all the swamis and brahmacaris should retire to India, for most of the local leaders are American, and the Yogoda textbook will soon be published. The Vedanta movement in America has proved itself a true branch of the Ramakrishna monastic order in India that seeks renunciation, or escape from the world, but the Yogoda Society, with its carefully planned organization, seeks to control even the future.

The Ramakrishna movement will most likely abide by itself in America as long as sufficient wistful Americans exist to support the kindly and sweet-tempered swamis that supply them with inner peace. But the Yogoda Society—who knows what it will do? For it both supplies and creates a demand. Seeking to penetrate Western culture, it adopts American forms and methods, which may gradually modify the message itself until it becomes a kind of New Thought, and the Hinduism called to America in the twentieth century by the Unitarian Congress joins the Hinduism introduced to America in the nineteenth century by the Unitarian Emerson.

* * *

In general, there are three main reasons for the persistence of these and other Hindu cults in America. First, their claim of universal authority is both novel and supreme, and consequently very impressive. While the Roman Catholic Church claims absolute dogmatic authority, it cannot deny that it springs from a single historical person, who lived less than two thousand years ago. But the dogma presented by the Hindus is supposed to be nothing less than a complete and universal summary of all possible religious principles existing from the beginning of time the world over. It thus seems all-embracing, all-tolerant, and all-supreme.[19] Hence we can readily accept it without critical effort. We can enjoy "universal scientific and philosophic truth" without being scientists or philosophers ourselves. We can attain religious satisfaction without the trouble of thinking out a special way

of life. We need not strive to search for the best, for
the best is regarded as all religion in general, and each
religion in particular as it suits our individual need. This
leads us to a second reason.

Their cultivation of the individual rather than society
fits in nicely with the American post-war mood of reaction
from social idealism, and most likely helps to account for
the rapid increase in Yogoda membership. The practice
of concentration and meditation, a religious duty so simple
that anyone can perform it, helps to relieve the spiritual
depression caused by the collapse of fond hopes for mankind, and provides an obviously sane and modest outlet
for religious fervor. Sacrificial devotion to social service
and reform, or strenuous inquiry into political, economic
and domestic problems may or may not be wise or possible—so runs the feeling—but self-culture is undoubtedly
good. This contemporary leaning towards the renunciation of the turbulent world of public affairs is naturally
encouraged by the dualistic, or ascetic, side of classical
Vedanta.[20]

Finally, their insistence on the essential oneness of the
individual with God is universally satisfying.[21] This
monistic side of classical Vedanta is in itself neither ascetic
nor deterministic, and it supports rather than opposes the
Western stress on science and social personality. While
it becomes pantheistic if God be conceived as impersonal,
it becomes theistic if God be conceived as personal. Hence
it is quite suitable for the typical Western life of creation.
On this account, we are not surprised to discover in the
adjustment of Hinduism to the creative culture of America
an increasing emphasis on the monistic conviction of the
oneness of the individual and society with God, and a
decreasing emphasis on the dualistic tradition of escape
from the world.[22] This movement from a world-denying
to a world-affirming position, which is fitful and slow in

the Ramakrishna cult, is more steady in many other Hindu orders in America, and glaringly rapid in the Yogoda society.

The most rapid movement of all, however, is found in the clean-cut work of A. K. Mozumdar,[23] an independent Christian of Hindu race and tradition, who has preached here and there in America for about twenty years. While Mozumdar's teaching is popular, it has unusual historic significance, for it shows us what happens when a thinker immersed in Hindu lore completely accepts a world-affirming position. What happens is an identification of the Hindu conception of a divine universal Self with the Hebrew conception of a divine creative Power. To Mozumdar the ultimate God is not uncreative Bliss, as in the view of Sankara, but creative Power, as in the Hebrew tradition. Yet this creative Power, he declares, is the same as the universal Self. Here the universal Self, we should note, is not a finite Ideal, as in Greek philosophy, but the infinite Substance of the world.

Mozumdar makes this synthesis on the basis of his faith in Jesus Christ. Whether Jesus was historically influenced by Hinduism, as many Hindus contend, we cannot at present determine, but what makes him more than an ordinary Hebrew prophet in his life and teaching is precisely the Hindu-like conviction, expressed as well as possible within the limits of Jewish conceptions, that God is the universal Self, or the personal Substance of man. Elaborating the same conviction, Spinoza declares that the God of creative Power is also the thinking Substance of man and the universe. While the synthesis of Jesus is implicit and popular, the synthesis of Spinoza is explicit and technical.

Like Spinoza, Mozumdar worships Jesus as the supreme religious genius. Like Spinoza again, he feels both Hindu and Hebrew influence. And like Spinoza in the third place, he accepts the monistic philosophy of modern science instead of the dualistic philosophy of ancient Greece. Unlike Jesus, both Spinoza and Mozumdar are explicit in their Hebrew-Hindu synthesis, but like Jesus and unlike Spinoza, Mozumdar uses a popular instead of a technical method, for he preaches, teaches and performs faith-healing. While his lectures, classes, lessons and correspondence courses subordinate the Hebrew interest in social justice to the Hindu interest in meditation and concentration, his philosophical position—as revealed in his numerous pamphlets and books on "The Messianic World Message"—is definitely Christian and opposed to many traditional Hindu conceptions, such as the equal value of all great religious geniuses, the illusory nature of the world, and the postponement of final salvation till the end of the cosmic process. Says he:

Jesus's teaching is the greatest and simplest revelation of God, and is different from other teachings of Truth. . . . He came to teach us that the human expression is not an illusion . . . but . . . a vital reality. . . . Instead of following a specific path to realize God, you let God direct your life. . . . It need not take you millions of years to dispel millions of years' accumulated darkness. It will take but a flash of light from God to light your entire mental life.[24]

Yet his Christian teaching is unusual because it rejects the traditional Greek dualism in favor of Hindu monism.

If man thinks and acts, is not the thinker . . . and actor . . . God? . . . If God is All-Life . . . then all lives are God. . . . The Creative-power is the very nature of the Being of the Creator; hence the Creative-power is God. . . . Life is the Creator, and It will never be reduced to the level of Its own creation. The creature will forever be ensouled with the Creative-activity, and move and act according to the inner impulse of the Creator. . . . By thinking with the mind of the One Life, you become conscious of being the Thinker. . . . At the back of your every action you should find Yourself. . . . You are spirit and therefore spiritual. . . . The Permanent Substance is underneath all forms. The forms are made of the Everlasting Substance. This knowledge sets a man free. . . .[25]

American religion, with its dualistic Greek notion of an ideal God up in heaven and an actual man down on earth, has come to a fork in the road. To the left lies a path trod by atheists, secularists, humanists and others, who seek to exalt man by getting rid of this sort of God. To the right lies a path trod by Hindus, Theosophists, Christian Scientists and others, who seek to exalt man by supporting him with a belief in his divine nature. The modern age has little use for the traditional dualism between the natural and the supernatural, and is moving towards pluralism on the one hand and monism on the other, towards the path of less religion and the path of more religion. Hinduism comes to America to point out the path of more religion.

SPELLING AND PRONUNCIATION

The Sanskrit words in the Index are spelled and marked according to the usage of the American Oriental Society. The reader unfamiliar with Sanskrit may avoid the most noticeable mistakes in pronunciation by pronouncing *a* as the *u* in *up*, *ā* as the *a* in *arm*, *c* as *ch*, *e* as the *ê* in *fête*, *ś* and *ṣ* as *sh*, and *th* as *t*. Proper names of modern Hindus are spelled as they usually appear in English, while the letters are marked for pronunciation.

NOTES

CHAPTER II

1. Müller, *Six Systems of Indian Philosophy*, p. 41, tr. *Rigveda* I, 164.46.

2. Hume, *Thirteen Principal Upanishads*, p. 71, tr. *Brihad-Aranyaka Upanishad* 1.3.28.

3. *Sacred Books of the East*, v. 34, p. 23; Sankara's comment on *Vedanta Sutras* 1.1.1. For most of my treatment of Sankara and Ramanuja I am indebted to M. H. Harrison's dissertation, *Monism and Pluralism in the Upanishads*, Faculty of Philosophy, Columbia University, 1928.

4. *Maitri* 6.22, and *Mundaka* 1.1.4.

5. *Sacred Books of the East*, v. 34, p. 14; Sankara's comment on *Vedanta Sutras* 1.1.1.

6. The same, v. 34, p. 43; comment on *V. S.* 1.1.4.

7. Sankara, *Vivekacudamani*, verses 18-27; comment on *Vedanta Sutras* 1.

8. Sankara's comment on *Brihadaranyaka Upanishad* 2.4.5.

9. Radhakrishnan, *Indian Philosophy*, v. 2, p. 636; quotation from Sankara's comment on *Vedanta Sutras* 1.1.4.

10. *Katha* 6.10-11; *Maitri* 6.18-29.

11. Garbe, article "Yoga" in *Encyclopedia of Religion and Ethics*, v. 12, p. 831; Das Gupta, *Yoga as Philosophy and Religion*, p. vii; Sankara's comment on *Vedanta Sutras* 2.1.2.

12. *Sacred Books of the East*, v. 34, p. 37; Sankara's comment on *Vedanta Sutras*, 1.1.4.

13. Sankara's first comment on *V. S.* 1.1.1.

14. *Sacred Books of the East*, v. 34, p. 365; comment on *V. S.* 2.1.1.

15. The same, v. 38, p. 20; comment on *V. S.* 2.3.9. Cf. v. 34, p. 290. This argument was not original with Sankara, as also the one from design, and he did not place primary reliance on them; but for all that, he did accept them.

16. The same, v. 34, p. 290.

17. Barnett, *The Heart of India*, p. 42-43.

18. The pluralistic theism of the *Katha* and *Svetasvatara Upanishads* is probably an outgrowth of the old Vedic polytheism transformed by the pantheism of the early *Upanishads*, yet without getting rid of inconsistency.

19. Radhakrishnan, *Indian Philosophy*, v. 2, p. 666.

20. Ramanuja gives the term *avidya* no technical status. To him, even error is a kind of knowledge of the real, and may be corrected by further knowledge of the same kind.

21. Thus God is an object of knowledge who can be defined in positive terms.

22. *Bhagavad Gita* 10.10.

23. To Vedic rites are added traditional Visnuite practices such as abstention from all but ceremonially clean foods, freedom from attachment to desire, repetition of scriptural passages, and virtuous behavior, including service to others.

24. *Sacred Books of the East*, v. 48, p. 135-40; Ramanuja's comment on *Vedanta Sutras* 1.1.1. Cf. p. 370: comment on *V. S.* 1.4.10; and p. 566: comment on *V. S.* 2.3.42.

25. The same, v. 48, p. 424; comment on *V. S.* 2.1.9.

26. The same, v. 48, p. 240; comment on *V. S.* 1.1.21.

CHAPTER III

1. Paramahansa means literally "great goose," but as a name of Visnu, it means "divine." It is a rare title, and higher than the usual "sri," or "honorable."

2. Madhavananda, *Life of Sri Ramakrishna*, p. vii.

3. Following Madhavananda, whose edition is based on the most complete Bengali *Life*.

4. Swami Saradananda, author of the most authentic *Life* (in Bengali), claims on the evidence of women friends of the mother, Chandra Devi, that the father Khudiram was away from his wife for about a year before the child was born.

5. Not Buddha-Gaya, but the more ancient Visnu-pada-Gaya of the Hindus, about seven miles to the south.

6. In the *Sraddha*, or "faith," ceremony.

7. The famous saying of Krishna, Visnu's *avatara* or incarnation.

8. Madhavananda, *Life of Sri Ramakrishna*, p. 68.

9. The same, p. 92.

10. The same, p. 102-3.

11. The same, p. 98-99.

12. The same, p. 124-25.

13. The bethrothal of a five year old girl is not unusual in India.

14. Krishna Chaitanya was a young Bengali ascetic of the sixteenth century who founded a new sect for the worship of Krishna and Radha, Krishna's favorite mistress, and won his success by an emotional tempest of devotion.

15. Madhavananda, *Life of Sri Ramakrishna*, p. 192.

16. The same, p. 179.

17. The same, p. 257.

18. See above, p. 34.

19. The same, p. 260.

20. The same, p. 263.

21. The same, p. 278.

22. The famous prayer the Muslim offers towards Mecca regularly five times a day.

23. The same, p. 283.

24. The same, p. 283.

25. The same, p. 338.

26. The same, p. 340.

27. Farquhar, *Modern Religious Movements in India*, p. 57; quotation from the *Sunday Mirror*, Calcutta, Oct. 23, 1881.

28. This and the following aphorisms are selected from Müller's *Ramakrishna*, Gupta's *The Gospel of Sri Ramakrishna*, and Abhedananda's *Sayings of Sri Ramakrishna*.

29. Madhavananda, *Life of Sri Ramakrishna*, p. 371.
30. See Dr. Ketkar's explanation below, p. 208.

CHAPTER IV

1. Following Virajananda, *Life of Swami Vivekananda*, p. 29.
2. The same, p. 105.
3. The same, p. 203.
4. The same, p. 210.
5. Madhavananda, *Life of Sri Ramakrishna*, p. 445.
6. Virajananda, *Life of Swami Vivekananda*, v. 1, p. 112.
7. Madhavananda, *Life of Sri Ramakrishna*, p. 723.
8. Virajananda, *Life of Swami Vivekananda*, v. 2, p. 25.
9. The same, v. 2, p. 25.
10. See above, p. 26.
11. Virajananda, *Life of Swami Vivekananda*, v. 2, p. 21.
12. The same, v. 2, p. 241-42.
13. The same, v. 2, p. 251.
14. The same, v. 2, p. 279.
15. See Nash, *The Message and Influence of Swami Vivekananda*, p. 742, and Madhavananda, *Complete Works of Swami Vivekananda*, v. 1, p. 1. Beautiful! But how true? Vivekananda was initiated as a monk by his master Ramakrishna, his master in turn by the monk Totapuri, who followed Sankara's teaching. Sankara lived in the ninth century after Christ. In the very same country of India, Gautama Buddha had established an order of monks in the sixth century before Christ, a full fifteen hundred years before Sankara. Vivekananda was speaking for Hinduism, not Buddhism. Then how could he speak in the name of "the most ancient order of monks in the world"? Indeed, how could he speak as a Hindu monk at all, after living in palatial hotels, sporting gaudy finery, and eating—of all things—*beef?* (See Christian Literature Society, *Swami Vivekananda and His Guru*, p. xxv.) And how can India be called *the* mother of religions, when she produced only four of the eleven religions of the world, and of these four Buddhism is hers no longer, while Jainism and Sikhism are offshoots of Hinduism?
16. See Reed, *Hinduism in England and America*, p. 170, and Madhavananda, *Complete Works of Swami Vivekananda*, v. 1, p. 18. The answer is, of course, that Christian missionaries have done, and are doing, and want to do wonders to save the starving bodies of India's poor, so often neglected by high caste Hindus. The majority of the five million Christians in India have come from those who were saved by missionaries in times of famine. And Christian missionaries have blazed the trail not only in mass education, but also in mass medical relief, establishing vast numbers of hospitals and dispensaries with money from America.
17. He practiced "wish-thinking." In all his preaching he prepared no addresses or notes. Says J. N. Farquhar, "he had no historical conscience whatsoever." See Farquhar, *Modern Religious Movements in India*, p. 204. Our Hindu speaker did his best without the facts. The teacher had called on him. He was not prepared, but he had to recite. So he bluffed. And the bluff worked, for the audience on the whole was more ignorant than he.
18. Nash, *Message and Influence of Swami Vivekananda*, p. 744-45.

19.   Christian Literature Society, *Swami Vivekananda and His Guru,*
p. iv.
20.   The same, p. iv.
21.   The same, p. iv.
22.   The same, p. vi.
23.   Virajananda, *Life of Swami Vivekananda,* v. 2, p. 359.
24.   About Greenacre see the same, v. 2, p. 353; Daggett, in *Missionary Review,* v. 35, p. 211, and Ingersoll, in *Arena,* v. 22, p. 484.
25.   Virajananda, *Life of Swami Vivekananda,* v. 2, p. 356.
26.   The same, v. 2, p. 370-77.   See above, p. 34-36.
27.   The same, v. 2, p. 381.
28.   The same, v. 2, p. 382.
29.   The same, v. 2, p. 382.
30.   The same, v. 2, p. 379.   The swami himself revealed somewhat the kind of people that flocked to hear him when he declared,
"Scarcely could I go to a meeting or society, but I found three quar-
ters of the women present had turned out their husbands and children.
It is so here, there, and everywhere."   From the *Brahmavadin,* 1897,
p. 251.
31.   The same, v. 2, p. 379.   See also Daggett, *Missionary Review,*
v. 35, p. 211.
32.   Not to be confused with the Hindu leader of the Yogoda Sat-
sanga Society, who has the same name.
33.   Virajananda, *Life of Swami Vivekananda,* v. 3, p. 86.
34.   For all these statements see Christian Literature Society, *Swami
Vivekananda and His Guru,* p. ii-iii; quotations from Vivekananda, *From
Columbo to Almora, Seventeen Lectures,* p. 12, 13, 25, 32-34, 47, 203.
Sceptical of Hindu boasts about America, Dr. Wilber W. White,
Secretary of the College Y. M. C. A. of Calcutta, wrote a letter to
many prominent men and women in America, asking for information.
The replies were unanimous in affirming that to the main body of Ameri-
cans, Swami Vivekananda was at most a passing fad, leaving no perma-
nent impression.   Some of the writers had only vaguely heard of him.
Others admitted he had made converts, but not from Christianity.   Said
Rev. B. Fay Mills, a lecturer and evangelist of New York:

> "Swami Vivekananda made a very pleasant impression on Ameri-
> cans at first.   I am afraid some of it was dissipated later.   He did
> not produce a ripple in the stream of Christian thought and progress.
> Except for a mild curiosity to see how far Hindu dogmas might be
> strained to suggest Christian ethics, I do not know that he produced
> any effect on American Christian thought and practice."

Said Dr. Lyman Abbott of Brooklyn, editor of the *Outlook:*

> "We have in the United States, especially in the great cities, con-
> siderable numbers of people who flock to see and hear the latest
> curiosity whether in art, music, literature or religion.   From these
> classes Swami Vivekananda has gathered considerable audiences,
> especially in Boston and Chicago."

Henry Watterson, editor of the *Courier-Journal* of Louisville, Kentucky,
saw in the Hindu boast good material for an editorial.   Said he:

> "That our readers may not be misled, it is necessary to explain

that Swami Vivekananda is not . . . a tropical fruit or . . . an idol, or an insect, but the title and name of a person who is supposed to have set on foot the conversion of the United States to Vedantism, or some other sort of Indian religion. . . . Possibly some hundreds of people have professed to believe in Hinduism, but these are not converts. They are mere dilletanti, who, having grown weary of a course of hypocritical adherence to Christianity, are seeking some new diversion and possible social distinction by professing conversion to a religion whose tenets they no more understand than they comprehend the religion which they have renounced. . . .

"Even if these few hundred men and women were in deadly earnest, it would not signify anything whatever. So many converts may be easily commanded in this country for any fantastical scheme under the name of religion that any one chooses to invent. There is an arrant fakir out in Illinois who claims to be Jesus Christ, who has captured a number of people by his transparent lies, and is running a harem which he calls Heaven, giving out that the children born there have the Holy Ghost as their father. That many of his disciples are in earnest is evinced by the fact that they have surrendered their property to him, and work for him like slaves. In various other parts of the country there are similar fakirs, teaching all sorts of follies, and devoutly believed in by small bands of foolish men and women, who accept their confident statements as divine revelations."

35. Virajananda, *Life of Swami Vivekananda*, v. 2, p. 15; Farquhar, *Modern Religious Movements in India*, p. 202.

36. This zeal for social welfare seems to have come from Christianity, not from his master Ramakrishna, who always felt a disgust for service.

37. Nash, *The Message and Influence of Swami Vivekananda*, p. 753.

38. Information supplied by Swami Bodhananda in person.

39. Bois, *The New Religions of America, Forum*, v. 77, p. 419-20.

40. Virajananda, *Life of Swami Vivekananda*, v. 2, p. 392.

41. The same, v. 2, p. 393.

42. Madhavananda, *Complete Works of Swami Vivekananda*, v. 1, p. 9.

43. Vivekananda has no justification in either Vedanta or Christianity for calling men "divinities". This is a rare kind of polytheism. He seems here to have made a weird combination of Hindu pantheism and Western personalism.

44. Farquhar, *Modern Religious Movements in India*, p. 357.

45. Urquhart, *Pantheism and the Value of Life*, p. 472.

46. The same, p. 475; quotations from Vivekananda, *Jnana Yoga*, p. 67.

47. The same, p. 476; quotation from Vivekananda, *Science and Philosophy of Religion*, p. 122.

48. Madhavananda, *Complete Works of Swami Vivekananda*, v. 1, p. 133. (*Raja Yoga*).

49. Urquhart, *Pantheism and the Value of Life*, p. 477.

50. The same, p. 477; quotation from Vivekananda, *Bhakti Yoga*, p. 1.

51. The same, p. 479; quotation from the same, p. 95.
52. The same, p. 482; quotation from Vivekananda, *Karma Yoga*, p. 134.

CHAPTER V

1. The information about the growth of the Vedanta Movement was obtained from Swami Bodhananda personally. See *Vedantists in America* by S. Bose in *Modern Review*, Calcutta, March, 1930, v. 47, no. 3, p. 309.
2. The information about Paramananda is obtained from his own little Boston pamphlet, *The Vedanta Centre.*
3. See Directory for addresses.
4. See above, p. 70.
5. See above, p. 84.
6. See above, p. 83.
7. *Ramakrishna Math and Mission Convention,* 1926, p. 235.
8. The same, p. 285-88, showing that no centers outside these two countries were represented at the great Belur Conference in 1926.
9. The same, p. 287; cf. p. 238.
10. See above, p. 70, 84.
11. This statement comes from Swami Bodhananda personally.
12. In the light of this answer we can now understand that intolerant, anti-Christian remark of a Vedanta member. (See above, p. 102.) He evidently assumed that the worthy Swami was attacking Christianity, when he was only attacking hypocrisy in the name of Christ. Moreover, his bigoted background must have kept him bigoted even after his conversion to Hindu ideals. But perhaps the simplest explanation is that intolerance will arise whenever dogma meets dogma. For all his supposed Hindu tolerance, the great Sankara pounced on the Sankhya position, and Ramanuja tried his best to make mincemeat of Sankara.
13. But the experience of God, curiously, is conceived as super-rational.
14. Madhavananda, *Complete Works of Swami Vivekananda,* v. 1. p. 365-81.
15. The same, v. 1, p. 423-24.
16. The same, v. 1, p. 45-46.
17. The same, v. 4, p. 141.
18. The same, v. 4, p. 263.
19. *Vedanta Monthly Bulletin,* v. 1, p. 129; "Healing Power of Breath."
20. The same, v. 1, p. 115.
21. In reply to the question, "What books do you consider sacred?" one of the swamis answered, "First the *Upanishads,* then the *Gita* and *Puranas,* then the sayings of Ramakrishna, then the works of Vivekananda". He did not mention the Christian Bible or any other non-Hindu book, although he claims to accept *all* religions as true. This indicates the actual dogmatic basis of the Ramakrishna cult in India and America.
22. The classical meaning of *Moksha* is liberation from the fetters of the world and absorption into transcendent bliss.
23. *Ramakrishna Math and Mission Convention,* p. 207-08.
24. Support comes from Sunday offerings, a membership fee of $15

a year, and free individual donations to the work and the swamis, who keep no accounts, but claim to take just enough for their modest needs.

25. *United States Census,* 1926, "Vedanta Society," p. 5.
26. Quoted in Virajananda, *Life of Swami Vivekananda,* v. 2 and 3.
27. See above, ch. 4, note 34.
28. According to the principle of *critical ownership* of any religious traditions, I joined the New York Vedanta Society, and became acquainted with the two swamis and several of the members and adherents. Then I sent out about 20 questionnaires to each of the five American centers, including New York, receiving 37 replies in all, from New York 6, San Francisco 7, Boston 11, and Portland (Oregon) 13. Owing to the pre-occupation of one of the swamis, no reply came from Los Angeles. Here is the questionnaire:

(1) Name and address (optional).
(2) Country of birth. (3) Age. (4) Sex. (5) Married?
(6) Nationality or race. (7) Occupation.
(8) Parents' religion (specify denomination).
(9) Of what church were you ever, or are you still, an active member?
(10) How did you happen to become interested in Vedanta?
(11) Are you a member of any Vedanta society?
(12) About how much time and energy do you devote to Vedanta?
(13) In the light of Vedanta what system of belief or practice have you felt constrained to give up?
(14) What persons or books in all the world have appealed to you most?
(15) What methods of Vedanta do you use? Jnana, Raja, Bhakti or Karma?

29. See above, p. 100.
30. Information from picture postcards published by the San Francisco Society. See also Drury, in *Missionary Review,* v. 44, p. 281-83.
31. See especially the work of another American woman, E. A. Reed, *Hinduism in England and America,* in which Mrs. Daggett's reports are reflected, and Hinduism warmly denounced.
32. Most likely the work of Baba Bharati.
33. See above, p. 78.
34. See above, p. 80.
35. Daggett, in *Missionary Review,* v. 35, p. 214.
36. *Literary Digest,* v. 45, p. 64.
37. See above, p. 92.
38. Madhavananda, *Complete Works of Swami Vivekananda,* v. 1, p. 119.
39. The same, v. 1, p. 137.
40. Prepared by Swami Jnanesvarananda.
41. This is the wall, or *rang,* that Ramakrishna used to visualize so vividly. See above, p. 48.
42. The rite of the *Kundalini* is not mentioned in the classic *Raja Yoga* of Patanjali, and I find no evidence that it was advocated by Sankara, although he may have known it, for the *Tantra* works of the Saktist cult in which it is found may have been extant in his time. He did, however, accept the rite of *Pranayama,* developed on the basis of

Patanjali, 1.34. See Vivekananda's comment in the *Complete Works. . . .* p. 139, 223.

43. This rather mechanical combination of *Prana* and *Kundalini* indicates their separate origin. Each is supposed to be an infinite power!

44. See above, p. 48. Each lotus has its special name, number, location, color, number of petals, shape of central opening, and presiding element.

45. The information in this paragraph was obtained from Swami Jnanesvarananda personally. It applies to the system as practiced at the present time.

46. Madhavananda, *Complete Works of Swami Vivekananda,* v. 1. p. 123.

47. See above, p. 92, also Vivekananda's *Raja Yoga,* chapter on *Prana.*

48. Madhavananda, *Complete Works of Swami Vivekananda,* v. 1, p. 134.

49. See above, p. 101.

50. The same, v. 1, p. 148-50.

51. January-April, 1927, p. 15.

52. Vivekananda, *Raja Yoga,* beginning of Chapter III.

53. Madhavananda, *Complete Works of Swami Vivekananda,* v. 1, p. 152.

54. See above, p. 106.

Chapter VI

1. From the *East-West* Magazine, November-December, 1928, p. 15-16. The information contained in this whole chapter has been checked by Swami Yogananda in person, just as the chapter on the Ramakrishna movement was approved by Swami Bodhananda.

2. *East-West,* September-October, 1927, p. 20.

3. See Vivekananda, *Raja Yoga,* ch. 2, verse 1, and comment.

4. *East-West,* January-April, 1927, p. 5.

5. *East-West,* first issue, November-December, 1925. The chart used is now published in America as *Psychological Chart.* Another school has now been established at Gidni, Bengal.

6. The report of this Congress—the seventh—is recorded in the book, *New Pilgrimages of the Spirit.*

7. This and the following quotations are from *East-West,* November-December, 1925, p. 7-11.

8. The Swami wants it understood that this fee is used mainly to support the work, and is not a fixed amount, no one being denied the privilege of the course on account of poverty.

9. *East-West,* January-April, 1927, p. 43.

10. The same, May-June, 1927, p. 14.

11. Yogananda, *The Science of Religion,* p. 60.

12. The same, p. 72.

13. The same, p. 73-76.

14. The same, p. 80.

15. The same, p. 49.

16. The same, p. 60-61. Verses similar to this sentence appear in the Bible in *John* 3:14 and 12:32.

17. The same, p. 73.

18. The same, p. 82. Cf. article of Nicolai Husted in *East-West*, May-June, 1928, p. 6, where the allegorical method is used in its "*moral*" form.

19. See above, ch. 5, p. 122-27 and note 42.

20. Chapter 5.

21. This notion goes back to the *Chandogya Upanishad*. "When the life has left it, this body dies. The life does not die." See above, p. 32. The same notion is very prominent in Plotinus.

22. Pages 10-11.

23. Page 37. Note the adoption of modern psychological terms.

24. Pages 40, 42-43, 44-47, 53-54.

25. Vivekananda, *Raja Yoga*, ch. 3, verse 4 and comment. Here the word is not *samgama* but *samyama*. See above, p. 122, 129.

26. The same, ch. 1, verses 30-31.

27. According to the old-fashioned method, we would know God perfectly by contacting Him. The idea of knowing God only by serving Him seems to be an American addition.

28. The Swami wants it understood that he is willing to give his course *free* in any educational institution that will pay its expenses. For other methods of concentration and healing, see Barrett, *Man: His Making and Unmaking*, p. 108. Until the Swami defines his aim with more single-minded consistence, Western educational institutions may not care to consider his system. I have tried the course, and found it helpful in several ways, especially in improving the quality of sleep by previously inducing a state of mental peace, and in offering new ways of "suggestion". But while I accept elements out of it, its lack of united appeal deters me from accepting it as a whole.

29. *East-West*, January-April, 1927, p. 34.

30. The same, May-June, 1927, p. 11.

31. Theosophy has a similar theory. Cf. Vivekananda, *Raja Yoga*, ch. 3, verse 18.

32. *East-West*, September-October, 1926, p. 5.

33. The same, January-February, 1928, p. 3.

34. Dale Stewart in *East-West*, September-October, 1927, p. 10.

35. *East-West*, March-April, 1926, p. 24.

36. The same, p. 20.

37. While the facts of the yogi's trance experience need not be doubted, the hypothesis of reincarnation is at last as doubtful as the hypothesis of disembodied spirits to explain the "manifestations" studied by the Society for Psychical Research. It is always possible to account for the facts in other ways. Yet the spiritualistic hypothesis may be, in certain cases, the simpler, more fruitful and picturesque.

38. Here the dualism between God and the soul in practical life is quite striking.

39. The doctrine of reincarnation, however, is not the only explanation for the pre-existence of the soul.

40. Modern science does not admit that the circumstances are exactly the same, and claims great significance for apparently trifling differences at the start.

41. *East-West*, November-December, 1928, p. 5-7. The teachings of the swami on some other subjects come from sources still wider

apart. At the beginning he said in line with American tradition that he believed in "common sense education, free from all mysticism," but now he teaches "Contacting Cosmic Consciousness." He accepts the *Gita* doctrine of *meritless* works, yet preaches "reincarnation till freedom is won through *merit*." (East-West March-April, 1926, p. 21.) With Sankara he states that true religion transcends all cults, creeds and ceremonies, yet in line with American procedure he is busy establishing a new cult with non-compulsory creeds such as "the medulla oblongata is the mouth of God" (*East-West,* September-October, 1927, p. 7), and technical ceremonies such as facing "North or East" while practicing meditation. (*Scientific Healing Affirmations,* p. 42.)

He believes in the solitary spiritual Self, yet gives his support to the utilitarian dogma, "the greatest good for the greatest number." After telling us in Western fashion that pain is one of man's best friends, because it warns him of danger, he insists on the Eastern teaching that "pain is a man-made Delusion," for "the consciousnes of man is made of God and is pain-proof." (*East-West,* May-June 1928, p. 4.) With the East he says we know God only by meditation; with the West, we know God only by service.

42. Swami Dhirananda, the associate and disciple of Swami Yogananda, holds less to Schopenhauerian renunciation and Stoic resignation, and more to Hegelian evolutionism. Demand great things, he says to America in his *Philosophic Insight.* No demand is too great to be fulfilled if you are fit for it. Great men not only make demands—they exist to create new and fresh demands. Not wealth, but vanity is bad. The business man is of the same caste as the preacher. But remember that Soul is All, the base and atmosphere of success. The good things of the world cannot be enjoyed without the "sauce" of the higher knowledge of the Soul. So reverence the Soul that crowns your activity with success. Expand into the Universal Soul, be broadminded, tolerant, liberal, appreciating even where you cannot agree.

Then he apologizes for the law of *karma,* and seeks to heal the longstanding dualism between this formal law and the formless God. The rigid law of cause and effect whether in nature or man, he says, is no bar to our trust in the Soul. Although 75 per cent of our conduct may be due to past cause and effect, 25 per cent is in our own power of free will which is moved by final causes. The motive of Eternal Good that is embodied in the Cosmic Law is in every atom, and in us too. The universal reason is always ready to save its own property, the world. As the past is within the Soul, so is the future. The fascination of the unknown is only the fascination of progress in self-discovery, the growth and blossoming of our own unknown into the known. This Self-development is the reason for evolution.

43. *Yogoda,* p. 47.

44. This information about methods was obtained from Yogananda in person, as well as from official literature.

45. *Brahmacari* Nerod is the resident teacher.

46. There is a center in Scotland and in Mexico, and there are three *Brahmacarya* Residential Schools for Boys in Bengal. In Washington there are two centers, one of which is "Afro-American." A list of centers is given in the Directory.

47. Yogananda claims about 25,000 Yogoda students of all kinds.

In the 12 American centers, however, his secretary estimates about 3,000 contributing members, from among whom I received 50 replies: from St. Paul 1, Detroit 1, Washington 3, Pittsburgh 3, Cincinnati 5, Philadelphia 6, Minneapolis 7, Boston 7, Buffalo 17, and one from the Newark group, making 51 in all. Three centers did not respond, one because it failed to receive the letters. The questionnaire is as similar as possible to the one for Vedanta. See above, ch. 5, note 28.

48. Ferguson, *Confusion of Tongues*, p. 317-18.
49. *Yogoda*, middle insert.

CHAPTER VII

1. See Daggett, *Missionary Review*, v. 35, p. 210-14; *Literary Digest*, v. 45, p. 64.
2. Information supplied by Miss Stephanie M. Worletsek, president of the Benares League at St. Paul, and secretary of the Yogessar Class at St. Paul, 670 Charles Street, St. Paul, Minnesota.
3. See Ferguson, *Confusion of Tongues*, p. 312.
4. See Book List, Chapter V.
5. *General Prospectus*, N. Y., 1928, p. 3-4.
6. *Special Bulletin No. 3, A List of Current Hindu Books on India*, is a valuable bibliography.
7. Ellinwood, *Homiletic Review*, v. 28, p. 497.
8. Natesan, G. A., ed., *Ramanand to Ram Tirath*, p. 244. Wording altered.
9. The same, p. 251-54. Italics mine.
10. The same, p. 254.
11. The same, p. 255.
12. See Thompson, *Rabindranath Tagore*, and Maitra, S., "*Rabindranath and Bergson*," in the *Calcutta Review*, May 1926, p. 189-205.
13. Ketkar, *Hinduism: Its Formation and Future*, p. 157.
14. See his similar Upton Lectures, delivered in Manchester College, Oxford, and published as *The Hindu View of Life*.
15. Radhakrishan, *The Hindu View of Life*, p. 79.
16. The same, p. 91.
17. The same, p. 22.
18. The same, p. 23. Italics mine.
19. The same, p. 34.
20. Published as *Hindu Mysticism*.
21. The same, p. 17.
22. The same, p. viii.
23. At 6039: in the Nelson Evans Studio.
24. Maitra, *Hinduism: the World Ideal*, p. vii.
25. Coomaraswamy, *The Dance of Siva*, p. 56.
26. The same, p. 1.
27. The same, p. 2.
28. This is consistent with the classic view that the world itself is illusion.
29. The same, p. 12.
30. The same, p. 16.
31. Ferguson, *Confusion of Tongues*, p. 308-12.
32. The New York *Times* of May 6th, 1929, on page 27 mentions

such a one by the name of Hernam Singh, possibly not a Hindu, but a Sikh.

33. *Confusion of Tongues,* p. 302, 312.

34. From a certain green-colored Los Angeles newspaper of about March 7, 1929.

35. See above, p. 185.

36. Information obtained from his former private secretary.

37. Das Gupta, *Hindu Mysticism,* p. vii.

38. For immigration in general see the *American Review of Reviews,* v. 37, p. 604-05, May 1908; R. K. Das, *Hindustani Workers on the Pacific Coast,* Berlin, W. de Gruyter and Co., 1923; California State Board of Control, *California and the Oriental,* Sacramento, Calif. State Printing Office, 1920; R. E. Chase and Sakharam Ganesh, *The Eligibility of Hindus for American Citizenship,* Los Angeles, Printed by Parker, Stone and Baird Co., 1926; G. Mukerji, "The Hindu in America," *Overland,* (n. s.), v. 51, p. 303-08, Ap.; E. M. Wherry, "The Hindu Immigrant in America," *Missionary Review,* v. 30, p. 918, Dec., 1907. One of the Hindu professors is S. L. Joshi, Professor of Comparative Religion and Hindu Philosophy at Dartmouth. Another is Sudhindra Bose, Professor in the State University of Iowa.

39. *Literary Digest,* July 13, 1912.

40. Nicholson, "Sufiism." *ERE,* v. 12, p. 11.

41. Sykes, *History of Persia,* v. 1, p. 459.

42. Dhalla, *Zoroastrian Theology,* p. 358.

43. Farquhar, *Modern Religious Movements in India,* p. 218.

44. The same, p. 227.

45. The same, p. 271.

46. Atkins, *Modern Religious Cults and Movements,* p. 132.

47. According to A. K. Swihart, a research student in Columbia University in 1929, Mrs. Eddy's doctrine is like Sankara's illusionism, only more extreme.

48. Page 234.

49. Yogananda's statements have been checked by Swihart, who finds no error in them. Mrs. Eddy's second reference is to p. 35-36 of Wilkin's translation of the *"Bhagvat-Geeta"* (ch. 2, verses 14-16), London, 1785. References are found to appear in editions 19, 20, 23 and 26, the only editions available in the New York Public Library, and so may very likely be found in all editions up to the 33rd, as Yogananda claims.

50. Page 7.

51. See Bellwald, *Christian Science and the Catholic Faith,* p. 68-70.

52. Christy, "Emerson's Debt to the Orient," *Monist.* v. 38, p. 43.

53. The same, p. 47. Here spelled "Narayena."

54. The same, p. 45.

55. The same, p. 56.

56. The same, p. 63.

57. See above, p. 24, 28-29, 32.

58. The same, p. 61.

59. Atkins, p. 125.

60. The same, p. 128.

61. Ferguson, *Confusion of Tongues,* p. 163.

62. Atkins, p. 108-09.

63. Weber, *History of Philosophy*, p. 266.

64. Rawlinson, *Intercourse between India and the Western World*, p. 142-43. Cf. p. 138, 140-41.

65. See also Harding, *Prabuddha Bharata*, Calcutta, March, 1928, article "Vedanta and Christian Science," and March, 1929, article "Vedanta and New Thought."

66. Curiously, Theosophy and Christian Science were also founded simultaneously, in the year 1875.

67. Atkins, p. 225-26.

68. The same, p. 223.

69. The same, p. 224.

70. Ferguson, p. 158.

71. Atkins, p. 223. Ferguson, p. 168. According to the U. S. *Census of Religious Bodies of* 1926, Divine Science in that year had 22 churches with 3,466 members, who contributed $158,000 for the support of the work, including $11,000 for benevolence. Seventeen of the churches reported Sunday Schools.

72. Ferguson, p. 216.

73. The same, p. 217.

74. The Nautilus magazine has been published since 1896 from Holyoke, Massachusetts by Mrs. Elizabeth Towne, a New Thought leader who defines New Thought after the manner of Vivekananda's definition of religion as "the fine art of recognizing, realizing, and manifesting the God of the individual." She writes such books as *Just How to Wake up the Solar Plexus, Just How to Concentrate,* and *Just How to Cook Meals.*

75. Marden is also a New Thought leader who preaches the "Gospel of Getting On," and writes such books as *The Victorious Life, He Can who Thinks He Can, The Victorious Attitude, Self Improvement,* and *Be Good to Yourself.* See Ferguson, p. 174, and Atkins, p. 236.

76. One of the followers of New Thought, associated with Quimby and the Dressers. See Ferguson, p. 166, 169.

77. The same, p. 217.

78. Ferguson, p. 279-83.

79. Inge, *Plotinus*, v. 1, p. 74, 109.

80. Windelband, *History of Ancient Philosophy*, p. 365.

81. See Whittaker, *The Neo-Platonists*, ch. 10, for this and the following statements.

82. See also Workman, *Christian Thought to the Reformation*, p. 197, 221, 227, and Harnack, *History of Dogma*, v. 6, p. 179, 185.

83. Spinoza was influenced by Bruno and Maimonides.

84. Fluegel, *Philosophy, Qabbala, Vedanta*, p. 75.

85. Weber, *History of Philosophy*, p. 587-88.

86. Fluegel, p. 222; quoting Schlegel, *Language and Philosophy*, p. 471.

87. The same, p. 187.

88. The same, p. 221; quoting Jones, *Works*, Calcutta ed., v. 1, p. 20, 125, 127.

89. The same, p. 191.

90. The same, p. 222.

91. See Aiyar, *The Theosophist*, v. 35, p. 232.

92. In the *Missionary Review of the West*, October 1917, p. 786. See also the *Hindu Missionary*, July 2, 1917—July 23, 1924, organ of reformed Hinduism, ed. by Gajanan Bhaskar Vaidya, c/o Vaidya Bros., Thakurdwar, Bombay. Society founded July 5, 1917.

93. In the *Literary Digest*, "A Hindu View of Christian Defeat," v. 46, p. 133.

94. *Hinduism and Buddhism*, v. 1, p. 191.

95. Quoted in Close, *The Revolt of Asia*, p. 252.

96. See Close, *The Revolt of Asia*.

97. See Atkins, *Modern Religious Cults and Movements*, ch. 2.

98. Rowe, *History of Religion in the United States*, ch. 8-10.

CHAPTER VIII

1. See above, p. 34, 70.
2. See above, p. 73.
3. See above, p. 142, 167, 176.
4. See above, p. 73-75, 142-45.
5. See above, p. 17, 20.
6. See above, p. 83, 102, 106, 113, 133.
7. See above, p. 117, 174, 228-36.
8. See above, p. 176.
9. See above, p. 118, 173-76.
10. See above, p. 119, 176.
11. See above, p. 160, 162-63.
12. See above, p. 107, 113, 133.
13. See above, p. 113, 166, 243.
14. See above, p. 75, 111, 140, 155.
15. Quoted in Bois, *Forum*, v. 77, p. 416.
16. See above, p. 99-100, 109-12, 160, 164, 166.
17. See above, p. 159-71.
18. See above, p. 114-16, 172-76.

19. In America, Leo C. Robertson, for example, sees value in every step of Vedanta. In particular, he shows that its original monism is not solipsistic, as many Westerners believe, but realistic. "According to the solipsist, what appears to be other finite selves like himself are in reality merely his experience. There are no other selves, only he exists. Now the Vedantist, in affirming the sole reality of the Atman, does not say that other selves are merely his experience, that there is naught beyond his present self and its experience. What he does is to identify himself with other selves, and even further with all else." See the *Monist*, v. 26, p. 234. In his high estimate of Vedanta, Robertson seems to follow Paul Deussen, who is a well-known Vedanta enthusiast. While Max Müller is not so devoted, he is generous and somewhat uncritical in his sympathy. See his *India, What Can It Teach Us?* For an appreciative study of the meaning of Hinduism as functioning in India itself, see J. B. Pratt's *India and Its Faiths*, ch. 21.

20. Horatio W. Dresser, one of the founders of the New Thought movement, admits that Vedanta induces a desirable peace and tranquillity, but is quick to point out its failure to stress the values of purpose and personality on which Western culture in the long run so strongly insists.

See "An Interpretation of Vedanta," *Arena,* v. 22, p. 489-508. W. S. Urquhart, in the final chapter of his book *The Vedanta and Modern Thought,* takes essentially the same position. The main value of Vedanta, he says, is to produce a feeling of "religious contentment" with its "emphasis on the community of nature between the human and the divine" (p. 222-23). But he laments its negation of the positive characters of social personality, and agrees with Tagore that "Flight from the world is flight from God." (p. 230).

21. William Tully Seeger admires Vedanta for its genuine monism, which he declares to be "the vital value of the Hindu God-idea". The "identity of the Universal God with the Monad," he contends, does not necessarily imply the loss of the self-consciousness of the one in the other, but simply shows that the humanist symbols of father and son cannot suffice for the person that has persisted in penetrating the heart of religion. "The religion of the Divine Self is sure to make its way, because it will, while upholding individualism, place it firmly upon a higher basis having nothing in common with selfish motives . . . and declare that every normally developed soul has the latent power to win and *must* win its own freedom, especially the freedom from the control of the 'natural man.' " See the *Hibbert Journal,* v. 5, p. 75-76, 84. No doubt an individualistic monism is implicit in Vedanta, but it seems that until the present it has never become explicit, on account of its persistent dualism. Either the monism swallows up the individualism as in Sankara, or the individualism rebels again the monism, as in Ramanuja.

22. It is only this dualistic side of Vedanta that leads to "hazy mysticism and scientific futilty". The monistic side leads to scientific universality and artistic loveliness. As Paul Carus says, the intrinsic grandeur, beauty and truth of Vedanta lies in its claim that all is God, which Emerson made so famous and attractive. "God reveals Himself in hammer and anvil, in action and reaction, in energy of all kinds, in good and evil, in the aspiration of the worm that crawls in the dust, and in the heaven-inspired prophet who longs for the beyond that he beholds in his vision." See the *Monist,* v. 26, p. 299. S. P. Rice, of the Indian Civil Service, holds a similar critical view of Vedanta. While the religion dominant in Hindu philosophy has value, he says, it lacks detailed accuracy and motive power. See the *Asiatic Review* (n. s.), v. 19, p. 87-108.

23. Address the Messianic Publishing Co., 1001 Armour Ave., Los Angeles, Calif., E. Schurra, editor, Tel., Capitol 1826, for a list of his books and other information.

24. *The Conquering Man,* Los Angeles, Messianic Publishing Co., 1001 Armour Ave., 1929, p. 58, 84, 85, 22.

25. *The Life of Man,* p. 1, 3, 7, 27, and *The Conquering Man,* **p. 41.**

BOOK LIST

CHAPTER I

Andrews, C. F. *Mahatma Gandhi's Ideas.* N. Y., Macmillan, 1930.

Archer, W. *India and the Future.* London, Hutchinson, 1917.

Besant, Annie. *India, Bond or Free?* N. Y., Putnams, 1926.

Buck, C. H. *Faiths, Fairs and Festivals of India.* Calcutta, Thacker, 1917.

Cape, J., and H. Smith. *An Indian Commentary.* N. Y., Garrat, 1930.

Datta, S. K. *The Desire of India.* London, Young People's Missionary Movement, 1908.

Field, Harry. *After Mother India.* New York, Harcourt, 1930.

Fisher, F. B. *India's Silent Revolution.* N. Y., Macmillan, 1919.

Fuller, Sir Bampfylde. *Studies in Indian Life and Sentiment.* London, Murray, 1910.

Gandhi, M. K. *The Story of My Experience with Truth.* Ahmedabad, Navajivan Press, 1927.

Ganesh, ed. *Mahatma Gandhi: His Life, Writings and Speeches.* Madras, Ganesh, 1921.

Gray, R. M., and M. C. Parekh. *Mahatma Gandhi.* Calcutta, Association Press, 1928.

Holland, W. E. *The Goal of India.* London, United Council of Missionary Education, 1917.

Howells, G. *The Soul of India.* London, Clark, 1923.

Jones, J. P. *India: Its Life and Thought.* N. Y., Macmillan, 1915.

Macnicol, Nicol. *The Making of Modern India.* N. Y., Oxford University Press, 1924.

Mookerji, R. *The Fundamental Unity of India.* N. Y., Longmans. 1914.

Rai, L. *Young India.* N. Y., Huebsch, 1917.

——*Unhappy India.* Calcutta, Banna, 1928.

Ranken, G. P. "The Material Side of Hinduism," *Edinburgh Review,* CCXL, 65-79.

Ronaldshay, L. J. *The Heart of Aryavarta.* London, Constable, 1925.

Smith, V. C. *The Oxford Student's History of India,* 4th ed. N. Y., Oxford University Press, 1924.

Sunderland, J. T. *India in Bondage.* N. Y., Copeland, 1930.

Van Tyne, C. H. *India in Ferment.* N. Y., Appleton, 1923.

Walker, F. D. *India and Her People.* London, United Council for Missionary Education, 1922.

Wood, Ernest. *An Englishman Defends Mother India.* Madras, Ganesh, 1930.

Woolacott, J. A. *India on Trial.* London, Macmillan, 1930.

CHAPTER II

Baijnath, Lala. *Hinduism: Ancient and Modern.* Meerut, Vaishya Hitkari Office, 1905.

Ballantyne, J. R., tr. *The Vedantasara.* London, Christian Literature Society, 1898.

Barnett, L. D. *The Heart of India.* London, Murray, 1913.

Beck, L. Adams. *The Story of Oriental Philosophy.* N. Y., Cosmopolitan Book Corporation, 1928.

Bhattacharya, J. N. *Hindu Castes and Sects.* Calcutta, Thacker, 1896.

——*Studies in Vedantism.* University of Calcutta, 1909.

Burway, M. W. *Glimpses of the Bhagawat Gita and the Vedanta Philosophy.* Bombay, Burway, 1916.

Crooke, W. "Hinduism," *Encyclopedia of Religion and Ethics,* VI, 686-715.

Dasgupta, S. *History of Indian Philosophy.* N. Y., Macmillan, 1922.

——*Yoga as Philosophy and Religion.* N. Y., Dutton, 1924.

Deussen, P. *The Philosophy of the Upanishads.* Tr. by A. S. Gedden. Edinburgh, Clark, 1906.

——*Outlines of Indian Philosophy,* Vol. I. Berlin, Curtius, 1907.

——*The System of the Vedanta.* Tr. by Charles Johnston. Chicago, Open Court, 1912.

Eliot, Sir Charles. *Hinduism and Buddhism.* London, Arnold, 1921. 3 Vol.

Farquhar, J. N. *Modern Religious Movements in India.* N. Y., Macmillan, 1915.

——*An Outline of the Religious Literature of India.* N. Y., Oxford University Press, 1920.

Frazer, R. W. *Indian Thought, Past and Present.* N. Y., Stokes. 1915.

Garbe, R. "Yoga," *Encyclopedia of Religion and Ethics,* XII.

Ghate, V. S. "Sankaracharya," *Encyclopedia of Religion and Ethics,* XI.

Griswold, H. D. *Brahman.* N. Y., Macmillan, 1900.

——*The Religion of the Rig Veda.* N. Y., Oxford University Press, 1923.

Guenon, René. *Man and His Becoming, According to the Vedanta.* Tr. by C. J. Whiteley. London, Rider.

Hume, R. E., tr. *The Thirteen Principal Upanishads.* N. Y., Oxford University Press, 1921.

Jacob, G. A., tr. *The Vedantasara,* 3d ed. London, Paul, 1891.

Keith, A. B. *Buddhist Philosophy in India and Ceylon.* N. Y., Oxford University Press, 1923.

——*The Religion and Philosophy of the Vedas and Upanishads,* Harvard University Press, 1925. 2 Vols.

Khedkar, R. V. *A Handbook of the Vedanta Philosophy and Religion.* Kolhapur (India), Shri Venkateshwar Press, 1911.

——*Adwaitism and the Religions of the East.* Kolhapur (India), Shri Venkateshwar Press, 1915.

Kirtikar, V. J. *Studies in Vedanta.* Bombay, Taraporewala, 1924.

Macdonell, A. A. "Indian Buddhism," *Encyclopedia of Religion and Ethics,* VII.

Macnicol, Nicol. *Indian Theism.* N. Y., Oxford University Press, 1915.

Majumdar, S. *The Vedanta Philosophy.* Barisal (Bengal), 1929.

Monier-Williams, Sir Monier. *Brahmanism and Hinduism.* N. Y., Macmillan, 1891.

Müller, F. M. *Three Lectures on the Vedanta Philosophy.* N. Y., Longmans, 1901.

Narahari, Sri. *Bodhasar, a Treatise on Vedanta.* Tr. by Svami Dayanand. Benares (India), 1906. ...

Oman, J. C. *The Mystics, Ascetics and Saints of India.* London, Unwin, 1903.

Pantulu, J. R. "The Scheme of Hindu Life," *South Indian Association Journal* (Madras, 1913), IV, 111-129.

Radhakrishnan, S. *Indian Philosophy.* London, Allen and Unwin. Vol. 1, 1923; Vol. 2, 1927.

Rau, M. S., and K. A. Aiyar. *The Panchadasi of Vidyaranya.* Srirangam (India), Sri Vani Vilas Press, 1912.

Rhys-Davids, T. W. "Buddhism," *Encyclopedia Britannica,* 11th ed., IV.

Sarkar, K. L. *The Hindu System of Religious Science and Art.* Calcutta, Sarkar, 1890.

Sastri, K. *An Introduction to the Adwaita Philosophy.* University of Calcutta, 1924.

Saunders, K. J. *Epochs in Buddhist History.* University of Chicago Press, 1921.

Shastri, P. D. *The Doctrine of Maya.* London, Luzac, 1911.

Seshacharri, V. C. *The Upanishads and Sri Sankara's Commentary.* Madras, 1898-1901. 5 Vols.

Sircar, M. *The System of Vedantic Thought and Culture.* University of Calcutta, 1925.

Sukhtankar, V. A. *The Teachings of Vedanta According to Ramanuja.* Vienna, Holzhausen, 1908.

Thibaut, G. *The Vedanta Sutras with the Commentary of Sankaracharya.* In *Sacred Books of the East.* N. Y., Oxford University Press. Vols. 34 and 38, 1896.

——*The Vedanta Sutras with the Commentary of Ramanuja.* Vol. 48, 1904.

Tripathi, M. S. *A Sketch of the Vedanta Philosophy,* 2d ed. Bombay, 1901.

Underhill, M. M. *The Hindu Religious Year.* N. Y., Oxford University Press, 1921.

CHAPTER III

Abhedananda, Swami. *The Sayings of Sri Ramakrishna.* N. Y., Vedanta Society, 1903.

Brahmananda, Swami. *Words of the Master.* San Francisco, Vedanta Society.

Gupta, M. N. *The Gospel of Sri Ramakrishna.* Madras, 1912.

"M." *The Gospel of Ramakrishna.* Calcutta, Advaita Ashrama Publishing Department (28 College Street Market).

Macdonell, A. A. "Ramakrishna," *Encyclopedia of Religion and Ethics,* X.

Madhavananda, Swami, ed. *The Life of Sri Ramakrishna.* Almora (India), Advaita Ashrama, 1925.

Majumdar, P. C. "Paramahansa Ramakrishna," reprint from *Theistic Quarterly Review,* October, 1897. Calcutta, Udbodhan Office (Baghbazar), 1915.

Müller, F. M. *Ramakrishna: His Life and Sayings.* N. Y., 1899.

Nivedita, Sister (Margaret E. Noble). *The Master as I Saw Him.* London, Longmans, 1910.

Saradananda, Swami. *Sri Ramakrishna, the Great Master.* Madras, Ramakrishna Math (Mylapore), 1920.

Vedanta Society, ed. *Sri Ramakrishna's Teachings.* San Francisco, Vedanta Society. 2 Vols.

CHAPTER IV

Bannerjea, D. N. *India's Nation Builders.* (Chapter on Swami Vivekananda, p. 128-145).

Bois, J. (Jules-Bois). "The New Religions of America: V—Hindu Cults," *Forum,* LXXVII, 413-422.

Christian Literature Society. *Swami Vivekananda and His Guru*. London, 1897.

Dictionary of American Biography, Vol. 1. "Barrows, J. H."

Goodspeed, G. S. *The World's First Parliament of Religions*. Chicago, 1895.

Jones, J. L. *A Chorus of Faith*. Chicago, Unity Publishing Co., 1893.

Madhavananda, Swami, ed. *The Complete Works of the Swami Vivekananda*. Almora (India), Advaita Ashrama, 1921-1924. 7 Vols.

Nash, J. V. "The Message and Influence of Vivekananda," *Open Court*, XXXIX, 740-754.

Natesan, G. A., ed. *Speeches and Writings of Swami Vivekananda*. Madras, Natesan.

Ramakrishna Mission. *The Life and Teaching of Swami Vivekananda*. Dacca (India), Paresnath Chakrabarti, 1904.

Sastri, K. S. "The Life and Teaching of Swami Vivekananda," *Brahmavadin* (Madras), XI, 17-32, 81-103. (Cf. IX, 121-126, XVI, 235-243, 301-307).

Thompson, E. W. *The Teaching of Swami Vivekananda*. Madras, M. E. Publishing House, 1898.

Virajananda, Swami, ed. *The Life of Swami Vivekananda*. Almora (India), Advaita Ashrama, 1924-1928.

Vivekananda, Swami. *Raja Yoga*. N. Y., Baker and Taylor, 1899.

——*Karma Yoga*. N. Y., Baker and Taylor, 1901.

——*My Master*. N. Y., Baker and Taylor, 1901.

[For complete works of Swami Vivekananda see Literature of the Ramakrishna Movement in Book List under Chapter V.]

CHAPTER V

Abhedananda, Swami. "The Word and the Cross in Ancient India," *Brahmavadin* (Madras), VI, 237-250.

——"The Religion of the Hindus," *Brahmavadin*, VI, 363-374, 413-444.

——"Swami Vivekananda and His Work," *Brahmavadin*, VIII, 328-347.

——"The Correct Interpretation of Vedanta," *Arena*, XXIII, 218-224.

Alexander, F. J. *Hours of Meditation*, 3d ed. San Francisco, Vedanta Ashrama, 1907.

Alexander, Mrs. Gross. "Hinduism in America," *Methodist Quarterly Review*, July, 1912.

Atkinson, W. W. (Yogi Ramacharaka). *Fourteen Lessons in Yogi Philosophy and Oriental Occultism*. Chicago, Yogi Publishing Society, 1904.

——*The Hatha Yoga*. Chicago, Yogi Publishing Society, 1904.

——*Advanced Course in Yogi Philosophy and Oriental Occultism*. Chicago, Yogi Publishing Society, 1905.

——*A Series of Lessons in Raja Yoga*. Chicago, Yogi Publishing Society, 1906.

——*A Series of Lessons in Gnani Yoga*. Chicago, Yogi Publishing Society, 1907.

——*The Hindu-Yogi Science of Breath*. Chicago, Yogi Publishing Society, 1909.

Avalon, Arthur (Sir J. G. Woodroffe), ed. *The Principles of Tantra*. London, Luzac, 1914-1916. 2 Vols.

——*Tantric Texts*. Calcutta, Sanskrit Printing Depositories, 1913-1918. 7 Vols.

——*The Serpent Power.* London, Luzac, 1919.
Bodhananda, Swami. *Lectures on the Vedanta Philosophy.* N. Y., Knickerbocker Press, 1928.
Daggett, M. P. "The Heathen Invasion of America," *Hampton-Columbian,* XXVII, 399-411. Also *Current Literature,* LI, 538-540; *Missionary Review,* XXXV, 210-214. Same content in "Strange Gods of American Women," *Literary Digest,* XLV, 64.
Drury, C. M. "Hinduism in the United States," *Missionary Review,* XLIV, 281-283.
Ellinwood, F. F. "A Hindu Missionary in America," *Homiletic Review,* XXVIII, 400-406, 494-499.
——"Vedantism in America," *Current Literature,* XXXI, 102.
Farnsworth, E. C., and Swami Abhedananda. "Vedanta Philosophy," *Arena,* XXIII, 212.
Fuller, J. F. *Yoga: a Study of the Mystical Philosophy of the Brahmans and Buddhists.* London, Rider, 1925.
Hartmann. *Yoga Practice in the Roman Catholic Church.* Chicago, Theosophical Press.
Ingersoll, A. J. "The Swamis in America," *Arena,* XXII, 482-488.
Madhavananda, Swami. Almora (India), Advaita Ashrama.
——*Sri Krishna and Uddhava,* 1924.
——*Vivekachudamani of Sri Sankaracharya,* 2d ed.
Mukerji, A. P. *The Doctrine and Practice of Yoga.* Chicago, Yogi Publishing Society, 1923.
——*Spiritual Consciousness.* Chicago, Yogi Publishing Society.
——*Yoga Lessons.* Chicago, Yogi Publishing Society.
Natesan, G. A., ed. *The Mission of Our Master.* Madras, Natesan.
Noble, M. E. (Sister Nivedita). *Kali the Mother.* London, Swann, 1900.
——*Religion and Dharma.* London, Longmans, 1910.
——*The Master as I Saw Him.* London, Longmans, 1910. Also in *Hibbert Journal,* IX, 431-435.
——*The Web of Indian Life.* London, Heinemann, 1914.
Paramananda, Swami. *Patanjali for Western Readers.* Chicago Theosophical Press.
Ramakrishna Math, ed. *Ramakrishna Math and Mission Convention.* Belur (Bengal, India), The Math, 1926.
Reed, E. A. *Hinduism in Europe and America.* N. Y., Putnam, 1914.
Saradananda, Swami. *Sri Ramakrishna, the Great Master.* Madras, Ramakrishna Math (Mylapore), 1920.
——*Stray Thoughts in Religion and Literature.* N. Y., Vedanta Society.
Sinha, H. N. "Nadisodhana, or, The Purification of the Nerves," *Brahmavadin* (Madras), IX, 571-584, 627-637, 695-706.
——"Asuniyama, or, The Control of the Psychic Prana," *Brahmavadin,* IX, 762-774; X, 17-31, 75-89, 148-157, 192-200.
United States Census of Religious Bodies. *The Vedanta Society.* Washington, Government Printing Office, 1928.
Vishita, B. *Practical Yoga.* Chicago, Advanced Thought Publishing Co.
Waldo, Ellen, *Vedanta Philosophy.* N. Y., Vedanta Society, 1897.
Wase, C. *Inner Teaching and Yoga.* Philadelphia, David McKay.
Wells, A. A. *True and False Yoga.* Chicago Theosophical Press.
Wood, E. *Raja Yoga.* Chicago Theosophical Press.

Woodroffe, Sir J. G. (Arthur Avalon). *Shakti and Maya.* N. Y., Oxford University Press, 1917.
——*Shakti, or, The World as Power.* London, 1920.

LITERATURE PUBLISHED BY THE RAMAKRISHNA MOVEMENT IN AMERICA
The Following Literature is for Sale at the San Francisco Vedanta Society:

Works of Swami Vivekananda

Complete Works, 7 ▼.	*East and West*
Raja-Yoga	*India and Her Problems*
Jnana-Yoga	*Mother India*
Bhakti-Yoga	*My Master*
Karma-Yoga	*Harvard Address* (on Vedanta)
*Inspired Talks**	*Christ the Messenger*
Religion of Love	*Chicago Addresses*
Science and Philosophy of Religion	*The Atman*
	The Cosmos
Religion and Philosophy	*The Ideal of a Universal*
Realization and Its Methods	*Religion*
Study of Religion	*The Real and Apparent Man*
Thoughts on Vedanta	*Women of India*

(*All the works after *Inspired Talks* are pamphlets)

Works of Swami Abhedananda

Philosophy of Work	*How to Be a Yogi*
Reincarnation	*Great Saviors of the World*
Spiritual Unfoldment	*Self-Knowledge*
Divine Heritage of Man	*Nine Lectures*

Complete Works
(Single Lectures)

Woman's Place in Hindu Religion	*Religion of the Hindus*
The Relation of Soul to God	*Who Is the Savior of Souls?*
Spiritualism and Vedanta	*Does the Soul Exist after Death?*
Simple Living	*Scientific Basis of Religion*
Unity and Harmony	*Divine Communion*
Way to the Blessed Life	*The Word and the Cross in Ancient India*
Cosmic Evolution	
Philosophy of Good and Evil	*Christian Science and Vedanta*
Motherhood of God	*Why a Hindu Is a Vegetarian*

Works of Swami Trigunatita
Essential Doctrines of Hinduism   *Health*

Works of Swami Prakashananda
Inner Consciousness   *Universality of Vedanta*

Mystery of Human Vibration

Works of Swami Prabhavananda

Dynamic Religion	*Super-Conscious Vision*
Sub-Conscious Mind and Its Control	*Cosmology*

Works of Sister Nivedita

An Indian Study of Life and Death	*Siva and Buddha*
Notes on Some Wanderings with Swami Vivekananda	*Notes from an Eastern Home*
	Cradle Tales of Hinduism

(For other works see above)

Photographs

Christ in Yoga Posture
Sri Ramakrishna
Swami Vivekananda

Views of Temples of India
Views of the Hindu Temple, San Francisco

Other Swamis

The Following Literature Is for Sale at the Boston and Los Angeles Vedanta Centres:

Works of Swami Paramananda

Rhythm of Life (Poems)
The Vigil (Poems)
Soul's Secret Door (Poems)
Books of Daily Thoughts and Prayers

The Path of Devotion (in French also)
The Way of Peace and Blessedness
Vedanta in Practice
Reincarnation and Immortality

Practical Series

Concentration and Meditation
Faith as a Constructive Force
Self-Mastery

Creative Power of Silence
Spiritual Healing
Secret of Right Activity

Comparative Study Series

Emerson and Vedanta
Plato and Vedic Idealism

Christ and Oriental Ideas

Booklets and Pamphlets

Problem of Life and Death
Universal Ideal of Religion
Power of Thought
Principles and Purpose of Vedanta

Glorifying Pain and Adversity
Science and Practice of Yoga
Yoga and Christian Mystics
Civilization and Spiritualization

Prayer Cards I-IV

Works of Swami Ramakrishnananda

The Search After Happiness
The Path to Perfection

True Self of Man
Wisdom and Devotion

Works of Sister Devamata

Sri Ramakrishna and His Disciples

Days in an Indian Monastery

Pamphlets

The Practice of Devotion
The Indian Mind and Indian Culture
Sleep and Samadhi
Robert Browning and the Vedanta

Eastern and Western Religious Ideals
Development of the Will
What Is Maya?
Health and Healing

Magazines of the Ramakrishna Movement

(Present)

Message of the East, the Vedanta Monthly, La Crescenta (Los Angeles Co., Calif.), Ananda Ashrama, 1911-date.
Prabuddha Bharata (Awakened India), Calcutta, 182A, Muk-

taram-Babu St., 1897-date (monthly).
Vedanta Kesari, Madras, Sri Ramakrishna Math (Mylapore), 1913-date (monthly).

(Past)

Brahmavadin (The way of Brahman), Madras, 1895-date (fortnightly: apparently merged

with the *Vedanta Kesari* monthly in 1913).
The Pacific Vedantist, San Fran-

cisco, Vedanta Society, v. 1 only, 1902.

The Star of the East, Melbourne (Australia), July, 1910-Dec., 1911; later, *The Vedanta Universal Messenger*, Jan.-Dec., 1912.

Vedanta Magazine, the Monthly Bulletin, New York, Vedanta Society, v. 1-5, 1905-1909.

Voice of Freedom, San Francisco, Vedanta Society, v. 1-7, 1909-1916.

CHAPTER VI

Barrett, E. B. *Man, His Making and Unmaking.* N. Y., Thomas Seltzer, 1925.

Gabrilowitsch, C. *Why Be Nervous?* N. Y., Harper, 1927.

New Pilgrimages of the Spirit. Proceedings and Papers of the Pilgrim Tercentenary Meeting of the International Congress of Free Christian and Other Religious Liberals held at Boston and Plymouth, Oct. 3-7, 1920. Boston, Beacon Press, 1923.

Vivekananda, *Raja Yoga*, New York, Vedanta Society.

LITERATURE OF THE YOGODA SAT-SANGA SOCIETY OF AMERICA

The Following Literature is for Sale at the Yogoda Book Dept., 3880 San Rafael Ave., Los Angeles:

East-West Magazine

Works by Swami Yogananda

Yogoda, 1923; 9th ed., 1928.

Scientific Healing Affirmations, 1924; 3rd ed., 1926.

Psychological Chart, 1925; 9th ed., 1926.

Science of Religion, 1924; 5th ed., 1926.

Songs of the Soul, 1925; 5th ed., rev. and enlarged, 1926.

Songs for Piano (Sheet Music), *Song of Brahma, My Soul Is Marching On, Om Song.*

Yogoda Correspondence Course, 1925; 2d printing.

A Work by Swami Dhirananda

Philosophic Insight, 2d ed., 1926.

Works by Brahmacharee Nerode

Teachings of the East   *On the Wings of Bliss*

Photographs of Swami Yogananda

CHAPTER VII

Aiyar, K. N. "Professor Bergson and Hindu Vedanta," *Theosophist* (Madras), XXXV, 215-234.

Atkins, G. G. *Modern Religious Cults and Movements.* N. Y., Revell, 1923.

Baijnath, Lala. "Modern Hindu Religion and Philosophy," *Transactions of the Ninth International Congress of Orientalists*, London, 1892. I, 141-173.

Bellwald, A. M. *Christian Science and the Catholic Faith.* N. Y., Macmillan, 1922.

Buchanan, A. F. "The West and the Hindu Invasion," *Overland* (n. s.) LI, 308-313.

Carrington. *Higher Psychic Development.* N. Y., Dodd, 1920.

Cheyne, T. K. *The Reconciliation of Races and Religions.* London, Black, 1914.

Christy, A. E. "Emerson's Debt to the Orient," *Monist*, XXXVIII, 38-64.

Close, Upton. *The Revolt of Asia.* N. Y., Putnam, 1927.

Coomaraswamy, A. K. *The Dance of Siva.* N. Y., Sunwise Turn, 1918.

Daggett, M. P. "The Heathen Invasion," *Missionary Review,* XXXV, 538-540.

Dasgupta, S. *Hindu Mysticism.* Chicago, Open Court, 1927.

Dennett, Tyler. *The Democratic Movement in Asia.* N. Y., Association Press, 1918.

Desai, S. A. "Brahma: the Central Doctrine of Hindu Theology," *Hibbert Journal,* X, 561-580.

Dhalla, M. N. *Zoroastrian Theology.* N. Y., 1914.

Dresser, H. W. *A History of the New Thought Movement.* N. Y., Crowell, 1919.

Dutton, E. P., ed. *The Theosophical Movement.* N. Y., Dutton, 1925.

Farquhar, J. N. *A Primer of Hinduism.* N. Y., Oxford University Press, 1912.

——*The Crown of Hinduism.* N. Y., Oxford University Press, 1915.

——*Modern Religious Movements in India.* N. Y., Macmillan, 1915.

——"The Greatness of Hinduism," *Contemporary Review* (London), XCVII, 647-662.

Ferguson, C. W. *Confusion of Tongues.* N. Y., Doubleday, 1928.

Fleming, D. J. *Attitudes Towards Other Faiths.* N. Y., Association Press, 1928.

Fletcher, Ella. *The Law of Rhythmic Breath.* N. Y., Fenno, 1908.

Fluegel, M. *Philosophy, Qabbala and Vedanta.* Baltimore, Fluegel, 1902.

Gandhi, V. R. *India's Message to America.* N. Y., Hicks, 1894.

Ganesh, ed. *Swami Ram Tirtha: His Life and Teachings.* Madras, Ganesh, 1912. 2 Vol.

Garland, Marie (An Anglo-Saxon Mother). *Hindu Mind Training.* London, Longmans, 1917.

Harding, Madeleine. "Vedanta and Christian Science," *Prabuddha Bharata* (182A, Muktaram-Babu Street, Calcutta), March, 1928.

——"Vedanta and New Thought," *Prabuddha Bharata,* March, 1929.

Harnack, A. *History of Dogma.* Tr. by Neil Buchanan. Boston, Little, 1899. 7 Vol.

Hume, R. E. "Hinduism and the War," *American Journal of Theology,* XX, 31-44.

Inge, W. R. *The Philosophy of Plotinus.* N. Y., Longmans, 1918. 2 Vol.

Ketkar, S. V. *The History of Caste in India.* Ithaca (N. Y.), Taylor and Carpenter, 1909.

——*Hinduism: Its Formation and Future.* London, Luzac, 1911.

Kilmer, W. J. *The Human Atmosphere.* N. Y., Rebman.

Kingsland, W. *Anthology of Mysticism and Mystical Philosophy.* London, Methuen, 1929.

Krishna Sastri, G. *Democratic Hinduism.* Poona (India), Oriental Book Supply Agency, 1921.

Literary Digest, ed. "A Hindu Vision of Christian Defeat," *Literary Digest,* XLVI, 138.

Macdonell, A. A. *A History of Sanskrit Literature.* London, Heinemann, 1917.

MacKenna, Stephen, tr. *Plotinus.* London, Medici Society, 1924-1926.

Macnicol, Nicol. *Christianity and Hinduism.* N. Y., International Missionary Council, 1928.

Maitra, H. *Hinduism: the World Ideal.* N. Y., Temple Scott, 1922.

Martin, A. W. *The Fellowship of Faiths.* N. Y., Rowland, 1925.

Marvin, F. A. *India and the West.* N. Y., Longmans, 1927.

Massis, Henri. *Defense of the West.* Tr. by F. S. Flint. N. Y., Harcourt, 1928.

Natesan, G. A., ed. *Ramanand to Ram Tirath.* Madras, Natesan, 1926.

Nicholson, R. A. "Sufiism," *Encyclopedia of Religion and Ethics,* XII.

Patton, W. M. "Shi'ahs," *Encyclopedia of Religion and Ethics,* XI.

Radhakrishnan, S. *The Hindu View of Life.* London, Allen and Unwin, 1927.

——"The Ethics of the Bhagavad Gita and Kant," *International Journal of Ethics,* XXI, 465-475.

——"The Ethics of the Vedanta," *International Journal of Ethics,* XXIV, 168-183.

——"The Vedantic Approach to Reality," *Monist,* XXVI, 200-231.

——"The Heart of Hinduism," *Hibbert Journal,* XXI, 5-19.

——"Hindu Dharma," *International Journal of Ethics,* XXXIII, 1-22.

Rawlinson, H. G. *Intercourse between India and the Western World.* Cambridge University Press, 1916.

Rowe, H. K. *The History of Religion in the United States.* N. Y.. Macmillan, 1924.

Sarda, H. B. *Hindu Superiority.* Ajmer (India), Rajputana Printing Works, 1906.

Sarkar, B. K. "The Hindu View of Life," *Open Court,* XXXIII, 465-473.

Sen, N. N. *The International Ideal.* Calcutta, 1902.

Shastri, K. D. *Hindu Sexology in Spiritual Development.* Minneapolis, Indo-Aryan Publishing Co., 1917.

Singh, Puran. *The Story of Swami Rama.* Madras, Ganesh, 1924.

Sircar, M. N. *The System of Vedantic Thought and Culture.* University of Calcutta, 1925.

Sundararama Aiyar, K. *The Vedanta: Its Ethical Aspect.* Srirangam (India), Sri Vani Vilas Press, 1923.

Sykes, Sir Percy. *A History of Persia.* London, Macmillan, 1921. 2 Vol.

Tagore, R. N. *Sadhana.* N. Y., Macmillan, 1913.

——*Creative Unity.* London, Macmillan, 1922.

——"Towards Unity," *Sociological Review,* XVI, 90-102.

Thomas, F. W. "The Indian Ideas of Action," *Proceedings of the Aristotelian Society* (London), (n. s.) XVIII, 138-157.

Thompson, E. J. *Rabindranath Tagore: His Life and Work.* N. Y., Oxford University Press, 1921.

Vasu, S. C. *A Catechism of Hindu Dharma.* Allahabad (India), Panini Office, 1919.

Vaswani, T. L. *Sri Krishna, the Saviour of Humanity.* Madras, Ganesh, 1921.

——*The Aryan Ideal,* Madras, Ganesh, 1922.

Warman, E. B. *Hindu Philosophy in a Nutshell.* Chicago, McClurg, 1910.

Weber, A. *A History of Philosophy.* Tr. by Frank Thilly. N. Y., Scribners, 1896.

Whittaker, Thomas. *The Neo-Platonists.* London, Cambridge University Press, 1901.

Workman, H. B. *Christian Thought to the Reformation.* N. Y., Scribners, 1920.
Windelband, Wilhelm. *A History of Ancient Philosophy,* 3d ed. Tr. by H. E. Cushman. N. Y., Scribners, 1910.

Chapter VIII

Carus, Paul. "Vedantism, Its Intrinsic Worth and Vagaries," *Modist,* XXVI, 222, 298-307.
Deussen, Paul. *The System of the Vedanta.* Tr. by Charles Johnson. Chicago, Open Court, 1912.
Dresser, H. W. "An Interpretation of Vedanta," *Arena,* XXII, 489-500.
Müller, F. M. *India, What Can It Teach Us?* London, Longmans, 1883.
Pratt, J. B. *India and Its Faiths.* N. Y., Houghton, 1925.
Rice, S. P. "The Hindu Outlook on Life," *Asiatic Review* (London), (n. s.) XIX, 87-108.
Robertson, L. C. "The Conception of Brahma," *Monist,* XXVI, 232-44.
Seeger, W. T. "The Vital Value of the Hindu God-Idea," *Hibbert Journal,* V, 74.
Urquhart, W. S. *Vedanta and Modern Thought.* N. Y., Oxford University Press, 1928.

DIRECTORY

Vedanta Centers of the Ramakrishna Movement

New York
Vedanta Society, 34 East 71 St. Swami Bodhananda in charge.

Boston
The Vedanta Centre, 32 Fenway. Swami Paramananda in charge, assisted by Swami Akhilananda and Sister Daya.

Providence, R. I.
Vedanta Society, 381 Ives St. Swami Akhilananda in charge.

Los Angeles
Los Angeles Branch Centre, Music Art Studio Building, 233 South Broadway and 232 South Hill St., Rooms 427-428. Swami Paramananda in charge.

Pasadena, Calif.
Pasadena Branch Centre, 690 East Colorado St. Swami Paramananda in charge.

Hollywood, Calif.
Hollywood Branch Centre, 1946 Iver St. Swami Prabhavananda in charge.

La Crescenta, Los Angeles Co., Calif.
Ananda-Ashrama (Joy Retreat). Swami Paramananda in charge.

San Francisco
Vedanta Society, in the Hindu Temple, 2963 Webster St. Swami Madhavananda in charge, assisted by Swami Dayananda.

Portland, Ore.
Vedanta Society, Wheeldon Annex, Tenth and Salmon Sts. Swami Vividishananda in charge.

Chicago
Vedanta Society, 4454 N. Racine Ave. Swami Gnaneshwarananda (Jnanesvarananda) in charge.

287

YOGODA SAT-SANGA CENTERS

India

Brahmacarya Residential Schools for Boys, located at Ranchi and Puri, Bengal, India. The Maharaja of Kasimbazar is the patron of the Ranchi School.

Los Angeles, Calif.

Mount Washington Centre, National Headquarters, Yogoda Sat-Sanga Society of America, 3880 San Rafael Avenue, Los Angeles, Calif. Phone Garfield 6406.

Cleveland, Ohio

Leader, Upadeshak Panditji, 6614 Carnegie Avenue. Phone Prospect 3559. Thursday evening services at 507 Carnegie Hall.

Boston, Mass.

Leader, Dr. M. W. Lewis. Meetings at 543 Boylston Street.

Cincinnati, Ohio

Leader, Mr. Ranendra K. Das, 2559 Eden Avenue. Phone Avon 3186. Weekly meetings at Hotel Sinton.

Detroit, Mich.

Leader, Countess Elektra Rosanka, 561 Book Building. Secretary, Mrs. Maude Emerson, 49 Orchestra Place.

Minneapolis, Minn.

Leader, Mrs. Jenova Martin, 2915 Lyndale Avenue, N.

St. Paul, Minn.

Leader, Mr. George A. Young. Business address, 344 Minnesota St.

Pittsburgh, Pa.

R. J. Logan, Secretary, 714 Ardmore Boulevard, Wilkinsburg, Pa.

Washington, D. C.

Leader, Brahmacari Jotin, A.B. Several meetings weekly at 1424 K. Street N. W.

Washington, D. C.

Afro-American Yogoda Sat-Sanga Association. Leader, Mrs. Minnie C. Mayo, 123 T. Street N. W.

Buffalo, N. Y.

Leader, Mrs. Anna Krantz, 419 Wohlers Avenue.

Philadelphia, Pa.

Dr. A. D. Williams, Leader. Meetings at 200 West Johnson Street, Germantown.

Mexico

Yogoda Center of Progress; General Caly Mayor, in charge; Esq. Ave Coyoacan Y., Tacubaya, Col de Valle, Mexico, D. F.

Scotland

Yogoda Center of Progress. R. J. Calder, in charge. 14 Devon Square, Alloa, Scotland.

THE BENARES LEAGUE

The organization of Yogi Hari Rama, who has returned to India. 133 West 42d Place, Los Angeles, Calif.

THE APPLIED YOGA INSTITUTE OF AMERICA
and THE HINDU YOGA SOCIETY

President and Director, Sri Deva Ram Sukul, 232 East Erie St., Chicago, Ill.

YOGESSAR

The teaching of Swami Bhagwan Bissessar, P. O. B. 3, Oakland, Calif.

THE DHARMA MANDAL
(Aryan Religious Association)

Director, Mr. K. N. Das Gupta, Peace House, Fifth Ave. at 110th St., New York.

THE THREEFOLD MOVEMENT

The Union of East and West, The League of Neighbors, and The Fellowship of Faiths. Executives, Mr. K. N. Das Gupta, Mr. and Mrs. C. F. Weiler, Peace House, Fifth Ave. at 110th St., New York.

THE INTERNATIONAL SCHOOL OF VEDIC AND ALLIED RESEARCH

Director, Pandit J. C. Chatterji, Times Building, New York. Secretary, Dr. G. C. O. Haas.

THE HINDUSTAN ASSOCIATION OF AMERICA

General Secretary, Mr. Sudhir Bose, International House, 500 Riverside Dr., New York.

THE INDIA SOCIETY OF AMERICA

Director, Mr. H. G. Govil, Times Building, New York.

THE INDIA FREEDOM FOUNDATION, INC.

Director, Mr. S. N. Ghose, 31 Union Sq., New York.

INDEX

CPSIA information can be obtained
at www.ICGtesting.com
Printed in the USA
BVHW060011090722
641728BV00008B/423